Reading
Study Workbook

With Math Support

Prentice Hall
Physical
Science

Concepts in Action
With Earth and Space Science

PEARSON

Prentice
Hall

Boston, Massachusetts
Upper Saddle River, New Jersey

Reading and
Study Workbook
With Math Support

Prentice Hall
Physical
Science
Concepts in Action
With Earth and Space Science

Copyright © by Pearson Education, Inc., publishing as Pearson Prentice Hall, Boston, Massachusetts 02116. All rights reserved. Printed in the United States of America. This publication is protected by copyright, and permission should be obtained from the publisher prior to any prohibited reproduction, storage in a retrieval system, or transmission in any form or by any means, electronic, mechanical, photocopying, recording, or likewise. For information regarding permission(s), write to: Rights and Permissions Department, One Lake Street, Upper Saddle River, New Jersey 07458.

Pearson Prentice Hall™ is a trademark of Pearson Education, Inc.
Pearson® is a registered trademark of Pearson plc.
Prentice Hall® is a registered trademark of Pearson Education, Inc.

© Pearson Education, Inc., publishing as Pearson Prentice Hall. All rights reserved.

ISBN 0-13-166325-9

12 13 14 15   11 10 09 08

Contents

© Pearson Education, Inc., publishing as Pearson Prentice Hall. All rights reserved.

© Pearson Education, Inc., publishing as Pearson Prentice Hall. All rights reserved.

Chapter 1   Science Skills

Summary

1.1 What Is Science?

Science is a system of knowledge and the methods you use to find that knowledge. Science begins with curiosity and often ends with discovery. Curiosity provides questions but is usually not enough to arrive at scientific results. Methods such as observing and measuring provide ways to find answers. In some experiments, observations are qualitative, which means they are descriptive. In others, they are quantitative, which means they are numerical.

Technology is the use of knowledge to solve practical problems. The goal of science is to expand knowledge. The goal of technology is to apply that knowledge. Science and technology depend on each other. Advances in one lead to advances in the other.

The study of science is divided into social science and natural science. Natural science is generally divided into three branches:

- physical science,
- Earth and space science,
- life science.

The two main areas of physical science are chemistry and physics. Chemistry is the study of the makeup, structure, properties, and reactions of matter. Physics is the study of matter and energy and the interactions between the two through forces and motion.

The foundation of Earth science is geology, the study of the origin, history, and structure of Earth. The foundation of space science is astronomy, the study of the universe beyond Earth, including the sun, moon, planets, and stars.

The study of living things is known as biology, or life science.

The basic rules of nature can be thought of as the big ideas of physical science. These big ideas include

- space and time,
- matter and change,
- forces of motion,
- energy.

1.2 Using a Scientific Approach

An organized plan for gathering, organizing, and communicating information is called a scientific method. The goal of any scientific method is to solve a problem or to better understand an observed event.

Scientific investigations often begin with observations. An observation is information that you obtain through your senses. A next step often involves forming a hypothesis. A hypothesis is a proposed answer to a question.

For a hypothesis to be useful, it must be testable. Scientists perform experiments to test their hypotheses. In an experiment, any factor that can change is called a variable. A variable that causes change in another variable is called a manipulated variable. The responding variable is the variable that changes in response to the manipulated variable. A controlled experiment is an experiment in which only one variable, the manipulated variable, is deliberately changed at a time.

Based on the data produced by an experiment, scientists can draw a conclusion about whether the evidence supports or disproves the hypothesis. Once a hypothesis has been supported in repeated experiments, scientists can begin to develop a theory. A scientific theory is a well-tested explanation for a set of observations or experimental results.

© Pearson Education, Inc., publishing as Pearson Prentice Hall. All rights reserved.

Chapter 1   Science Skills

After repeated observations or experiments, scientists may arrive at a scientific law, which is a statement that summarizes a pattern found in nature. A scientific law describes an observed pattern in nature without attempting to explain it. The explanation of such a pattern is provided by a scientific theory.

A model is a representation of an object or event. Scientific models make it easier to understand things that might be too difficult to observe directly.

Whenever you work in your science laboratory, it's important to follow safety precautions at all times. The single most important rule for your safety is simple: Always follow your teacher's instructions and the textbook directions exactly.

1.3 Measurement

Scientists often work with very large or very small numbers. Instead of writing out all the zeroes in such numbers, you can use a shortcut called scientific notation. Scientific notation is a way of expressing a value as a product of a number between 1 and 10 and a power of 10. For example, the number 300,000,000 written in scientific notation is 3.0×10^8. Using scientific notation makes very large or very small numbers easier to work with.

Scientists use a set of measuring units called SI, or the International System of Units. SI is built on seven metric units, known as base units.

- the meter (m) for length
- the kilogram (kg) for mass
- the kelvin (K) for temperature
- the second (s) for time
- the mole (mol) for amount of substance
- the ampere (A) for electric current
- the candela (cd) for luminous intensity

Additional SI units, including volume and density, are called derived units. Derived units are made from combinations of base units.

The base unit for a given quantity is not always a convenient one to use. The measurement can be written in a more compact way using a metric prefix. A metric prefix indicates how many times a unit should be multiplied or divided by 10.

Precision is an assessment of how exact a measurement is. Significant figures are all the digits that are known in a measurement, plus the last digit that is estimated. The fewer the significant figures, the less precise the measurement is. The precision of a calculated answer is limited by the least precise measurement used in the calculation. Another important quality of measurement is accuracy, which is the closeness of a measurement to the actual value of what is being measured.

1.4 Presenting Scientific Data

A relationship in which the ratio of two variables is constant is a called a direct proportion. A relationship in which the product of two variables is a constant is called an inverse relationship.

A bar graph is often used to compare a set of measurements, amounts, or changes. A circle graph is a divided circle that shows how a part or share of something relates to the whole.

A crucial part of any scientific investigation is reporting the results. Scientists can communicate results by writing in scientific journals or speaking at conferences. Different scientists may interpret the same data differently. This is the basis for peer review, a process in which scientists examine other scientists' work.

© Pearson Education, Inc., publishing as Pearson Prentice Hall. All rights reserved.

Name _Karin Vieira_ Class _____ Date _10/8/09_

Section 1.1 What Is Science?
(pages 2–6)

This section describes the characteristics of science and technology. It also discusses the big ideas of physical science.

Reading Strategy (page 2)

Previewing Skim the section to find out what the main branches of natural science are. Complete the concept map based on what you have learned. For more information on this Reading Strategy, see the **Reading and Study Skills** in the **Skills and Reference Handbook** at the end of your textbook.

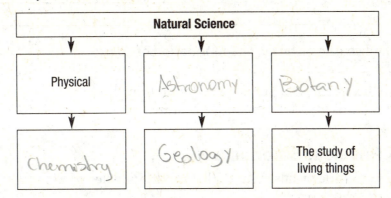

Natural Science
Physical | Astronomy | Botany
Chemistry | Geology | The study of living things

Science From Curiosity (pages 2–3)

1. Define science. _is a system of knowledge and the methods you use to find that knowledge._

2. The questions that lead to scientific discovery are provided by _curiosity_ .

3. Is the following sentence true or false? The results of every scientific experiment are quantitative. _False_

Science and Technology (page 3)

4. Is the following sentence true or false? The use of knowledge to solve practical problems is known as curiosity. _True_

5. How are science and technology related? _Science and technology are interdependent. Advances in one lead to advances in the other_

Branches of Science (page 4)

6. Name the two general categories that the study of science can be divided into.
   a. _Physical_   b. _Earth and space science_

7. Circle the letters of each branch of natural science.
   (a.) physical science   (b.) Earth and space science
   c. social science   (d.) life science

© Pearson Education, Inc., publishing as Pearson Prentice Hall. All rights reserved.

Chapter 1   Science Skills

8. Circle the letter of each sentence that is true about the field of chemistry.

    (a.) Chemists study reactions involving matter.

    b. Chemists study the composition of matter.

    (c.) Chemists study the structure of matter.

    (d.) Chemists study the properties of matter.

9. The study of matter, energy, and the interactions between the two through forces and motion is known as _Physics_.

10. Identify the topics that are included in the science of geology.
    Chemistry, physics, geology, astronomy and biology.

11. Is the following sentence true or false? The foundation of space science is astronomy. _True_

12. Scientists who study the origin and behavior of living things are called biologists, and the study of living things is known as _biology_.

The Big Ideas of Physical Science (pages 5–6)

13. Is the following sentence true or false? All of the important rules of nature have already been discovered. _False_

14. Circle the letter of each sentence that is true about the diameter of the observable universe.

    a. It is one hundred million meters.

    b. It is seven hundred billion meters.

    c. It is seven hundred million billion meters.

    d. It is seven hundred million billion billion meters.

15. Name the two characteristics of matter.

    a. _Volume_

    b. _mass_

16. The basic building blocks of matter are called _Atoms_.

17. Is the following sentence true or false? A force causes a change in time. _True_

18. Describe kinetic energy. _The energy of moving objects_

19. Two general types of energy are kinetic energy and _potential_ energy.

Science and Your Perspective (page 6)

20. Is the following sentence true or false? The scientific facts of today will not change in the future. _False_

© Pearson Education, Inc., publishing as Pearson Prentice Hall. All rights reserved.

Name _Kaun Vieira_ Class _8th_ Date _09/_

_1:3 - 1.4_

Section 1.2 Using a Scientific Approach
(pages 7–11)

This section describes scientific methods and how they are used to understand the world around you.

Reading Strategy (page 7)

Using Prior Knowledge Before you read, add to the web diagram what you already know about scientific methods. After you read the section, revise the diagram based on what you have learned. For more information on this Reading Strategy, see the **Reading and Study Skills** in the **Skills and Reference Handbook** at the end of your textbook.

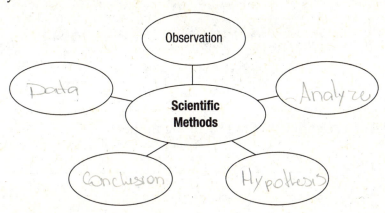

Scientific Methods (pages 7–9)

1. Identify the goal of any scientific method. _To solve a problem or to better understand an observed event._

2. Name three types of variables in an experiment.
   a. _manipulated v._ b. _responding v._ c. _controlled experiment_

3. Is the following sentence true or false? If the data from an experiment do not support your hypothesis, you can revise the hypothesis or propose a new one. _False_

4. How does a scientific theory differ from a hypothesis? _Hypothesis is a guess, not a theory_

Match the following vocabulary terms to the correct definition.

Definition	Vocabulary Terms
_C_ 5. Information that you obtain through your senses	a. theory
_b_ 6. A well-tested explanation for a set of observations	b. hypothesis
_a_ 7. A proposed answer to a question	c. observation

© Pearson Education, Inc., publishing as Pearson Prentice Hall. All rights reserved.

Chapter 1   Science Skills

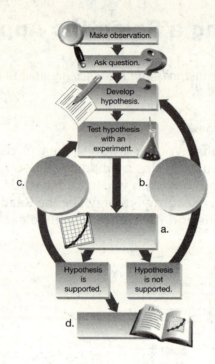

8. Complete the model of a scientific method by filling in the missing steps.

   a. _analyze data_   b. _Revise hypothesis_
   c. _Test hypothesis_   d. _Develop theory_

Scientific Laws (page 9)

9. Is the following sentence true or false? A scientific law attempts to explain an observed pattern in nature. _True_

10. All scientists may accept a given scientific law, but different scientists may have different _attempting_ to explain it.

Scientific Models (page 10)

11. Why do scientists use scientific models? _make it easier to understand things that might be too difficult to observe directly._

12. Circle the letters that correctly state what scientists do if data show that a model is wrong.

   a. Change the model.   b. Replace the model.
   c. Ignore the data.   d. Revise the data.

Working Safely in Science (page 11)

13. Circle the letters of safety precautions to follow whenever you work in a science laboratory.

   a. Study safety rules.   b. Never ask questions.
   c. Read all procedural steps.   d. Understand the procedure.

14. Why should you wash your hands after every experiment? _Because you maybe in contact with chemicals that you cannot see on your own._

© Pearson Education, Inc., publishing as Pearson Prentice Hall. All rights reserved.

Chapter 1   Science Skills

Section 1.3 Measurement
(pages 14–20)

This section discusses units of measurement, making and evaluating measurements, and calculations with measurements.

Reading Strategy (page 14)

Previewing Before you read the section, rewrite the green and blue topic headings in this section as questions in the table below. As you read, write answers to the questions. For more information on this Reading Strategy, see the **Reading and Study Skills** in the **Skills and Reference Handbook** at the end of your textbook.

Measurement
Why is scientific notation useful?
(a) is a way of expressing a value as the product of a number between 1 and 10 and a power of 10.
(b) makes very large or very small numbers easier to work with

Using Scientific Notation (pages 14–15)

1. Scientific notation expresses a value as the product of a number between 1 and 10 and _a power of 10_

2. Circle the letter of the value that is expressed as 3×10^8.

   a. 300   b. 300,000

   c. 30,000,000   (d.) 300,000,000

3. Why is scientific notation useful? _to make very large or very small numbers easier to work with._

SI Units of Measurement (pages 16–18)

4. Circle the letters of elements that are required for a measurement to make sense.

   a. scientific notation   b. numbers

   c. exponents   d. units

5. Is the following sentence true or false? Units in the SI system include feet, pounds, and degrees Fahrenheit. _____

Match the SI base unit with the quantity that is used to measure.

SI Base Unit	Quantity
_____ 6. meter	a. Mass
_____ 7. kilogram	b. Time
_____ 8. kelvin	c. Length
_____ 9. second	d. Temperature

© Pearson Education, Inc., publishing as Pearson Prentice Hall. All rights reserved.

Chapter 1   Science Skills

SI Prefixes			
Prefix	**Symbol**	**Meaning**	**Multiply Unit By**
giga-	G		1,000,000,000
mega-	M	million (10^6)	
kilo-	k	thousand (10^3)	1000
deci-	d		0.1
centi-		hundredth (10^{-2})	0.01
	m	thousandth (10^{-3})	0.001
	μ	millionth (10^{-6})	0.000001
nano-		billionth (10^{-9})	0.000000001

10. Complete the table of SI prefixes by filling in the missing information.

11. A ratio of equivalent measurements that is used to convert a quantity expressed in one unit to another unit is called a(n) _____ .

Limits of Measurement (page 19)

12. Circle the letter of each expression that has four significant figures.

   a. 1.25×10^4 b. 12.51

   c. 0.0125   d. 0.1255

13. Is the following sentence true or false? The precision of a calculated answer is limited by the least precise measurement used in the calculation. _____

14. Calculate the density if the mass of a solid material is measured as 15.00 grams and its volume is measured as 5.0 cm^3? Round off your answer to the proper number of significant figures.

   _____

15. Describe the difference between precision and accuracy. _____

   _____

   _____

Measuring Temperature (page 20)

16. Circle the letter of the base unit of temperature in SI.

   a. degree Fahrenheit (°F)   b. degree Celsius (°C)

   c. candela (cd)   d. kelvin (K)

17. Write the formula used to convert degrees Celsius to kelvins.

   _____

© Pearson Education, Inc., publishing as Pearson Prentice Hall. All rights reserved.

Chapter 1   Science Skills

Section 1.4 Presenting Scientific Data
(pages 22–25)

This section describes how scientists organize and communicate data.

Reading Strategy (page 22)

Comparing and Contrasting After you read this section, compare the types of graphs by completing the table. For more information on this Reading Strategy, see the **Reading and Study Skills** in the **Skills and Reference Handbook** at the end of your textbook.

Type of Graph	Description	Used For
Line graph		
Bar graph		
Circle graph		

Organizing Data (pages 22–24)

1. Circle the letters of tools that scientists use to organize their data.

   a. the Internet   b. newspapers

   c. tables   d. graphs

2. The simplest way to organize data is to present them in a(n) _____.

3. Circle the letter of the place on a line graph where the manipulated variable is generally plotted.

   a. the y-axis   b. the rise

   c. the x-axis   d. the run

4. On a line graph, the ratio of the change in the y-variable to the corresponding change in the x-variable is called the line's _____.

5. Circle the letters of the relationships that are direct proportions.

   a. distance traveled versus time at a constant speed

   b. the mass of a substance versus its volume

   c. the time to travel a given distance versus average speed

   d. the number of fingers in your classroom versus the number of people

© Pearson Education, Inc., publishing as Pearson Prentice Hall. All rights reserved.

6. Is the following sentence true or false? An inverse proportion is one in which the product of the two variables is constant. _____

7. Identify each data organizing tool shown below.

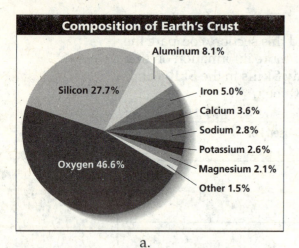

a.

Average Annual Precipitation for Selected U.S. Cities	
City	**Average Annual Precipitation (cm)**
Buffalo, N.Y.	98.0
Chicago, Ill.	91.0
Colorado Springs, Colo.	41.2
Houston, Tex.	117.0
San Diego, Calif.	25.1
Tallahassee, Fla.	166.9
Tucson, Ariz.	30.5

b.

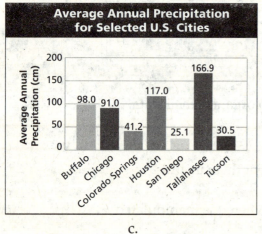

c.

Mass vs. Volume of Water

$$\text{Slope} = \frac{\text{Rise}}{\text{Run}} = \frac{5 \text{ g}}{5 \text{ cm}^3} = 1 \text{ g/cm}^3$$

Rise = 5 g

Run = 5 cm³

Mass (g)

Volume (cm³)

d.

a. _____   b. _____
c. _____   d. _____

Communicating Data (page 25)

8. Name two ways that scientists can report results of their experiments.

a. _____   b. _____

9. Is the following statement true or false? Scientists always interpret a given set of data the same way. _____

10. Why is peer review an important part of scientific research? _____

_____

© Pearson Education, Inc., publishing as Pearson Prentice Hall. All rights reserved.

Chapter 1   Science Skills

WordWise

Answer the questions by writing the correct vocabulary term in the blanks.
Use the circled letter in each term to find the hidden vocabulary word. Then
write a definition for the hidden word.

Clues	Vocabulary Terms
The study of matter, energy, and their interactions	_ Ⓞ _ _ _ _ _
The closeness of a measurement to the actual value of what is being measured	_ _ _ _ _ _ _ Ⓞ
A gauge of how exact a measurement is	Ⓞ _ _ _ _ _ _ _
The ratio of a vertical change to the corresponding horizontal change in a line	_ _ Ⓞ _ _
An instrument used to measure temperature	_ _ _ _ _ _ _ Ⓞ _ _
The use of knowledge to solve practical problems	_ _ _ Ⓞ _ _ _ _
A representation of an object or event	_ _ _ Ⓞ _
A system of knowledge and the methods used to find that knowledge	Ⓞ _ _ _ _ _ _
A statement that summarizes a pattern found in nature	_ _ _ _ _ _ Ⓞ _ _ _ _ _ _ _
Information that you obtain through your senses	_ _ Ⓞ _ _ _ _ _ _ _

Hidden word: _ _ _ _ _ _ _ _ _ _

Definition: _____

© Pearson Education, Inc., publishing as Pearson Prentice Hall. All rights reserved.

Chapter 1   Science Skills

Using Scientific Notation

Light travels through space at a speed of 3.00×10^8 meters per second. How long does it take for light to travel from the sun to Earth, which is a distance of 1.50×10^{11} meters?

Math Skill: Scientific Notation

You may want to read more about this **Math Skill** in the **Skills and Reference Handbook** at the end of your textbook.

1. Read and Understand

What information are you given?

Speed = 3.00×10^8 m/s

Total distance = 1.50×10^{11} m

2. Plan and Solve

What unknown are you trying to calculate?

Time = ?

What formula contains the given quantities and the unknown?

$$\text{Time} = \frac{\text{Total distance}}{\text{Average speed}}$$

Replace each variable with its known variable and known value.

$$\text{Time} = \frac{1.50 \times 10^{11} \text{ m}}{3.00 \times 10^8 \text{ m/s}}$$

$$= \frac{1.50}{3.00} \times (10^{11-8})(\text{m}/(\text{m}/s))$$

$$= 0.50 \times 10^3 \text{ s} = 5.00 \times 10^2 \text{ s}$$

3. Look back and check

Is your answer reasonable?

Yes, the number calculated is the quotient of distance and speed, and the units (s) indicate time.

Math Practice

On a separate sheet of paper, solve the following problems.

1. The flow of water in a stream is 210,000 liters per hour. Use scientific notation to calculate the amount of water that flows in a week (168 hours).

2. The density of a liquid is 8.03×10^{-1} kilogram per liter. What is the mass (in kg) of liquid in a full 100,000 liter tank?

3. How many balloons, each containing 6.02×10^{23} particles of helium gas, can be filled from a tank that contains 1.204×10^{25} helium particles?

© Pearson Education, Inc., publishing as Pearson Prentice Hall. All rights reserved.

Chapter 2   Properties of Matter

Summary

2.1 Classifying Matter

Matter that always has exactly the same composition, or makeup, is classified as a pure substance, or simply a substance. Every sample of a given substance has the same properties because a substance has a fixed, uniform composition. Substances can be classified into two categories—elements and compounds.

An element is a substance that cannot be broken down into simpler substances. An atom is the smallest particle of an element. An element has a fixed composition because it contains only one type of atom. No two elements have the same type of atom. At room temperature, most elements are solid. Chemists use symbols to represent elements. For example, C represents carbon, and Au represents gold.

A compound is a substance that is made from two or more simpler substances and can be broken down into those simpler substances. The properties of a compound differ from those of the substances it is made from. Properties change when elements join and form compounds. A compound always contains two or more elements joined in a fixed proportion. In water, for example, there are always two hydrogen atoms for each oxygen atom.

The properties of a mixture are less uniform than the properties of a substance. The properties of a mixture can vary because the composition of a mixture is not fixed. Mixtures can be classified by how well the parts of the mixture are distributed throughout the mixture.

- In a heterogeneous mixture, the parts of the mixture are noticeably different from one another.

- In a homogeneous mixture, the substances are so evenly distributed that it is difficult to tell one substance in the mixture from another. A homogeneous mixture appears to contain only one substance.

A mixture can be classified as a solution, a suspension, or a colloid. This classification is based on the size of a mixture's largest particles.

- A solution forms when substances dissolve and form a homogeneous mixture.
- A suspension is a heterogeneous mixture that separates into layers over time.
- A colloid contains some particles that are intermediate in size between the small particles in a solution and the larger particles in a suspension.

2.2 Physical Properties

A physical property is any characteristic of a material that can be observed or measured without changing the composition of the substances in the material. Viscosity, conductivity, malleability, hardness, melting point, boiling point, and density are examples of physical properties.

Viscosity is the tendency of a liquid to keep from flowing. The greater the viscosity, the slower the liquid moves. Thick liquids have a high viscosity, and thin liquids have a low viscosity.

A material's ability for allowing heat to flow through it is called conductivity. Materials that have high conductivity, such as metals, are called conductors. Malleability is the ability of a solid to be hammered without shattering. Most metals are malleable. Solids that shatter when struck are brittle.

© Pearson Education, Inc., publishing as Pearson Prentice Hall. All rights reserved.

Chapter 2   Properties of Matter

The hardness of two materials can be compared by seeing which of the materials can scratch the other. Diamond is the hardest known material.

The temperature at which a substance changes from solid to liquid is its melting point. The temperature at which a substance boils is its boiling point.

Density is the ratio of the mass of a substance to its volume. Density can be used to test the purity of a substance.

Knowing the physical properties of matter can be useful in the following ways:

• identifying a material
• choosing a material for a specific purpose
• separating the substances in a mixture

Scientists follow these steps in using properties to identify a material:

1. Decide which properties to test.

2. Do tests on a sample of the unknown.

3. Compare the results with the data reported for known materials.

Properties determine which materials are chosen for which uses.

Some properties can be used to separate mixtures. Filtration and distillation are two common separation methods. Filtration is a process that separates materials based on the size of their particles. Distillation is a process that separates substances in a solution based on their boiling points.

A physical change occurs when some of the properties of a material change, but the substances in the material remain the same. Some physical changes can be reversed, and some cannot be reversed.

2.3 Chemical Properties

A chemical property is any ability to produce a change in the composition of matter. Chemical properties can be observed only when the substances in a sample of matter are changing into different substances.

Flammability and reactivity are two examples of chemical properties. Flammability is a material's ability to burn in the presence of oxygen. Reactivity is the property that describes how readily a substance combines chemically with other substances. Oxygen is a highly reactive element, whereas nitrogen has an extremely low reactivity.

Oxygen reacts easily with most other elements. Rust forms when oxygen reacts with iron and water. A rusty chain or bolt is more likely to break than a new chain or bolt, because rust is weaker than iron.

A chemical change occurs when a substance reacts and forms one or more new substances. Three common types of evidence for a chemical change are

• change in color,
• the production of a gas,
• the formation of a precipitate, or a solid that separates from a liquid mixture.

Each of these changes is a clue that a chemical change has produced at least one new substance.

It is not always easy to tell a chemical change from a physical change. Even if you observe a color change, a gas, or a precipitate, you cannot be sure a chemical change has taken place. If different substances are present after the change takes place, then the change is chemical, not physical. If different substances are not present, then the change is physical, not chemical.

When matter undergoes a chemical change, the composition of the matter changes. When matter undergoes a physical change, the composition of the matter remains the same.

© Pearson Education, Inc., publishing as Pearson Prentice Hall. All rights reserved.

Chapter 2   Properties of Matter

Section 2.1 Classifying Matter
(pages 38–44)

*This section explains how materials are classified as pure substances
or mixtures. It discusses types of pure substances and mixtures.*

Reading Strategy (page 38)

Summarizing As you read, complete the classification of matter in
the diagram below. For more information on this Reading Strategy,
see the **Reading and Study Skills** in the **Skills and Reference
Handbook** at the end of your textbook.

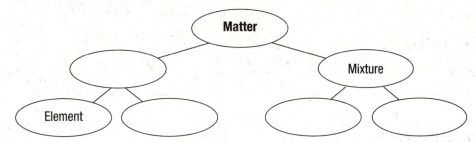

Pure Substances (page 39)

1. Is the following sentence true or false? Every sample of a pure
   substance has exactly the same composition and the same
   properties. _____

2. What are the two categories of pure substances?

   a. _____   b. _____

Elements (pages 39–40)

3. What is an element? _____

   _____

4. Is the following sentence true or false? The smallest particle of an
   element is an atom. _____

5. Why does an element have a fixed, uniform composition? _____

   _____

6. Circle the letter before each element that is a gas at room temperature.

   a. carbon   b. oxygen

   c. mercury   d. nitrogen

Match each element to its correct symbol.

Element	Symbol
_____ **7.** aluminum	a. C
_____ **8.** gold	b. Al
_____ **9.** carbon	c. Au

© Pearson Education, Inc., publishing as Pearson Prentice Hall. All rights reserved.

Chapter 2   Properties of Matter

Compounds (page 40)

10. What is a compound? _____

_____

11. Circle the letter of each sentence that is true about compounds.

   a. A compound always contains at least two elements.

   b. The substances that make up a compound are always joined in a fixed proportion.

   c. A compound has the same properties as the elements from which it is formed.

   d. A compound can be broken down into simpler substances.

Mixtures (pages 41–42)

12. Why do the properties of a mixture vary? _____

_____

13. A(n) _____ mixture is a mixture whose parts are noticeably different from one another.

14. Is the following sentence true or false? A homogeneous mixture is a mixture in which it is difficult to distinguish the substances from one another. _____

Solutions, Suspensions, and Colloids (pages 42–44)

15. A mixture can be classified as a solution, a suspension, or a colloid based on the size of its _____ particles.

16. Circle the letter of the term that identifies the homogeneous mixture that forms when sugar is dissolved in a glass of hot water.

   a. solution   b. suspension

   c. colloid   d. substance

17. Complete the table about solutions, suspensions, and colloids.

Solutions, Suspensions, and Colloids			
Type of Mixture	Relative Size of Largest Particles	Homogeneous or Heterogeneous?	Do Particles Scatter Light?
Solution			No
	Intermediate	Homogeneous	
	Large		Yes

18. Circle the letter before each example of a colloid.

   a. windshield wiper fluid   b. fog

   c. homogenized milk   d. muddy water

19. Is the following sentence true or false? If salt water is poured through a filter, the salt will be trapped on the filter.

_____

© Pearson Education, Inc., publishing as Pearson Prentice Hall. All rights reserved.

Chapter 2   Properties of Matter

Section 2.2 Physical Properties
(pages 45–51)

This section discusses physical properties and physical changes. It also explains how physical properties can be used to identify materials, select materials, and separate mixtures.

Reading Strategy (page 45)

Building Vocabulary As you read, write a definition for each term in the table below. For more information on this Reading Strategy, see the **Reading and Study Skills** in the **Skills and Reference Handbook** at the end of your textbook.

Defining Physical Properties	
Physical Property	**Definition**
Viscosity	
Malleability	
Melting Point	

Examples of Physical Properties (pages 45–47)

1. A physical property is any characteristic of a material that can be observed or measured without changing the _____ of the substances in the material.

2. Explain why a wooden spoon is a better choice than a metal spoon for stirring a boiling pot of soup. _____

    _____

3. Is the following sentence true or false? A liquid with a high viscosity flows more slowly than a liquid with a low viscosity at the same temperature. _____

4. Is the following sentence true or false? Discovering which of two materials can scratch the other is a way to compare the hardness of the materials. _____

Match each term to its definition.

Term	Definition
_____ 5. viscosity	a. The ability of a solid to be hammered without shattering
_____ 6. conductivity	b. The temperature at which a substance changes from a liquid to a gas
_____ 7. malleability	
_____ 8. melting point	c. The resistance of a liquid to flowing
_____ 9. boiling point	d. The ability to allow heat to flow
_____ 10. density	e. The ratio of the mass of a substance to its volume
	f. The temperature at which a substance changes from a solid to a liquid

© Pearson Education, Inc., publishing as Pearson Prentice Hall. All rights reserved.

Chapter 2   Properties of Matter

11. Which of the substances in the table below are gases at room temperature?

a. _____   b. _____   c. _____

Melting and Boiling Points of Some Substances		
Substance	Melting Point	Boiling Point
Hydrogen	−259.3°C	−252.9°C
Nitrogen	−210.0°C	−195.8°C
Ammonia	−77.7°C	−33.3°C
Octane (found in gasoline)	−56.8°C	125.6°C
Water	0.0°C	100.0°C
Acetic acid (found in vinegar)	16.6°C	117.9°C

Using Physical Properties (page 48)

12. Describe three steps that can be used to identify a material. _____

_____

_____

13. Is the following sentence true or false? Usually, people consider only one property when choosing a material. _____

Using Properties to Separate Mixtures (page 50)

14. Two processes that are commonly used to separate mixtures are _____ and _____.

15. Explain how filtration separates materials based on the size of their particles.

_____

_____

16. Explain why distillation works for converting seawater into fresh water.

_____

_____

_____

Recognizing Physical Changes (page 51)

17. Is the following sentence true or false? In a physical change, some of the substances in a material change, but the properties of the material stay the same. _____

18. Explain why the boiling of water is a physical change. _____

19. Circle the letter for each process that is a reversible physical change.

a. wrinkling a shirt   b. freezing water

c. cutting hair   d. peeling an orange

© Pearson Education, Inc., publishing as Pearson Prentice Hall. All rights reserved.

Chapter 2   Properties of Matter

Section 2.3 Chemical Properties
(pages 54–58)

This section discusses chemical properties and describes clues that may show that a chemical change has taken place.

Reading Strategy (page 54)

Relating Text and Visuals As you read, complete the table by finding examples of the clues for recognizing chemical changes in Figures 19 and 20. For more information on this Reading Strategy, see the **Reading and Study Skills** in the **Skills and Reference Handbook** at the end of your textbook.

Recognizing Chemical Changes	
Clue	**Example**
Change in color	
Production of gas	
Formation of precipitate	

Observing Chemical Properties (pages 54–55)

1. Is the following sentence true or false? The substances in paraffin do not change when a candle burns. _____

2. Circle the letters of the compounds formed when a candle burns.

   a. paraffin

   b. hydrogen

   c. water

   d. carbon

3. What is a chemical property? _____

   _____

4. Is the following sentence true or false? Flammability is a material's ability to burn in the presence of carbon dioxide. _____

5. The property that describes how readily a substance combines chemically with other substances is _____.

6. Circle the letter of each property that is a chemical property.

   a. hardness   b. density

   c. flammability   d. reactivity

7. Is the following sentence true or false? Nitrogen is a more reactive element than oxygen. _____

© Pearson Education, Inc., publishing as Pearson Prentice Hall. All rights reserved.

Chapter 2   Properties of Matter

8. Why isn't iron used to make coins? _____

_____

9. What is the benefit of pumping nitrogen gas into seawater that is stored in steel tanks? _____

_____

_____

Recognizing Chemical Changes (pages 56–57)

10. A(n) _____ change occurs when a substance reacts and forms one or more new substances.

11. What are three examples of chemical changes?

a. _____   b. _____

c. _____

12. Circle the letters of examples of evidence for a chemical change.

a. a change in color

b. a filter trapping particles

c. the production of a gas

d. the formation of a solid precipitate

Match each example to evidence of a chemical change.

Example	Chemical Change
_____ **13.** Lemon juice is added to milk.	a. the production of a gas
_____ **14.** A silver bracelet darkens when exposed to air.	b. the formation of a precipitate
_____ **15.** Vinegar is mixed with baking soda.	c. a change in color

Is a Change Chemical or Physical? (page 58)

16. Is the following sentence true or false? When iron is heated until it turns red, the color change shows that a chemical change has taken place. _____

17. When matter undergoes a chemical change, the composition of the matter _____.

18. When matter undergoes a physical change, the composition of the matter _____.

19. Complete the following table about chemical changes.

Chemical Changes		
Type of Change	Are New Substances Formed?	Example
Chemical		
Physical		

© Pearson Education, Inc., publishing as Pearson Prentice Hall. All rights reserved.

Chapter 2   Properties of Matter

WordWise

Answer the questions by writing the correct vocabulary term in the blanks. Use the circled letter in each term to find the hidden vocabulary word. Then, write a definition for the hidden word.

Clues	Vocabulary Terms
A mixture that results when substances dissolve to form a homogeneous mixture	Ⓞ _ _ _ _ _ _ _
A substance that can be broken down into two or more simpler substances	_ _ _ _ Ⓞ _ _
A change in which the composition of matter stays the same	_ _ Ⓞ _ _ _ _ _ _ _ _ _ _
A solid that forms and separates from a liquid mixture	_ _ _ _ Ⓞ _ _ _
A substance that cannot be broken down into simpler substances	Ⓞ _ _ _ _ _ _
The ability of a material for allowing heat to flow	_ _ Ⓞ _ _ _ _ _ _ _ _
A classification for matter that always has the same composition	_ _ _ _ Ⓞ _ _ _ _ _ _
The ability of a material to burn	_ _ _ _ _ _ _ _ Ⓞ _ _
A homogeneous mixture containing particles that scatter light	_ Ⓞ _ _ _ _ _
The temperature at which a substance changes from a liquid to gas	_ _ _ _ _ _ _ _ _ Ⓞ _

Hidden Term: _ _ _ _ _ _ _ _ _ _ _

Definition: _____

_____

© Pearson Education, Inc., publishing as Pearson Prentice Hall. All rights reserved.

Chapter 2   Properties of Matter

Melting and Boiling Points

Math Skill:
Data Tables

You may want to read more about this **Math Skill** in the **Skills and Reference Handbook** at the end of your textbook.

Melting and Boiling Points of Some Substances		
Substance	Melting Point	Boiling Point
Hydrogen	−259.3°C	−252.9°C
Nitrogen	−210.0°C	−195.8°C
Water	0.0°C	100.0°C
Acetic acid (found in vinegar)	16.6°C	117.9°C
Table salt	800.7°C	1465°C

Which of the substances in the table above are solids at a temperature of −40°C?

1. Read and Understand

What information are you given?

Temperature = −40°C

The melting and boiling points of five substances are listed in the table.

2. Plan and Solve

What unknown are you trying to find?

Which of the five substances are solids at −40°C?

What guideline can you use?

Any substance that is a solid at −40°C must have a melting point greater than −40°C.

Check the melting point of each substance in the table to find out whether it satisfies the guideline.

Water, acetic acid, and table salt are solids at −40°C.

3. Look Back and Check

Is your answer reasonable?

Because water, acetic acid, and table salt have melting points equal to or greater than 0°C, they will all be solids at a temperature well below 0°C.

Math Practice

On a separate sheet of paper, solve the following problems.

1. Which substance in the table is a liquid at 105°C? _____

2. Which substance in the table has a melting point closest to room temperature (20°C)? _____

3. Which substance in the table boils at the lowest temperature? _____

4. Which substance has the smallest temperature range as a liquid, hydrogen or nitrogen? _____

© Pearson Education, Inc., publishing as Pearson Prentice Hall. All rights reserved.

Chapter 3   States of Matter

Summary

3.1 Solids, Liquids, and Gases

Materials can be classified as solids, liquids, or gases, based on whether their shapes and volumes are definite or variable.

Solid is the state of matter in which materials have a definite shape and a definite volume. The term *definite* means that the shape and volume of a material do not easily change. Almost all solids have some type of orderly arrangement of particles at the atomic level.

Liquid is the state of matter in which a material has a definite volume but not a definite shape. A liquid always has the same shape as its container and can be poured from one container to another.

Gas is a state of matter in which a material has neither a definite shape nor a definite volume. A gas takes the shape and volume of its container.

On Earth, almost all matter exists in a solid, liquid, or gaseous state. But ninety-nine percent of all the matter in the universe exists in a state that is not common on Earth. At extremely high temperatures, matter exists as plasma. At extremely low temperatures, matter exists as a fifth state of matter called a Bose-Einstein condensate (BEC).

Kinetic energy is the energy an object has due to its motion. The faster an object moves, the greater its kinetic energy. The kinetic theory of matter says that all particles of matter are in constant motion.

The particles in a gas are never at rest. There are forces of attraction among the particles in all matter. In a gas, the attractions are too weak to have an effect. The constant motion of particles in a gas allows a gas to fill a container of any shape or size. The kinetic theory as applied to gases has three main points:

- Particles in a gas are in constant, random motion.

- The motion of one particle is unaffected by the motion of other particles unless the particles collide.
- Forces of attraction among particles in a gas can be ignored under ordinary conditions.

The particles in liquids also have kinetic energy. In a liquid, there is a kind of tug of war between the constant motion of particles and the attractions among particles. A liquid takes the shape of its container because particles in a liquid can flow to new locations. The volume of a liquid is constant because forces of attraction keep the particles close together.

Solids have a definite volume and shape because particles in a solid vibrate around fixed locations.

3.2 Gas Laws

Pressure is the result of a force distributed over an area. The SI unit of pressure is derived from SI units of force and area. When a force in newtons (N) is divided by an area in square meters (m^2), the unit of pressure is newtons per square meter (N/m^2). The SI unit for pressure, the pascal (Pa), is shorthand for newtons per square meter. One kilopascal (kPa) is equal to 1000 pascals.

Collisions between particles of a gas and the walls of the container cause the pressure in a closed container of gas. The more frequent the collisions, the greater the pressure of the gas is.

Factors that affect the pressure of an enclosed gas are its temperature, its volume, and the number of its particles.

- Raising the temperature of a gas will increase its pressure if the volume of the gas and the number of particles are constant, or the same.

© Pearson Education, Inc., publishing as Pearson Prentice Hall. All rights reserved.

Chapter 3   States of Matter

- Reducing the volume of a gas increases its pressure if the temperature of the gas and the number of particles are constant.
- Increasing the number of particles will increase the pressure of a gas if the temperature and the volume are constant.

Charles's law states that the volume of a gas is directly proportional to its temperature in kelvins if the pressure and the number of particles of the gas are constant. Charles's law can be expressed mathematically with T_1 and V_1 representing the temperature and volume of a gas before a change occurs. T_2 and V_2 represent the temperature and volume after a change occurs.

$$\frac{V_1}{T_1} = \frac{V_2}{T_2}$$

The temperatures must be expressed in kelvins.

Boyle's law states that the volume of a gas is inversely proportional to its pressure if the temperature and the number of particles are constant. Boyle's law can be expressed as follows:

$$P_1V_1 = P_2V_2$$

P_1 and V_1 represent the pressure and volume of a gas before a change occurs. P_2 and V_2 represent the pressure and volume of a gas after a change occurs.

Boyle's law and Charles's law can be combined into a single gas law that describes the relationship among the temperature, volume, and pressure of a gas when the number of particles is constant.

3.3 Phase Changes

When at least two states of the same substance are present, scientists describe each different state as a phase. A phase change is the reversible physical change that occurs when a substance changes from one state of matter to another.

Melting, freezing, vaporization, condensation, sublimation, and deposition are six common phase changes.

One way to recognize a phase change is by measuring the temperature of a substance as it is heated or cooled. The temperature of a substance does not change during a phase change.

During a phase change, energy is transferred between a substance and its surroundings. During an endothermic change (for example, melting), the system absorbs energy from its surroundings. During an exothermic change (for example, freezing), the system releases energy to its surroundings.

The arrangement of molecules in water becomes less orderly as water melts and more orderly as water freezes.

The phase change in which a substance changes from a liquid into a gas is vaporization. Vaporization is an endothermic process. Scientists note the difference between two vaporization processes—boiling and evaporation. Evaporation takes place at the surface of a liquid and occurs at temperatures below the boiling point. Evaporation is the process that changes a substance from a liquid to a gas at temperatures below the substance's boiling point. The greater the surface area of a container of water, the faster the water evaporates.

Condensation is the phase change in which a substance changes from a gas or vapor to a liquid. Condensation is an exothermic change.

Sublimation is the phase change in which a substance changes from a solid to a gas or vapor without changing to a liquid first. Sublimation is an endothermic change.

Deposition is the phase change in which a gas or vapor changes directly into a solid without first changing to a liquid. Deposition is an exothermic change and is the reverse of sublimation.

© Pearson Education, Inc., publishing as Pearson Prentice Hall. All rights reserved.

Chapter 3   States of Matter

Section 3.1 Solids, Liquids, and Gases
(pages 68–73)

This section explains how materials are classified as solids, liquids, or gases.
It also describes the behavior of these three states of matter.

Reading Strategy (page 68)

Comparing and Contrasting As you read about the states of matter,
replace each letter in the diagram below with one of these phrases:
definite volume, definite shape, variable volume, or *variable shape.* For more
information on this Reading Strategy, see the **Reading and Study Skills**
in the **Skills and Reference Handbook** at the end of your textbook.

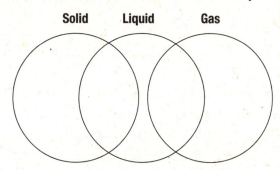

Describing the States of Matter (pages 68–70)

1. What are three common states of matter?

   a. _____ b. _____ c. _____

2. Is the following sentence true or false? The fact that a copper wire
   can be bent shows that some solids do not have a definite shape.

   _____

3. Circle the letter of each phrase that describes how particles at the
   atomic level are arranged within most solids.

   a. randomly arranged   b. packed close together

   c. arranged in a regular pattern   d. spaced far apart

4. Is the following sentence true or false? A liquid takes the shape of its
   container. _____

5. What is the state of matter in which a material has neither a definite
   shape nor a definite volume? _____

6. Compare and contrast the arrangement of particles at the atomic level for a liquid
   and a solid. _____

   _____

7. What determines the shape and volume of a gas? _____

   _____

8. On the sun, where temperatures are extremely high, matter exists in a state known
   as _____.

© Pearson Education, Inc., publishing as Pearson Prentice Hall. All rights reserved.

Name _____ Class _____ Date _____

9. The state of matter that can exist at extremely _____ temperatures is called a Bose-Einstein condensate.

10. Complete the table about states of matter.

States of Matter		
State	**Shape**	**Volume**
	Definite	
Liquid		
		Not definite

Kinetic Theory (page 71)

11. Describe kinetic energy. _____

_____

12. Circle the letter of the phrase that describes all particles of matter in the kinetic theory of matter.

   a. randomly arranged   b. constant temperature

   c. in constant motion   d. orderly arrangement

Explaining the Behavior of Gases (pages 72–73)

13. Is the following sentence true or false? There are forces of attraction among the particles in all matter. _____

14. Why can scientists ignore the forces of attraction among particles in a gas under ordinary conditions? _____

_____

_____

15. Is the following sentence true or false? Because of the constant motion of the particles in a gas, the gas has a definite shape and volume. _____

Explaining the Behavior of Liquids (page 73)

16. Do forces of attraction have a stronger effect on the behavior of the particles in a gas or in a liquid? _____

17. Circle the letter of each factor that affects the behavior of liquids.

   a. fixed location of particles

   b. constant motion of particles

   c. orderly arrangement of particles

   d. forces of attraction among particles

Explaining the Behavior of Solids (page 74)

18. Solids have a(n) _____ volume and shape because particles in a solid vibrate in _____ locations.

© Pearson Education, Inc., publishing as Pearson Prentice Hall. All rights reserved.

Chapter 3   States of Matter

Section 3.2 The Gas Laws
(pages 75–81)

This section discusses gas pressure and the factors that affect it. It also explains the relationships between the temperature, volume, and pressure of a gas.

Reading Strategy (page 75)

Identifying Cause and Effect As you read, identify the variables that affect gas pressure, and write them in the diagram below. For more information on this Reading Strategy, see the **Reading and Study Skills** in the **Skills and Reference Handbook** at the end of your textbook.

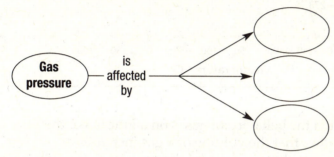

Pressure (pages 75–76)

1. What is pressure? _____

2. Circle the letter of each unit used to express amounts of pressure.

   a. newton   b. joule

   c. pascal   d. kilopascal

3. What causes the pressure in a closed container of gas? _____

_____

Factors that Affect Gas Pressure (pages 76–77)

4. Name the factors that affect the pressure of an enclosed gas.

   a. _____ b. _____ c. _____

5. Is the following sentence true or false? In a closed container, increasing the temperature of a gas will decrease the force with which particles hit the walls of the container. _____

6. What effect does raising the temperature of a gas have on its pressure, if the volume of the gas and the number of its particles are kept constant? _____

7. How does reducing the volume of a gas affect its pressure if the temperature of the gas and the number of particles are constant?

_____

_____

8. Increasing the number of particles of a gas will _____ its pressure if the temperature and the volume are constant.

© Pearson Education, Inc., publishing as Pearson Prentice Hall. All rights reserved.

Chapter 3   States of Matter

Charles's Law (page 78)

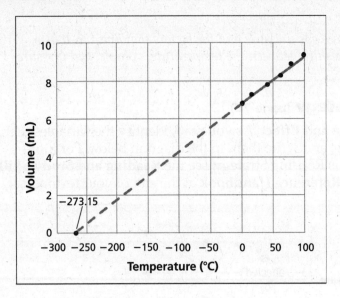

9. Jacques Charles recorded the behavior of gases on a graph like the one above. The data shows that the volume of a gas increases at the same rate as the _____ of the gas.

10. A temperature equal to 0 K on the Kelvin temperature scale is known as _____.

11. What does Charles's law state? _____

_____

Boyle's Law (page 79)

12. If the temperature and number of particles of gas in a cylinder do not change, and the volume of the cylinder is reduced by half, the pressure of the gas will be _____ as the original pressure.

13. Boyle's law states that there is an inverse relationship between the pressure and volume of a gas. Circle the letter of the correct expression of this relationship.

    a. $P_1V_1 = P_2V_2$

    b. $P_1V_2 = P_2V_1$

    c. $\dfrac{P_1}{V_1} = \dfrac{P_2}{V_2}$

    d. $P_1P_2 = V_1V_2$

The Combined Gas Law (pages 80–81)

14. Circle the letters of the factors that are included in the expression of the combined gas law.

    a. temperature   b. number of particles

    c. volume   d. pressure

© Pearson Education, Inc., publishing as Pearson Prentice Hall. All rights reserved.

Chapter 3   States of Matter

Section 3.3 Phase Changes
(pages 84–91)

This section explains what happens when a substance changes from one state of matter to another and describes six phase changes.

Reading Strategy (page 84)

Summarizing As you read, complete the description of energy flow during phase changes in the diagram below. For more information on this Reading Strategy, see the **Reading and Study Skills** in the **Skills and Reference Handbook** at the end of your textbook.

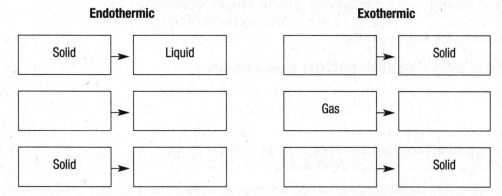

Characteristics of Phase Changes (pages 84–86)

1. What is a phase change? _____

_____

Match each term with the letter of the phase-change description that best describes it.

Term	**Phase-Change**
_____ **2.** freezing	a. Solid to gas
_____ **3.** sublimation	b. Liquid to gas
_____ **4.** condensation	c. Gas to solid
_____ **5.** melting	d. Liquid to solid
_____ **6.** deposition	e. Gas to liquid
_____ **7.** vaporization	f. Solid to liquid

8. What happens to the temperature of a substance during a phase change? _____

9. Is the following sentence true or false? The temperature at which a substance freezes is lower than the temperature at which it melts. _____

10. Circle the letter that describes the behavior of a substance during a phase change.

   a. neither absorbs nor releases energy   b. always absorbs energy

   c. always releases energy   d. either absorbs or releases energy

© Pearson Education, Inc., publishing as Pearson Prentice Hall. All rights reserved.

Chapter 3   States of Matter

11. A substance absorbs energy from its surroundings during a(n)
    _____ change.

12. The energy absorbed by one gram of ice as it melts is known as the
    _____ for water.

13. As water freezes, it releases heat to its surroundings. Freezing is an
    example of a(n) _____ change.

Melting and Freezing (page 88)

14. Is the following sentence true or false? Water molecules have a more
    orderly arrangement in ice than in liquid water. _____

15. When liquid water freezes, the average kinetic energy of its
    molecules _____, and the arrangement of the
    molecules becomes more orderly.

Vaporization and Condensation (pages 88–90)

16. Vaporization is the phase change in which a substance changes
    from a(n) _____ into a(n) _____.

17. The energy absorbed by one gram of water as it changes
    from its liquid phase into water vapor is known as the
    _____ for water.

18. Is the following sentence true or false? When water vapor collects
    above the liquid in a closed container, the pressure caused by the
    collisions of this vapor and the walls of the container is called
    vapor pressure. _____

19. The phase change in which a substance changes from a gas into a
    liquid is called _____.

20. Compare and contrast the processes of evaporation and boiling by
    completing the table below.

Evaporation and Boiling			
Process	**Phase Change**	**Where It Occurs**	**Temperature**
Evaporation			
Boiling			

21. Is the following sentence true or false? A gas absorbs energy as it
    changes into a liquid. _____

Sublimation and Deposition (page 91)

22. Dry ice can change directly from a solid to a gas without forming a
    liquid first. This process is an example of _____.

23. What is deposition? _____
    _____

© Pearson Education, Inc., publishing as Pearson Prentice Hall. All rights reserved.

Chapter 3   States of Matter

WordWise

Answer the questions by writing the correct vocabulary term in the blanks.
Use the circled letter in each term to find the hidden vocabulary word. Then,
write a definition for the hidden word.

Clues

What is the process that changes a
substance from a liquid to a gas below
the substance's boiling point?

Which gas law states that the
volume of a gas is directly
proportional to its temperature?

What is the phase change in which a
substance changes directly from a gas
to a solid?

In what state does matter have
both a definite shape and a definite
volume?

What is the phase change in which
a substance changes from a gas to
a liquid?

What is the phase change in which
a substance changes directly from a
solid to a gas?

During what type of phase change
does a substance release energy to
its surroundings?

During what type of phase change
does a substance absorb energy from
its surroundings?

Vocabulary Terms

_ _ _ Ⓞ _ _ _ _ _ _ _ _

_ _ _ Ⓞ _ _ _ ' _ _ _ _ _

_ Ⓞ _ _ _ _ _ _ _ _

Ⓞ _ _ _ _

_ _ _ _ _ _ Ⓞ _ _ _ _ _

_ Ⓞ _ _ _ _ _ _ _ _ _

_ _ _ _ _ _ Ⓞ _ _ _

Ⓞ _ _ _ _ _ _ _ _ _ _

Hidden Term: _ _ _ _ _ _ _ _

Definition: _____

_____

© Pearson Education, Inc., publishing as Pearson Prentice Hall. All rights reserved.

Chapter 3   States of Matter

The Combined Gas Law

A gas in a cylinder has a pressure of 235 kPa at a volume of 5.00 L. The volume is reduced to 1.25 L. The temperature does not change. Find the new pressure of the gas.

Math Skill: Calculating with Significant Figures

You may want to read more about this **Math Skill** in the **Skills and Reference Handbook** at the end of your textbook.

1. Read and Understand

What information are you given?

$V_1 = 5.00$ L $V_2 = 1.25$ L $P_1 = 235$ kPa

2. Plan and Solve

What unknown are you trying to calculate? P_2

What expression can you use?

$$\frac{P_1 V_1}{T_1} = \frac{P_2 V_2}{T_2}$$

Cancel out the variable that does not change and rearrange the expression to solve for P_2.

$$P_1 V_1 = P_2 V_2 \qquad P_2 = \frac{P_1 V_1}{V_2}$$

Replace each variable with its known value.

$$P_2 = 235 \text{ kPa} \times \frac{5.00 \text{ L}}{1.25 \text{ L}} = 940 \text{ kPa}$$

3. Look Back and Check

Is your answer reasonable?

The volume of a gas is inversely proportional to its pressure if the temperature and number of particles are constant. The volume decreased by a factor of four, from 5.00 L to 1.25 L. The answer, 940 kPa, is four times the original pressure, 235 kPa.

Math Practice

On a separate sheet of paper, solve the following problems. The number of particles remains constant for all problems.

1. A gas has a pressure of 340 kPa at a volume of 3.20 L. What happens to the pressure when the volume is increased to 5.44 L? The temperature does not change.

2. A gas has a pressure of 180 kPa at a temperature of 300 K. At what temperature will the gas have a pressure of 276 kPa? The volume does not change.

3. At 47°C, a gas has a pressure of 140 kPa. The gas is cooled until the pressure decreases to 105 kPa. If the volume remains constant, what will the final temperature be in kelvins? In degrees Celsius?

© Pearson Education, Inc., publishing as Pearson Prentice Hall. All rights reserved.

Chapter 4   Atomic Structure

Summary

4.1 Studying Atoms

The ancient Greek philosopher Democritus believed that all matter consisted of extremely small particles that could not be divided. He called these particles atoms from the Greek word *atomos*, which means "uncut" or "indivisible." Aristotle did not think there was a limit to the number of times matter could be divided.

By the 1800s, scientists had enough data from experiments to support an atomic model of matter. The English scientist John Dalton developed a theory to explain why the elements in a compound always join in the same way. Dalton proposed that all matter is made up of individual particles called atoms, which cannot be divided. The main points of Dalton's theory are as follows.

- All elements are composed of atoms.
- All atoms of the same element have the same mass, and atoms of different elements have different masses.
- Compounds contain atoms of more than one element.
- In a particular compound, atoms of different elements always combine in the same way.

In the model of atoms based on Dalton's theory, the elements are pictured as solid spheres. Each type of atom is represented by a tiny, solid sphere with a different mass.

J. J. Thomson used an electric current to learn more about atoms. Before Thomson's experiments, the accepted model of atoms was a solid ball of matter that could not be divided into smaller parts. Thomson's experiments provided the first evidence that atoms are made of even smaller particles. In Thomson's model of the atom, negative charges were evenly scattered throughout an atom filled with a positively charged mass of matter.

In 1899, Ernest Rutherford discovered that uranium gives off fast-moving particles that have a positive charge. He named them alpha particles. From the results of experiments conducted by Rutherford's student, Ernest Marsden, Rutherford concluded that the positive charge of an atom is not evenly spread throughout the atom. It is concentrated in a very small, central area that Rutherford called the nucleus. The nucleus is a dense, positively charged mass located in the center of the atom.

Rutherford proposed a new model of the atom. According to Rutherford's model, all of an atom's positive charge is concentrated in its nucleus.

4.2 The Structure of an Atom

Protons, electrons, and neutrons are subatomic particles.

- A proton is a positively charged subatomic particle that is found in the nucleus of an atom. Each proton is assigned a charge of 1+.
- An electron is a negatively charged subatomic particle that is found in the space outside the nucleus. Each electron has a charge of 1−.
- A neutron is a neutral subatomic particle that is found in the nucleus of an atom.

Protons, electrons, and neutrons can be distinguished by mass, charge, and location in an atom. Protons and neutrons have almost the same mass. The mass of about 2000 electrons would equal the mass of a proton. Electrons have a charge that is equal in size to the charge of a proton, but the charges of electrons and protons are opposite.

© Pearson Education, Inc., publishing as Pearson Prentice Hall. All rights reserved.

Chapter 4   Atomic Structure

The atoms of any given element always have the same number of protons. The atomic number of an element equals the number of protons in an atom of that element. Atoms of different elements have different numbers of protons. Each positive charge in an atom is balanced by a negative charge because atoms are neutral. So the atomic number of an element also equals the number of electrons in an atom.

The mass number of an atom is the sum of the protons and neutrons in its nucleus. Therefore, the number of neutrons in an atom equals the mass number minus the atomic number.

Isotopes are atoms of the same element that have different numbers of neutrons and different mass numbers. Isotopes of an element have the same atomic number but different mass numbers because they have different numbers of neutrons.

For example, every atom of oxygen has 8 protons. Some oxygen atoms have 8 neutrons and a mass number of 16. Some oxygen atoms have 9 neutrons and a mass number of 17. To distinguish one isotope from another, the isotopes are referred to by the mass number. The two oxygen isotopes, then, are referred to as oxygen-16 and oxygen-17.

With most elements, it is hard to notice any differences in the physical or chemical properties of their isotopes. Hydrogen is an exception.

4.3 Modern Atomic Theory

Niels Bohr, a Danish physicist, developed a model of the atom that focused on the electrons. A description of the arrangement of electrons in an atom is the centerpiece of the modern atomic model. In Bohr's model, electrons move with constant speed in fixed orbits around the nucleus, as planets move in fixed orbits around the sun.

Each electron in an atom has a certain amount of energy. The possible energies that electrons in an atom can have are called energy levels. An electron can move from one energy level to another when the atom gains or loses energy.

An electron can move up energy levels if it gains the right amount of energy. On the other hand, an electron can move down energy levels if it loses the right amount of energy. The size of the jump between energy levels determines the amount of energy gained or lost.

Scientists improved Bohr's model as new discoveries were made. Today, scientists know that electrons do not move like planets around the sun. An electron cloud is a visual model of the most likely locations for electrons in an atom. The cloud is denser where the chances of finding an electron are high. Scientists use the electron cloud model to describe the possible locations of electrons around the nucleus.

The electron cloud represents all the orbitals in an atom. An orbital is a region of space around the nucleus where an electron is likely to be found. An electron cloud is a good description of how electrons behave in their orbitals. The level in which an electron has the least energy has only one orbital. Higher energy levels have more than one orbital. The maximum number of electrons in an energy level is twice the number of orbitals of that energy level. Each orbital can contain two electrons at most.

A configuration is an arrangement of objects in a given space. An electron configuration is the arrangement of electrons in the orbitals of an atom. The most stable electron configuration is the one in which the electrons are in orbitals with the lowest possible energies. When all the electrons in an atom have the lowest possible energies, the atom is said to be in its ground state.

© Pearson Education, Inc., publishing as Pearson Prentice Hall. All rights reserved.

Chapter 4   Atomic Structure

Section 4.1 Studying Atoms
(pages 100-105)

This section discusses the development of atomic models.

Reading Strategy (page 100)

Summarizing As you read, complete the table about atomic models. For more information on this Reading Strategy, see the **Reading and Study Skills** in the **Skills and Reference Handbook** at the end of your textbook.

Atomic Models		
Scientist	**Evidence**	**Model**
	Ratio of masses in compounds	
	Deflected beam	
Rutherford		Positive, dense nucleus

Ancient Greek Models of Atoms (page 100)

1. Democritus named the smallest particles of matter _____ because they could not be divided.

2. List the four elements that Aristotle included in his model of matter.

   a. _____   b. _____

   c. _____   d. _____

Dalton's Atomic Theory (page 101)

3. Is the following sentence true or false? John Dalton gathered evidence for the existence of atoms by measuring the masses of elements that reacted to form compounds. _____

4. What theory did Dalton propose to explain why the elements in a compound always join in the same way? _____

   _____

5. Circle the letters of the sentences that represent the main points of Dalton's theory of atoms.

   a. All elements are composed of atoms.

   b. In a particular compound, atoms of different elements always combine the same way.

   c. All atoms have the same mass.

   d. Compounds contain atoms of more than one element.

© Pearson Education, Inc., publishing as Pearson Prentice Hall. All rights reserved.

Chapter 4   Atomic Structure

Thomson's Model of the Atom (pages 102–103)

6. Objects with like electric charges _____, and objects with opposite electric charges _____.

7. What happened to the beam when Thomson placed a pair of charged metal plates on either side of the glass tube? _____

_____

8. Thomson concluded that the particles in the glowing beam had a(n) _____ charge because they were attracted to a positive plate.

9. Is the following sentence true or false? Thomson's experiments provided the first evidence for the existence of subatomic particles.
_____

10. Describe Thomson's model. _____

_____

Rutherford's Atomic Theory (pages 104–105)

11. What is an alpha particle? _____

_____

12. Fill in the table to show what Rutherford hypothesized would happen to the paths of alpha particles as they passed through a thin sheet of gold.

Rutherford's Hypothesis	
Most particles would travel _____ from their source to a screen that lit up when struck.	Particles that did not pass straight through would be _____ _____

13. Circle the letters of the sentences that describe what happened when Marsden directed a beam of particles at a piece of gold foil.

  a. Fewer alpha particles were deflected than expected.

  b. More alpha particles were deflected than expected.

  c. None of the alpha particles were deflected.

  d. Some alpha particles bounced back toward the source.

14. Circle the letter of the sentence that states what Rutherford concluded from the gold foil experiment.

  a. An atom's negative charge is concentrated in its nucleus.

  b. Thomson's model of the atom was correct.

  c. An atom's positive charge is concentrated in its nucleus.

  d. An atom's positive charge is spread evenly throughout the atom.

© Pearson Education, Inc., publishing as Pearson Prentice Hall. All rights reserved.

Chapter 4   Atomic Structure

Section 4.2 The Structure of an Atom
(pages 108–112)

This section compares the properties of three subatomic particles. It also discusses atomic numbers, mass numbers, and isotopes.

Reading Strategy (page 108)

Monitoring Your Understanding Before you read, list in the table shown what you know about atoms and what you would like to learn. After you read, list what you have learned. For more information on this Reading Strategy, see the **Reading and Study Skills** in the **Skills and Reference Handbook** at the end of your textbook.

What I Know About Atoms	What I Would Like to Learn	What I Have Learned

Properties of Subatomic Particles (pages 108–109)

1. What are three subatomic particles?
   a. _____ b. _____ c. _____

2. Circle the letter that identifies a subatomic particle with a positive charge.
   a. nucleus   b. proton
   c. neutron   d. electron

3. Why did Chadwick conclude that the particles produced by his experiment were neutral in charge? _____
   _____
   _____

Comparing Subatomic Particles (pages 109–110)

4. Circle the letters of properties that vary among subatomic particles.
   a. color   b. mass
   c. charge   d. location in the atom

5. Circle the letter of the expression that accurately compares the masses of neutrons and protons.
   a. mass of 1 neutron = mass of 1 proton
   b. mass of 2000 neutrons = mass of 1 proton
   c. mass of 1 electron = mass of 1 proton
   d. mass of 1 neutron = mass of 1 electron

© Pearson Education, Inc., publishing as Pearson Prentice Hall. All rights reserved.

Chapter 4   Atomic Structure

Atomic Number and Mass Number (page 110)

6. Is the following sentence true or false? Two atoms of the same element can have different numbers of protons. _____

7. What is an atomic number? _____

_____

_____

8. Circle the letters that identify quantities that are always equal to an element's atomic number.

   a. number of nuclei

   b. number of protons

   c. number of neutrons

   d. number of electrons

9. Is the following sentence true or false? Two different elements can have the same atomic number. _____

10. What is the mass number of an atom? _____

_____

_____

11. Complete the equation in the table below.

Number of neutrons = _____ − _____

Isotopes (page 112)

12. Every atom of a given element has the same number of _____ and _____.

13. Every atom of a given element does not have the same number of _____.

14. What are isotopes? _____

_____

_____

15. All oxygen atoms have 8 protons. Circle the letter of the number of neutrons in an atom of oxygen-18.

   a. 8   b. 9

   c. 10   d. 18

16. Is the following sentence true or false? Isotopes of oxygen have different chemical properties. _____

17. Water that contains hydrogen-2 atoms instead of hydrogen-1 atoms is called _____.

© Pearson Education, Inc., publishing as Pearson Prentice Hall. All rights reserved.

Chapter 4   Atomic Structure

Section 4.3 Modern Atomic Theory
(pages 113–118)

This section focuses on the arrangement and behavior of electrons in atoms.

Reading Strategy (page 113)

Sequencing After you read, complete the description in the flow chart below of how the gain or loss of energy affects electrons in atoms. For more information on this Reading Strategy, see the **Reading and Study Skills** in the **Skills and Reference Handbook** at the end of your textbook.

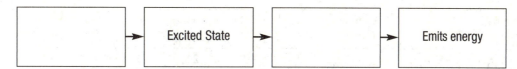

Bohr's Model of the Atom (pages 113–116)

1. Circle the letter of the sentence that tells how Bohr's model of the atom differed from Rutherford's model.

   a. Bohr's model focused on the nucleus.

   b. Bohr's model focused on the protons.

   c. Bohr's model focused on the neutrons.

   d. Bohr's model focused on the electrons.

2. Is the following sentence true or false? In Bohr's model of the atom, electrons have a constant speed and move in fixed orbits around the nucleus. _____

3. What can happen to an electron in an atom when the atom gains or loses energy? _____

   _____

4. What evidence do scientists have that electrons can move from one energy level to another? _____

   _____

5. Is the following sentence true or false? When electrons release energy, some of the energy may be released as visible light.

   _____

Electron Cloud Model (page 116)

6. Is the following sentence true or false? Bohr's model was correct in assigning energy levels to electrons. _____

7. When trying to predict the locations and motions of electrons in atoms, scientists must work with _____.

8. What is an electron cloud? _____

   _____

© Pearson Education, Inc., publishing as Pearson Prentice Hall. All rights reserved.

Chapter 4   Atomic Structure

9. Is the following sentence true or false? Scientists use the electron cloud model to describe the exact location of electrons around the nucleus. _____

Atomic Orbitals (page 117)

10. Is the following sentence true or false? An orbital is a region of space around the nucleus where an electron is likely to be found. _____

11. An electron model is a good approximation of _____ .

Use this table to answer questions 12 and 13.

Energy Level	Number of Orbitals	Maximum Number of Electrons
1	1	2
2	4	8
3	9	18
4	16	32

12. Higher energy levels have _____ orbitals than lower energy levels do.

13. What is the relationship between the number of orbitals and the maximum number of electrons in an energy level? _____

_____

Electron Configurations (page 118)

14. What is an electron configuration? _____

_____

15. Circle the letter of the number of energy levels needed for a lithium atom's three electrons when the atom is in its ground state.

   a. zero   b. one

   c. two   d. three

16. Is the following sentence true or false? An excited state is less stable than a ground state. _____

17. Circle the letters of each sentence that is true when all of the electrons in an atom are in orbitals with the lowest possible energies.

   a. The electrons are in the most stable configuration.

   b. The electrons are in an unstable configuration.

   c. The atom is in an excited state.

   d. The atom is in its ground state.

© Pearson Education, Inc., publishing as Pearson Prentice Hall. All rights reserved.

Chapter 4   Atomic Structure

WordWise

Solve the clues to determine which vocabulary terms from Chapter 4 are hidden in the puzzle. Then find and circle the terms in the puzzle. The terms may occur vertically, horizontally, or diagonally.

```
e  m  a  s  s  n  u  m  b  e  r  u  n
n  l  o  r  b  i  t  a  l  x  a  p  i
r  e  e  n  l  t  p  t  s  p  b  k  s
g  n  a  c  a  s  r  d  c  r  h  l  o
b  e  l  d  t  g  o  f  l  s  g  a  t
l  r  t  s  o  r  t  g  r  n  b  t  o
n  g  z  b  m  o  o  p  l  q  d  c  p
p  y  q  p  i  u  n  n  m  a  s  s  e
s  l  n  m  c  n  n  u  c  l  e  u  s
t  e  u  e  n  d  r  i  o  l  k  m  r
r  v  c  l  u  s  v  a  b  t  o  p  k
z  e  l  x  m  t  w  e  s  r  n  u  e
p  l  e  m  b  a  r  l  e  t  a  b  d
b  s  a  q  e  t  z  o  c  m  r  n  k
r  t  s  i  r  e  h  j  n  s  f  l  t
```

Clues   **Hidden Words**

Dense, positively charged mass in the center of an atom   _____

Positively charged subatomic particle found in the nucleus   _____

Neutral subatomic particle found in the nucleus   _____

Number of protons in an atom of an element   _____

Sum of the protons and neutrons in the nucleus of an atom   _____

Atoms of the same element having different numbers of neutrons _____

Possible energies that electrons in an atom can have   _____

Visual model of the most likely locations for electrons in an atom _____

Region of space where an electron is likely to be found   _____

Term for an atom whose electrons have the lowest possible energies _____

© Pearson Education, Inc., publishing as Pearson Prentice Hall. All rights reserved.

Chapter 4   Atomic Structure

Electrons and Orbitals

Use the table on page 117 of your textbook to find the
ratio of the maximum number of electrons to the number
of orbitals for each of four energy levels.

Math Skill:
Ratios and Proportions

You may want to read
more about this **Math
Skill** in the **Skills and
Reference Handbook**
at the end of your
textbook.

1. Read and Understand

What information are you given?
   The number of orbitals and the maximum number
   of electrons per energy level

2. Plan and Solve

What unknown are you trying to calculate?
   The ratio of the maximum number of electrons to
   the number of orbitals in energy levels 1 through 4

*What mathematical expression can you use to calculate
the unknown?*

$$\frac{\text{maximum number of electrons}}{\text{number of orbitals}}$$

Level 1: $\frac{2}{1} = \frac{2}{1}$ Level 3: $\frac{18}{9} = \frac{2}{1}$

Level 2: $\frac{4}{2} = \frac{2}{1}$ Level 4: $\frac{32}{16} = \frac{2}{1}$

3. Look Back and Check

Is your answer reasonable?
   The ratio is the same for all four energy levels. Also, each
   orbital can contain only two electrons.

Math Practice

On a separate sheet of paper, solve the following problems.

1. Calculate the maximum number of electrons for energy levels
   5 and 6. Energy level 5 contains 25 orbitals; energy level 6
   contains 36 orbitals.

2. Energy level 7 can contain a maximum of 98 electrons. How many
   orbitals are there in energy level 7?

3. A sodium atom has 11 electrons. How many orbitals in a sodium
   atom contain electrons?

© Pearson Education, Inc., publishing as Pearson Prentice Hall. All rights reserved.

Chapter 5   The Periodic Table

Summary

5.1 Organizing the Elements

An organized table of the elements is one of the most useful tools in chemistry. The placement of elements on the table shows the link between the atomic structure of elements and their properties.

In the 1860s, a Russian chemist named Dmitri Mendeleev discovered a strategy for organizing all the elements known at that time. Mendeleev arranged the elements into rows in order of increasing mass. This arrangement put elements with similar properties in the same column. Within a column, the masses of elements increased from top to bottom.

Mendeleev's chart was an example of a periodic table. A periodic table is an arrangement of elements in columns, based on a set of properties that repeat from row to row.

When Mendeleev made his table, many elements had not yet been discovered. He had to leave spaces in his table for those elements. Mendeleev inferred that the empty spaces in his table would be filled by new elements. He used the properties of elements located near the blank spaces in his table to predict properties for undiscovered elements. Some scientists used the predictions to help in their search for undiscovered elements.

As new elements were discovered, their properties were remarkably similar to the properties that Mendeleev had predicted the elements would have. The close match between Mendeleev's predictions and the actual properties of new elements showed how useful his periodic table could be.

5.2 The Modern Periodic Table

In the modern periodic table, elements are arranged by increasing atomic number (number of protons). Each row in the periodic table is called a period. The number of elements per period varies because the number of available orbitals increases from energy level to energy level.

Each column on the periodic table is called a group. The elements within each group have similar properties. Properties of elements repeat in a predictable way when atomic numbers are used to arrange elements into groups. The elements in a group have similar electron configurations. Therefore, members of a group in the periodic table have similar chemical properties. This pattern of repeating properties displayed by elements on the periodic table is called the periodic law.

There are four pieces of information for each element on the periodic table:

- name
- symbol
- atomic number
- atomic mass

The atomic mass is a value that depends on two factors—how common an element's isotopes are in nature and the masses of those isotopes.

In order to compare the masses of atoms, scientists chose one isotope to serve as a standard. Scientists assigned 12 atomic mass units to the carbon-12 atom, which has 6 protons and 6 neutrons. An atomic mass unit (amu) is defined as one twelfth the mass of a carbon-12 atom. On the periodic table, the atomic mass of an element is given in atomic mass units.

© Pearson Education, Inc., publishing as Pearson Prentice Hall. All rights reserved.

Chapter 5   The Periodic Table

The periodic table presents three different ways to classify elements:

- Elements are classified as solids, liquids, or gases, based on their states at room temperature. The symbols for solids are black, for liquids are purple, and for gases are red.
- Elements are divided into those that occur naturally and those that do not. The symbols for elements that do not occur naturally are white.
- Elements are classified as metals, nonmetals, and metalloids. Metals are located on the left, nonmetals are on the right, and metalloids are in between.

Metals are elements that are good conductors of electric current and heat. Except for mercury, metals are solid at room temperature. Most metals are malleable. Many metals are ductile—they can be drawn into thin wires.

The metals in groups 3 through 12 are called transition metals. Transition metals form a bridge between the elements on the left and right sides of the table. One property of many transition metals is their ability to form compounds with distinctive colors.

Nonmetals are elements that are poor conductors of heat and electric current. Many nonmetals are gases at room temperature. All the gases on the periodic table are nonmetals.

Metalloids are elements with properties that fall between those of metals and nonmetals. For example, a metalloid's ability to conduct electric current varies with temperature.

Across a period from left to right, elements become less metallic and more nonmetallic in their properties.

5.3 Representative Groups

A valence electron is an electron that is in the highest occupied energy level of an atom. These electrons play a key role in chemical reactions. Elements in a group have similar properties because they have the same number of valence electrons.

The elements in Group 1A are called alkali metals. The alkali metals include lithium, sodium, potassium, rubidium, cesium, and francium. These metals have a single valence electron, and they are extremely reactive. Because they are so reactive, alkali metals are found in nature only in compounds. Not all the elements in a group are equally reactive. The reactivity of alkali metals increases from the top of Group 1A to the bottom.

The elements in Group 2A are called alkaline earth metals. The alkaline earth metals include beryllium, magnesium, calcium, strontium, barium, and radium. All alkaline earth metals have two valence electrons. Metals in Group 2A are harder than metals in Group 1A. Differences in reactivity among the alkaline earth metals are shown by the ways they react with water. Calcium, strontium, and barium react easily with cold water. Magnesium will react with hot water. No change appears to occur when beryllium is added to water.

Group 3A contains the metalloid boron, the well-known metal aluminum, and three less familiar metals (gallium, indium, and thallium). All these elements have three valence electrons. Aluminum is the most abundant metal in Earth's crust. It is often found combined with oxygen in a mineral called bauxite.

Group 4A contains a nonmetal (carbon), two metalloids (silicon and germanium), and two metals (tin and lead). Each of these elements has four valence electrons. Life on Earth would not exist without carbon. Except for water, most of the compounds in your body contain carbon. Silicon is the second most abundant element in Earth's crust.

© Pearson Education, Inc., publishing as Pearson Prentice Hall. All rights reserved.

Chapter 5   The Periodic Table

Group 5A contains two nonmetals (nitrogen and phosphorus), two metalloids (arsenic and antimony), and one metal (bismuth). Group 5A includes elements with a wide range of physical properties. Despite their differences, all the elements in Group 5A have five valence electrons. Nitrogen is used to produce fertilizers. Besides nitrogen, fertilizers often contain phosphorus.

Group 6A has three nonmetals (oxygen, sulfur, and selenium), and two metalloids (tellurium and polonium). All the elements in Group 6A have six valence electrons. Oxygen is the most abundant element in Earth's crust.

The elements in Group 7A are called halogens. The halogens include four nonmetals (fluorine, chlorine, bromine, and iodine) and one metalloid (astatine). Each halogen has seven valence electrons. Fluorine and chlorine are gases, bromine is a liquid, and iodine and astatine are solids. Despite their physical differences, the halogens have similar chemical properties.

The elements in Group 8A are called noble gases. The noble gases include helium, neon, argon, krypton, xenon, and radon. Helium has two valence electrons. Each of the other noble gases has eight valence electrons. The noble gases are colorless and odorless and extremely unreactive.

© Pearson Education, Inc., publishing as Pearson Prentice Hall. All rights reserved.

Chapter 5   The Periodic Table

Section 5.1 Organizing the Elements
(pages 126–129)

This section explains how Mendeleev organized elements into a periodic table. It also discusses the predictions he made about undiscovered elements and how the discovery of those elements supported his version of the table of the table.

Reading Strategy (page 126)

Identifying Main Ideas As you read, complete the table by identifying the main idea for each topic. For more information on this reading strategy, see the **Reading and Study Skills** in the **Skills and Reference Handbook** at the end of your textbook.

Topic	Main Idea
Mendeleev's proposal	
Mendeleev's prediction	
Evidence supporting Mendeleev's table	

The Search for Order (page 126)

1. Is the following sentence true or false? The first elements to be identified were mainly gases. _____

2. As the number of known elements grew, so did the need to organize them into groups based on their _____.

3. Circle the letter of each category that the French chemist Antoine Lavoisier used to classify elements.

    a. gases   b. metals

    c. liquids   d. nonmetals

Mendeleev's Periodic Table (pages 127–129)

4. Is the following sentence true or false? Mendeleev needed to organize information about 63 elements. _____

5. Mendeleev's strategy for classifying elements was modeled on a(n) _____.

6. Circle the letter of each type of information Mendeleev knew about each element.

    a. name

    b. number of protons

    c. relative mass

    d. properties

© Pearson Education, Inc., publishing as Pearson Prentice Hall. All rights reserved.

Chapter 5   The Periodic Table

7. Mendeleev arranged the elements into rows in order of
_____ so that elements with similar properties
were in the same column.

8. Is the following sentence true or false? A periodic table is an
arrangement of elements in columns, based on a set of properties
that repeat from row to row. _____

Group I	Group II	Group III	Group IV	Group V	Group VI	Group VII	Group VIII
H = 1							
Li = 7	Be = 9.4	B = 11	C = 12	N = 14	O = 16	F = 19	
Na = 23	Mg = 24	Al = 27.3	Si = 28	P = 31	S = 32	Cl = 35.5	Fe = 56, Co = 59, Ni = 59, Cu = 63.
K = 39	Ca = 40	— = 44	Ti = 48	V = 51	Cr = 52	Mn = 55	
(Cu = 63)	Zn = 65	— = 68	— = 72	As = 75	Se = 78	Br = 80	Ru = 104, Rh = 104, Pd = 106, Ag = 108.
Rb = 85	Sr = 87	Yt = 88	Zr = 90	Nb = 94	Mo = 96	— = 100	
(Ag = 108)	Cd = 112	In = 113	Sn = 118	Sb = 122	Te = 125	I = 127	
Cs = 133	Ba = 137	Di = 138	Ce = 140	—	—	—	— — — —
(—)	—	—	—	—	—	—	Os = 195, Ir = 197, Pt = 198, Au = 199.
—	—	Er = 178	La = 180	Ta = 182	W = 184	—	
(Au = 199)	Hg = 200	Tl = 204	Pb = 207	Bi = 208			
—	—	—	Th = 231	—	U = 240		

9. Mendeleev published the table above in 1872. Why did Mendeleev leave some
locations in his periodic table blank? _____
_____

10. Circle the letters of two elements that have similar properties.

    a. zinc (Zn)   b. chlorine (Cl)

    c. nitrogen (N)   d. bromine (Br)

11. How did Mendeleev decide where to place arsenic (As) and selenium (Se)?
_____
_____

12. Is the following sentence true or false? Mendeleev was the first
scientist to arrange elements in a periodic table. _____

13. Describe a test for the correctness of a scientific model. _____
_____

14. Mendeleev used the _____ located near the spaces
in his table to predict properties for undiscovered elements.

15. The close match between Mendeleev's predictions and the actual
properties of new elements showed _____.

16. Circle the letter of each element that was discovered after Mendeleev
published his periodic table that supported Mendeleev's predictions
and provided evidence validating the table.

    a. gallium   b. scandium

    c. germanium   d. aluminum

© Pearson Education, Inc., publishing as Pearson Prentice Hall. All rights reserved.

Chapter 5   The Periodic Table

Section 5.2 The Modern Periodic Table
(pages 130–138)

This section explains the organization of the modern periodic table and discusses the general properties of metals, nonmetals, and metalloids.

Reading Strategy (page 130)

Previewing Before you read, complete the table by writing two questions about the periodic table on pages 132–133. As you read, write answers to your questions. For more information on this reading strategy, see the **Reading and Study Skills** in the **Skills and Reference Handbook** at the end of your textbook.

Questions About the Periodic Table	
Question	Answer

The Periodic Law (pages 131–133)

1. Is the following sentence true or false? In the modern periodic table, elements are arranged by increasing number of protons.

   _____

2. Explain why the number of elements per period varies. _____

   _____

3. Properties of elements repeat in a predictable way when atomic numbers are used to arrange elements into groups. This pattern of repeating properties is called the _____.

Atomic Mass (page 134)

4. Label the four types of information supplied for chlorine in the diagram.

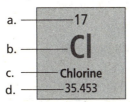

a. ————— 17
b. ————— Cl
c. ————— Chlorine
d. ————— 35.453

   a. _____   b. _____
   c. _____   d. _____

© Pearson Education, Inc., publishing as Pearson Prentice Hall. All rights reserved.

Chapter 5   The Periodic Table

5. Define atomic mass. _____

_____

6. Circle the letter of each sentence that is true about a carbon-12 atom.

   a. It has 6 protons and 6 neutrons.

   b. Scientists assigned a mass of 6 atomic mass units to the carbon-12 atom.

   c. It is used as a standard for comparing the masses of atoms.

   d. An atomic mass unit is defined as one twelfth the mass of a carbon-12 atom.

7. Is the following sentence true or false? Most elements exist as a mixture of two or more isotopes. _____

8. The mass of an atom of chlorine-37 is _____ than the mass of an atom of chlorine-35.

9. Is the following sentence true or false? All values are equally important in a weighted average. _____

Classes of Elements (pages 135–136)

10. Name the three categories into which elements are classified based on their general properties.

    a. _____

    b. _____

    c. _____

11. Is the following sentence true or false? All metals react with oxygen in the same way. _____

12. An important property of transition elements is their ability to form compounds _____.

13. Circle the letter of each sentence that is true about nonmetals.

    a. Nonmetals are poor conductors of heat and electric current.

    b. Many nonmetals are gases at room temperature.

    c. Some nonmetals are extremely reactive and others hardly react at all.

    d. Nonmetals that are solids tend to be malleable.

Variation Across a Period (page 138)

14. Across a period from left to right, the elements become _____ metallic and _____ nonmetallic in their properties.

15. Circle the letter of each Period 3 element that is highly reactive.

    a. sodium   b. silicon

    c. chlorine   d. argon

© Pearson Education, Inc., publishing as Pearson Prentice Hall. All rights reserved.

Chapter 5   The Periodic Table

Section 5.3 Representative Groups
(pages 139–145)

This section discusses how the number of valence electrons affects the properties of elements. It also describes properties of elements in Groups 1A through 8A.

Reading Strategy (page 139)

Monitoring Your Understanding As you read, record an important fact about each element listed in the table. For more information on this reading strategy, see the **Reading and Study Skills** in the **Skills and Reference Handbook** at the end of your textbook.

Element	Important Fact
Magnesium	
Aluminum	
Chlorine	

Valence Electrons (page 139)

1. An electron that is in the highest occupied energy level of an atom is a(n) _____ electron.

2. Elements within a group have the _____ number of valence electrons.

The Alkali Metals (page 140)

3. The reactivity of alkali metals _____ from the top of Group 1A to the bottom.

4. Sodium is stored under oil because it _____.

The Alkaline Earth Metals (page 141)

5. Differences in reactivity among alkaline earth metals are shown by the way they react with _____.

Find and match two properties to each element listed.

Alkaline Earth Metal	Property
_____ 6. magnesium	a. Helps build strong teeth and bones
_____ 7. calcium	b. Helps plants produce sugar
	c. Is used to make lightweight bicycle frames
	d. Is the main ingredient in limestone

© Pearson Education, Inc., publishing as Pearson Prentice Hall. All rights reserved.

Chapter 5   The Periodic Table

The Boron Family (page 142)

8. List the four metals in Group 3A.

   a. _____   b. _____

   c. _____   d. _____

9. Circle the letter of each sentence that is true about aluminum.

   a. It is the most abundant metal in Earth's crust.

   b. It is often found combined with oxygen in bauxite.

   c. It is more reactive than sodium and magnesium.

   d. It is a good conductor of electric current.

The Carbon Family (page 142)

10. List the two metalloids in Group 4A.

    a. _____   b. _____

11. Except for water, most of the compounds in your body contain

    _____.

The Nitrogen Family (page 143)

12. List the nonmetals in Group 5A.

    a. _____   b. _____

13. Name two elements in the nitrogen family that are contained
    in fertilizer.

    a. _____   b. _____

The Oxygen Family (page 143)

14. List the nonmetals in Group 6A.

    a. _____   b. _____   c. _____

15. Name the most abundant element in Earth's crust.

    _____

The Halogens (page 144)

16. List the four nonmetals in Group 7A.

    a. _____   b. _____

    c. _____   d. _____

17. Halogens have similar _____ properties but
    different _____ properties.

The Noble Gases (page 145)

18. Name three characteristics of noble gases.

    a. _____   b. _____   c. _____

19. How can an element that does not react easily with other elements
    be useful? _____

    _____

© Pearson Education, Inc., publishing as Pearson Prentice Hall. All rights reserved.

Chapter 5   The Periodic Table

WordWise

Match each definition with the correct term by writing the definition's number in the grid. When you have filled in all the boxes, add up the numbers in each column, row, and the two diagonals. Hint: The sum should be 15 in each case.

Definitions

1. An arrangement of elements in columns based on a set of properties that repeat from row to row

2. A pattern of repeating properties that occurs when atomic numbers are used to arrange elements into groups

3. One twelfth the mass of a carbon-12 atom

4. Elements that are good conductors of heat and electric current

5. Elements that form a bridge between the elements on the left and right sides of the periodic table

6. Elements that are poor conductors of heat and electric current

7. Elements with properties that fall between those of metals and nonmetals

8. An electron that is in the highest occupied energy level of an atom

9. Colorless, odorless, and extremely unreactive gases

diagonal
= _____

nonmetals _____	periodic table _____	valence electron _____	= _____
metalloids _____	transition metals _____	atomic mass unit _____	= _____
periodic law _____	noble gas _____	metals _____	= _____

= _____   = _____   = _____

diagonal
= _____

© Pearson Education, Inc., publishing as Pearson Prentice Hall. All rights reserved.

Chapter 5   The Periodic Table

Calculating Average Atomic Mass

Carbon has two stable isotopes. Carbon-12 has an assigned atomic mass of 12.0000 and a percentage in nature of 98.93%. The atomic mass of carbon-13 is 13.0034 and its percentage in nature is 1.070%. What is the average atomic mass for carbon?

Math Skill: Percents and Decimals

You may want to read more about this **Math Skill** in the **Skills and Reference Handbook** at the end of your textbook.

1. Read and Understand

What information are you given?

carbon-12: atomic mass = 12.0000, % in nature = 98.93
carbon-13: atomic mass = 13.0034, % in nature = 1.070

2. Plan and Solve

What unknown are you trying to calculate?

Average atomic mass for carbon = ?

What equation can you use?

(atomic mass C-12) (% C-12) + (atomic mass C-13) (% C-13)
= average atomic mass of C

Convert the percentages to decimals and multiply the atomic mass of each isotope by the decimal representing its percentage in nature.

(12.0000) (0.9893) = 11.8716 rounded to 11.87
(13.0034) (0.01070) = 0.1391364 rounded to 0.1391

Add the products of the two multiplications to find the average atomic mass for carbon.

11.87 + 0.1391 = 12.0091 rounded to 12.01

3. Look Back and Check

Is your answer reasonable?

Because almost all the carbon atoms in nature are carbon-12 atoms, the average atomic mass of carbon (12.01) is close to the atomic mass of carbon-12 (12.0000).

Math Practice

On a separate sheet of paper, solve the following problems.

1. The element boron has two stable isotopes. Boron-10 has an atomic mass of 10.0129 and a percentage in nature of 19.78% The atomic mass of boron-11 is 11.0093 and its percentage in nature is 80.22% What is the average atomic mass for boron?

2. Nitrogen has two stable isotopes, nitrogen-14 and nitrogen-15. Nitrogen-14 has an atomic mass of 14.0031. Its percentage in nature is 99.63%. What is the percentage in nature of nitrogen-15?

© Pearson Education, Inc., publishing as Pearson Prentice Hall. All rights reserved.

Chapter 6   Chemical Bonds

Summary

6.1 Ionic Bonding

The chemical properties of elements depend on an element's electron configuration. When the highest occupied energy level of an atom is filled with electrons, the atom is stable and not likely to react.

The chemical properties of an element depend on the number of valence electrons. An electron dot diagram is a model of an atom in which each dot represents a valence electron.

Elements that do not have complete sets of valence electrons tend to react. Some elements achieve stable electron configurations through the transfer of electrons between atoms. Each atom ends up with a more stable arrangement than it had before the transfer.

When an atom gains or loses an electron, the number of protons is no longer equal to the number of electrons. The atom is not neutral. An atom that has a net positive or negative electric charge is called an ion. An ion with a negative charge is an anion. An ion with a positive charge is a cation.

When an anion and a cation are close together, a chemical bond forms between them. A chemical bond is the force that holds atoms or ions together as a unit. An ionic bond is the force that holds cations and anions together. An ionic bond forms when electrons are transferred from one atom to another.

Cations form when electrons gain enough energy to escape from atoms. The amount of energy used to remove an electron is called ionization energy.

Compounds that contain ionic bonds are ionic compounds. Ionic compounds can be represented by chemical formulas. A chemical formula shows what elements a compound contains and the ratio of the atoms or ions of those elements in the compound.

Solids whose particles are arranged in a lattice structure are called crystals. The shape of an ionic crystal depends on the arrangement of ions in its rigid framework, or lattice. Crystals are classified into groups based on their shape. The properties of an ionic compound can be explained by the strong attractions among ions within a crystal lattice.

6.2 Covalent Bonding

A covalent bond is a chemical bond in which two atoms share a pair of valence electrons. When two atoms share one pair of electrons, the bond is called a single bond.

A molecule is a neutral group of atoms that are joined together by one or more covalent bonds. The attractions between the shared electrons and the protons in each nucleus hold the atoms together in covalent bonds. A chemical formula can be used to describe the molecules of an element as well as a compound.

When two atoms share two pairs of electrons, the bond is called a double bond. When two atoms share three pairs of electrons, the bond is called a triple bond.

In a molecule of an element, the atoms that form covalent bonds have the same ability to attract an electron. In a molecule of a compound, electrons are not always shared equally. A covalent bond in which electrons are not shared equally is called a polar covalent bond. When atoms form a polar covalent bond, the atom with the greater attraction for electrons has a partial negative charge. The other atom has a partial positive charge.

© Pearson Education, Inc., publishing as Pearson Prentice Hall. All rights reserved.

Chapter 6   Chemical Bonds

If a molecule that contains a polar covalent bond has only two atoms, it will be polar. When a molecule has more than two atoms, it may be polar or nonpolar. The type of atoms in a molecule and the molecule's shape are factors that determine whether a molecule is polar or nonpolar.

In a molecular compound, forces of attraction hold molecules together in a liquid or solid. Attractions between polar molecules are stronger than attractions between nonpolar molecules. Attractions among nonpolar molecules are weaker than attractions among polar molecules.

6.3 Naming Compounds and Writing Formulas

The name of an ionic compound must distinguish the compound from other ionic compounds containing the same elements. The formula of an ionic compound describes the ratio of the ions in the compound.

A compound made from only two elements is a binary compound. The names of binary compounds—such as sodium chloride—have a predictable pattern: the name of the cation followed by the name of the anion. The name for the cation is the name of the metal without any change: sodium atom and sodium ion. The name for the anion uses part of the name of the nonmetal with the suffix –ide: chlorine atom and chloride ion.

The alkali metals, alkaline earth metals, and aluminum form ions with positive charges equal to the group number. For example, the symbol for a calcium ion is Ca^{2+}, and the symbol for an aluminum ion is Al^{3+}.

Many transition metals form more than one type of ion. When a metal forms more than one ion, the name of the ion contains a Roman numeral to indicate the charge — for example, a copper(II) ion.

A covalently bonded group of atoms that has a positive or negative charge and acts as a unit is a polyatomic ion. Most simple polyatomic ions are anions. Sometimes there are parentheses in a formula that includes polyatomic ions. For example, the formula for iron(III) hydroxide is $Fe(OH)_3$.

If you know the name of an ionic compound, you can write its formula. Place the symbol of the cation first, and follow that with the symbol of the anion. Use subscripts to show the ratio of the ions in the compound.

Molecular compounds have names that identify specific compounds and formulas that match those names. The name and formula of a molecular compound describe the type and number of atoms in a molecule of the compound.

The general rule in naming molecular compounds is that the most metallic element appears first. The name of the second element is changed to end in the suffix –ide, as in carbon dioxide.

When writing molecular formulas, write the symbols for the elements in the order the elements appear in the name. The prefixes indicate the number of atoms of each element in the molecule. The prefixes appear as subscripts in the formula.

6.4 The Structure of Metals

In a metal, valence electrons are free to move among the atoms. In effect, the metal atoms become cations surrounded by a pool of shared electrons. A metallic bond is the attraction between a metal cation and the shared electrons that surround it. The cations in a metal form a lattice that is held in place by strong metallic bonds between the cations and the surrounding valence electrons.

© Pearson Education, Inc., publishing as Pearson Prentice Hall. All rights reserved.

Chapter 6   Chemical Bonds

The mobility of electrons within a metal lattice explains some of the properties of metals. The ability to conduct an electric current is an important property of metals. An electric current can be carried through a metal by the free flow of the shared electrons. Another important property of metals is malleability. The lattice in a metal is flexible compared to the rigid lattice in an ionic compound.

An alloy is a mixture of two or more elements, at least one of which is a metal. Alloys have the characteristic properties of metals.

The first important alloy was bronze. In its simplest form, bronze contains only copper and tin. Both are relatively soft metals. Mixed together in bronze, the metals are much harder and stronger than either metal alone. Scientists can design alloys with specific properties by varying the types and amounts of elements in an alloy.

Steel is an alloy of iron that contains small quantities of carbon and other elements. The carbon atoms form bonds with neighboring iron atoms. These bonds make the lattice harder and stronger than a lattice that contains only iron. The properties of any particular type of steel depend on which elements other than iron and carbon are used and how much of those elements are included.

© Pearson Education, Inc., publishing as Pearson Prentice Hall. All rights reserved.

Chapter 6   Chemical Bonds

Section 6.1 Ionic Bonding
(pages 158–164)

This section describes the formation of ionic bonds and the properties of ionic compounds.

Reading Strategy (page 158)

Sequencing As you read, complete the concept map to show what happens to atoms during ionic bonding. For more information on this Reading Strategy, see the **Reading and Study Skills** in the **Skills and Reference Handbook** at the end of your textbook.

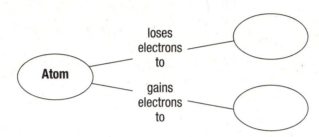

Stable Electron Configurations (page 158)

1. Describe the type of electron configuration that makes an atom stable and not likely to react. _____

_____

_____

2. Describe an electron dot diagram. _____

_____

Ionic Bonds (pages 159–161)

3. Some elements achieve stable electron configurations through the transfer of _____ between atoms.

4. By losing one valence electron, a sodium atom achieves the same electron arrangement as an atom of _____.

5. Circle the letter that states the result of a sodium atom transferring an electron to a chlorine atom.

   a. Each atom ends up with a more stable electron arrangement.

   b. The sodium atom becomes more stable, but the chlorine atom becomes less stable.

   c. The chlorine atom becomes more stable, but the sodium atom becomes less stable.

   d. Each atom ends up with a less stable electron arrangement.

6. Is the following sentence true or false? An ion is an atom that has a net positive or negative electric charge. _____

7. An ion with a negative charge is called a(n) _____.

© Pearson Education, Inc., publishing as Pearson Prentice Hall. All rights reserved.

8. An ionic bond forms when _____ are transferred from one atom to another.

9. Is the following sentence true or false? The lower the ionization energy, the easier it is to remove an electron from an atom. _____

Ionic Compounds (pages 161–164)

10. Circle the letter of each piece of information provided by the chemical formula of an ionic compound.

    a. which elements the compound contains

    b. the charge on each ion in the compound

    c. how the ions are arranged in the compound

    d. the ratio of ions in the compound

11. Circle the letter of the correct answer. The formula for magnesium chloride is $MgCl_2$. The charge on the magnesium ion is 2+. What is the charge on each chloride ion?

    a. 2−   b. 1−

    c. 0   d. 1+

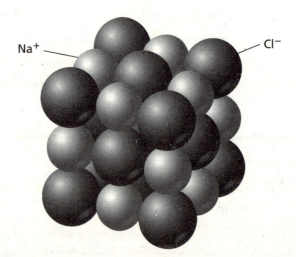

12. Look at the arrangement of ions in a sodium chloride crystal. How many sodium ions surround each chloride ion in this three-dimensional structure?

    a. 3   b. 4

    c. 6   d. 8

13. The shape of an ionic crystal depends on _____.

14. Identify two factors that determine the arrangement of ions in an ionic crystal.

    a. _____   b. _____

15. Is the following sentence true or false? The attractions among ions within a crystal lattice are weak. _____

© Pearson Education, Inc., publishing as Pearson Prentice Hall. All rights reserved.

Chapter 6   Chemical Bonds

Section 6.2 Covalent Bonding
(pages 165–169)

This section discusses the formation of covalent bonds and the factors that determine whether a molecule is polar or nonpolar. It also discusses attractions between molecules.

Reading Strategy (page 165)

Relating Text and Visuals As you read the section, look closely at Figure 9. Complete the table by describing each type of model shown. For more information on this Reading Strategy, see the **Reading and Study Skills** in the **Skills and Reference Handbook** at the end of your textbook.

Molecular Models	
Model	**Description**
Electron dot	
Structural formula	
Space-filling	
Electron cloud	

Covalent Bonds (pages 165–167)

1. Describe a covalent bond. _____

_____

2. Circle the letters of molecular models that show orbitals of atoms overlapping when a covalent bond forms.

    a. electron dot   b. structural formula

    c. space-filling   d. electron cloud

3. Describe a molecule. _____

_____

4. Is the following sentence true or false? In a covalent bond, the atoms are held together by the attractions between the shared electrons and the protons in each nucleus. _____

5. Circle the correct answer. Nitrogen has five valence electrons. How many pairs of electrons must two nitrogen atoms share in order for each atom to have eight valence electrons?

    a. zero   b. one

    c. two   d. three

© Pearson Education, Inc., publishing as Pearson Prentice Hall. All rights reserved.

Chapter 6   Chemical Bonds

Unequal Sharing of Electrons (pages 167–168)

6. In general, elements at the _____ of a group have a greater attraction for electrons than elements at the _____ of a group have.

7. In a hydrogen chloride molecule, the shared electrons spend more time near the _____ atom than near the _____ atom.

8. Describe a polar covalent bond. _____

_____

_____

9. When atoms form a polar covalent bond, the atom with the greater attraction for electrons has a partial _____ charge.

10. Is the following sentence true or false? In a molecule of a compound, electrons are always shared equally by both atoms.

_____

11. Circle the letter of each factor that determines whether a molecule is polar or nonpolar.

   a. the number of atoms in the molecule

   b. the type of atoms in the molecule

   c. the number of bonds in the molecule

   d. the shape of the molecule

CO_2

H_2O

12. Compare the shapes of carbon dioxide and water molecules. Circle the letter of the polar molecule.

   a. carbon dioxide   b. water

13. Is the following sentence true or false? In a water molecule, the hydrogen side of the molecule has a partial positive charge, and the oxygen side has a partial negative charge.

_____

Attraction Between Molecules (page 169)

14. Water has a higher boiling point than carbon dioxide because attractions between polar molecules are _____ than attractions between nonpolar molecules.

15. Is the following sentence true or false? Attractions among nonpolar molecules explain why nitrogen can be stored as a liquid at low temperatures and high pressures. _____

© Pearson Education, Inc., publishing as Pearson Prentice Hall. All rights reserved.

Chapter 6   Chemical Bonds

Section 6.3 Naming Compounds and Writing Formulas
(pages 170–175)

This section explains how to name and write formulas for ionic and molecular compounds.

Reading Strategy (page 170)

Predicting Before you read, predict the meaning of the term *polyatomic ion,* and write your prediction in the table. After you read, if your prediction was incorrect, revise your definition. For more information on this Reading Strategy, see the **Reading and Study Skills** in the **Skills and Reference Handbook** at the end of your textbook.

Vocabulary Term	Before You Read	After You Read
Polyatomic ion		

Describing Ionic Compounds (pages 171–173)

1. Is the following sentence true or false? The name of an ionic compound must distinguish the compound from other ionic compounds containing the same elements. _____

2. What information is provided by the formula for an ionic compound? _____

_____

3. Circle the letter of the word that describes a compound made from only two elements.

   a. ionic   b. binary

   c. diatomic   d. polar

4. Is the following sentence true or false? Names of anions are formed by placing the suffix *-ide* after part of the name of the nonmetal. _____

5. When a metal forms more than one ion, the name of the ion contains a Roman numeral to indicate the _____ on the ion.

6. What is a polyatomic ion? _____

_____

7. Is the following sentence true or false? Because all compounds are neutral, the total charges on the cations and anions in the formula of an ionic compound must add up to zero. _____

© Pearson Education, Inc., publishing as Pearson Prentice Hall. All rights reserved.

Chapter 6   Chemical Bonds

8. Circle the letter of the correct answer. The formula for sodium sulfide is Na_2S. The sodium ion has a charge of 1+. What must the charge on the sulfide ion be?

   a. 1+   b. 0

   c. 1−   d. 2−

Some Polyatomic Ions			
Name	**Formula**	**Name**	**Formula**
Ammonium	NH_4^+	Acetate	$C_2H_3O_2^-$
Hydroxide	OH^-	Peroxide	O_2^{2-}
Nitrate	NO_3^-	Permanganate	MnO_4^-
Sulfate	SO_4^{2-}	Hydrogen sulfate	HSO_4^-
Carbonate	CO_3^{2-}	Hydrogen carbonate	HCO_3^-
Phosphate	PO_4^{3-}	Hydrogen phosphate	HPO_4^{2-}

9. Circle the letter that identifies the number of ammonium ions needed to form a compound with one phosphate ion.

   a. one   b. two

   c. three   d. four

Describing Molecular Compounds (pages 174–175)

10. What information is provided by the name and formula of a molecular compound? _____

    _____

    _____

11. Describe the general rule for naming molecular compounds. _____

    _____

    _____

12. Is the following sentence true or false? The formula for a molecular compound is written with the symbols for the elements in the same order as the elements appear in the name of the compound.

    _____

13. Circle the letter that identifies the method of naming the number of atoms in molecular compounds.

    a. prefix   b. suffix

    c. number   d. symbol

14. In the formula of a molecular compound, the number of atoms of an element in the molecule is represented by a(n)

    _____.

© Pearson Education, Inc., publishing as Pearson Prentice Hall. All rights reserved.

Chapter 6   Chemical Bonds

Section 6.4 The Structure of Metals
(pages 176–181)

This section discusses metallic bonds and the properties of metals. It also explains how the properties of an alloy are controlled.

Reading Strategy (page 176)

Relating Cause and Effect As you read, complete the concept map to relate the structure of metals to their properties. For more information on this Reading Strategy, see the **Reading and Study Skills** in the **Skills and Reference Handbook** at the end of your textbook.

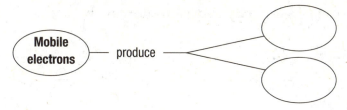

1. Circle the letter of the metal with the highest melting point.

   a. gold   b. vanadium

   c. titanium   d. tungsten

2. Is the following sentence true or false? The properties of a metal are related to bonds within the metal. _____

Metallic Bonds (pages 176–177)

3. Describe a metallic bond. _____

_____

4. The cations in a metal form a lattice. What holds the lattice in place? _____

_____

5. Is the following sentence true or false? The more valence electrons a metal has, the stronger its metallic bonds will be. _____

Explaining Properties of Metals (page 177)

6. Some of the properties of metals can be explained by the _____ of the electrons within a metal lattice.

7. Name two important properties of metals that can be explained by metallic bonding.

   a. _____   b. _____

Alloys (pages 178–181)

8. Circle the letter of the percentage of gold in jewelry that is labeled 18-karat gold.

   a. 18 percent   b. 50 percent

   c. 75 percent   d. 100 percent

© Pearson Education, Inc., publishing as Pearson Prentice Hall. All rights reserved.

Chapter 6   Chemical Bonds

9. Is the following sentence true or false? When a metal such as copper is mixed with gold, the gold becomes softer.
_____

10. Describe an alloy. _____
_____

11. How do the hardness and strength of bronze compare to the hardness and strength of copper alone and tin alone? _____
_____
_____

12. Name two factors that scientists can vary to design alloys with specific properties.
   a. _____
   b. _____

13. Complete the following table.

Comparing Bronze and Brass			
Alloy	**Component Metals**	**Comparative Hardness of Bronze and Brass**	**Comparative Speed of Weathering**
Bronze	Copper, tin		Weathers more slowly
Brass		Softer	

14. When carbon is added to iron, the lattice becomes _____ than a lattice that contains only iron.

15. Circle the letters of the elements that all types of steel contain.
   a. carbon   b. chromium
   c. iron   d. manganese

16. Circle the letters of each correct description of stainless steel.
   a. Stainless steel contains more carbon than chromium.
   b. Chromium forms an oxide that protects stainless steel from rusting.
   c. Stainless steel is more brittle than steels that contain more carbon.
   d. Stainless steel contains more than 3 percent carbon by mass.

17. Explain why pure aluminum is not the best material for the body of a plane.
_____
_____

18. What type of alloy is used to make airplane parts that need to be extremely lightweight? _____

© Pearson Education, Inc., publishing as Pearson Prentice Hall. All rights reserved.

Chapter 6   Chemical Bonds

WordWise

Unscramble the terms from the following list to fit each of the clues given below.

claimlet   ecumelol   levoctan
lorpa   loyal   marfulo
mooctyliap   nocii   nonia
odbn   starscly   tonica

Clues   **Vocabulary Terms**

A type of bond that holds cations and anions together   _____

A type of bond in which two atoms share a pair of   _____
valence electrons

A neutral group of atoms that are joined together by   _____
one or more covalent bonds

A term describing a covalent bond in which electrons   _____
are not shared equally

An ion that contains a covalently bonded group of atoms   _____

An ion with a negative charge   _____

An ion with a positive charge   _____

A notation that shows what elements a compound   _____
contains and the ratio of the atoms or ions of these
elements in the compound

Solids whose particles are arranged in a lattice structure   _____

A mixture of two or more elements, at least one of which   _____
is a metal

A type of bond that exists between a metal cation and the   _____
shared electrons that surround it

The force that holds atoms or ions together   _____

© Pearson Education, Inc., publishing as Pearson Prentice Hall. All rights reserved.

Chapter 6   Chemical Bonds

Writing Formulas for Ionic Compounds

What is the ratio of the ions in magnesium iodide?
What is the formula for magnesium iodide?

Math Skill:
Ratios and
Proportions

You may want to read more about this **Math Skill** in the **Skills and Reference Handbook** at the end of your textbook.

1. Read and Understand

What information are you given?

The name of the compound is magnesium iodide.

2. Plan and Solve

List the symbols and charges for the cation and anion.

Mg ion has a charge of 2+ and I ion has a charge of 1−.

Determine the ratio of ions in the compound.

Mg with a 2+ charge needs two I ions, each with a charge of 1−.
The ratio of the ions in the compound is 1 to 2.

Write the formula for magnesium iodide.

MgI_2

3. Look Back and Check

Is your answer reasonable?

Each magnesium atom loses two electrons and each iodine atom gains one electron. So there should be a 1-to-2 ratio of magnesium ions to iodide ions.

Math Practice

On a separate sheet of paper, solve the following problems.
Refer to Figures 16, 17, and 19 to help you solve the problems.

1. What is the formula for magnesium fluoride?

2. What is the formula for iron(III) chloride?

3. What is the formula for mercury(II) sulfide?

4. What is the formula for potassium dichromate?

5. What is the formula for barium nitrate?

© Pearson Education, Inc., publishing as Pearson Prentice Hall. All rights reserved.

Chapter 7   Chemical Reactions

Summary

7.1 Describing Reactions

In a chemical reaction, the substances that undergo change are called reactants. The new substances formed as a result of that change are called products.

During a chemical reaction, the reactants change into products. To describe the burning of coal, you can write the reactants and products as chemical formulas.

$$C + O_2 \longrightarrow CO_2$$

Now you have a chemical equation. A chemical equation represents a chemical reaction in which the reactants and products are written as formulas.

During a chemical reaction, the mass of the products is always equal to the mass of the reactants. The law of conservation of mass states that mass is neither created nor destroyed in a chemical reaction.

In order to show that mass is conserved during a reaction, a chemical equation must be balanced. In a balanced chemical equation, the number of atoms on the left side of the equation equals the number of atoms on the right. You can balance a chemical equation by changing the coefficients, which are the numbers that appear before the formulas.

Because chemical reactions often involve large numbers of small particles, chemists use a counting unit called the mole to measure amounts of a substance. A mole (mol) is an amount of a substance that contains approximately 6.02×10^{23} particles of that substance. This number is known as Avogadro's number.

The mass of one mole of a substance is called a molar mass. For an element, the molar mass is the same as its atomic mass expressed in grams. Once you know the molar mass of a substance, you can convert moles of that substance into mass or a mass of that substance into moles.

In chemical reactions, the mass of a reactant or product can be calculated by using a balanced chemical equation and molar masses of the reactants and products. The chemical equation tells you how to relate amounts of reactants to amounts of products.

7.2 Types of Reactions

Some general types of chemical reactions are

- synthesis reactions,
- decomposition reactions,
- single-replacement reactions,
- double-replacement reactions, and
- combustion reactions.

A synthesis reaction is a reaction in which two or more substances react to form a single substance. The reactants may be either elements or compounds. The general equation for a synthesis reaction is

$$A + B \longrightarrow AB$$

The opposite of synthesis is decomposition. A decomposition reaction is a reaction in which a compound breaks down into two or more simpler substances. The reactant in a decomposition reaction must be a compound. The products may be elements or compounds. The general equation for a decomposition reaction is

$$AB \longrightarrow A + B$$

A single-replacement reaction is a reaction in which one element takes the place of another element in a compound. Single-replacement reactions have the general form

$$A + BC \longrightarrow B + AC$$

© Pearson Education, Inc., publishing as Pearson Prentice Hall. All rights reserved.

Chapter 7   Chemical Reactions

A double-replacement reaction is one in which two different compounds exchange positive ions and form two new compounds. The general form of a double-replacement reaction is

$$AB + CD \longrightarrow AD + CB$$

A combustion reaction is one in which a substance reacts rapidly with oxygen, often producing heat and light.

A reaction in which electrons are transferred from one reactant to another is called an oxidation-reduction reaction, or redox reaction. Any process in which an element loses electrons during a chemical reaction is called oxidation. A reactant is oxidized if it loses electrons. The process in which an element gains electrons during a chemical reaction is called reduction. A reactant is said to be reduced if it gains electrons.

7.3 Energy Changes in Reactions

Chemical energy is the energy stored in the chemical bonds of a substance. Chemical reactions involve the breaking of chemical bonds in the reactants and the formation of chemical bonds in the products.

During a chemical reaction, energy is either released or absorbed. A chemical reaction that releases energy to its surroundings is called an exothermic reaction. In exothermic reactions, the energy released as the products form is greater than the energy required to break the bonds in the reactants.

A chemical reaction that absorbs energy from its surroundings is called an endothermic reaction. In endothermic reactions, more energy is required to break the bonds in the reactants than is released when the products form.

In both exothermic reactions and endothermic reactions, the total amount of energy before and after the reaction is the same. This principle is known as the law of conservation of energy.

7.4 Reaction Rates

Any change that happens over a period of time can be expressed as a rate. A reaction rate is the rate at which reactants change into products over time. Reaction rates tell you how fast a reaction is going.

Chemical reactions involve collisions between particles of reactants. If collisions occur more frequently, the reaction rate increases. Factors that affect reaction rates include

- temperature,
- surface area,
- concentration,
- stirring, and
- catalysts.

Increasing the temperature of a substance causes its particles to move faster, on average. Particles that move faster are more likely to collide and also more likely to react. If the number of collisions that produce reactions increases, then the reaction rate increases.

An increase in surface area increases the exposure of reactants to one another. Increasing the surface area of a reactant tends to increase the reaction rate.

You can also increase the exposure of reactants to each other by stirring them. Stirring the reactants usually increases the reaction rate.

Another way you can change the reaction rate is to change the concentration of the reactants. Concentration refers to the number of particles in a given volume. The more reacting particles that are present in a given volume, the more opportunities there are for collisions of those particles. The reaction rate is faster.

Sometimes you can change a reaction rate by using catalysts. A catalyst is a substance that affects the reaction rate without being used up in the reaction.

© Pearson Education, Inc., publishing as Pearson Prentice Hall. All rights reserved.

Chapter 7   Chemical Reactions

7.5 Equilibrium

Equilibrium is a state in which the forward and reverse paths of a change take place at the same rate. When opposing physical changes take place at the same rate, a physical equilibrium is reached. When a physical change does not go to completion, a physical equilibrium is established between the forward and reverse changes.

When opposing chemical changes take place at the same rate, a chemical equilibrium is reached. Most chemical reactions are reversible to some extent. A reversible reaction is a reaction in which the reactants can change into products and the products can change into reactants at the same time. When a chemical reaction does not go to completion, a chemical equilibrium is established between the forward and reverse reactions.

Chemical equilibria can change depending on the conditions of the reaction. When a change is introduced to a system in equilibrium, the equilibrium shifts in the direction that relieves the change. This rule is known as Le Châtelier's principle.

© Pearson Education, Inc., publishing as Pearson Prentice Hall. All rights reserved.

Chapter 7   Chemical Reactions

Section 7.1 Describing Reactions
(pages 192–198)

This section discusses the use of chemical equations and how to balance them. It also demonstrates the use of calculations in chemistry.

Reading Strategy (page 192)

Monitoring Your Understanding Preview the Key Concepts, topic headings, vocabulary, and figures in this section. List two things you expect to learn. After reading, state what you learned about each item you listed. For more information on this Reading Strategy, see the **Reading and Study Skills** in the **Skills and Reference Handbook** at the end of your textbook.

What I Expect to Learn	What I Learned

Chemical Equations (pages 192–193)

1. Is the following sentence true or false? The new substances formed as a result of a chemical reaction are called products. _____

2. Circle the letter of each sentence that is a correct interpretation of the chemical equation $C + O_2 \longrightarrow CO_2$.

   a. Carbon and oxygen react and form carbon monoxide.

   b. Carbon and oxygen react and form carbon dioxide.

   c. Carbon dioxide yields carbon and oxygen.

   d. The reaction of carbon and oxygen yields carbon dioxide.

3. Is the following sentence true or false? The law of conservation of mass states that mass is neither created nor destroyed in a chemical reaction. _____

4. Circle the letter of the correct answer. According to the equation $C + O_2 \longrightarrow CO_2$, how many carbon atoms react with 14 molecules of oxygen to form 14 molecules of carbon dioxide?

   a. 1   b. 7

   c. 14   d. 28

5. In the reaction represented by the equation $C + O_2 \longrightarrow CO_2$, the mass of carbon dioxide produced equals _____

   _____.

© Pearson Education, Inc., publishing as Pearson Prentice Hall. All rights reserved.

Chapter 7   Chemical Reactions

Balancing Equations (pages 194–195)

6. Is the following sentence true or false? A chemical equation must be balanced in order to show that mass is conserved during a reaction. _____

7. Circle the letter of the name given to the numbers that appear before the formulas in a chemical equation.

    a. subscripts   b. mass numbers

    c. atomic numbers   d. coefficients

8. Is the following sentence true or false? Because the equation $N_2H_4 + O_2 \longrightarrow N_2 + H_2O$ has two nitrogen atoms on each side, the equation is balanced. _____

Counting With Moles (pages 195–196)

9. Chemists use a counting unit called a(n) _____ to measure amounts of a substance because chemical reactions often involve large numbers of small particles.

10. Circle the letter of the correct answer. If one carbon atom has an atomic mass of 12.0 amu and one oxygen atom has an atomic mass of 16.0 amu, what is the molar mass of carbon dioxide?

    a. 28.0 amu   b. 44.0 amu

    c. 28.0 g   d. 44.0 g

11. Circle the letter of the correct answer. To convert grams of carbon dioxide to moles of carbon dioxide, you must multiply by which conversion factor?

    a. $\dfrac{44.0 \text{ g CO}_2}{1 \text{ mol CO}_2}$ b. $\dfrac{1 \text{ mol CO}_2}{44.0 \text{ g CO}_2}$

    c. $\dfrac{28.0 \text{ g CO}_2}{1 \text{ mol CO}_2}$ d. $\dfrac{1 \text{ mol CO}_2}{28.0 \text{ g CO}_2}$

Chemical Calculations (pages 197–198)

12. Complete the table.

Formation of Water			
Equation	$2H_2$ +	O_2 $\longrightarrow$	$2H_2O$
Amount	2 mol	1 mol	
Molar Mass	2.0 g/mol		18.0 g/mol
Mass (Moles × Molar Mass)		32.0 g	36.0 g

13. Circle the letter of the correct answer. One mole of oxygen has a mass of 32 grams. What is the mass of four moles of oxygen?

    a. 128 g   b. 144 g

    c. 128 amu   d. 144 amu

© Pearson Education, Inc., publishing as Pearson Prentice Hall. All rights reserved.

Chapter 7   Chemical Reactions

Section 7.2 Types of Reactions
(pages 199–205)

This section discusses how chemical reactions are classified into different types.

Reading Strategy (page 199)

Previewing Skim the section and begin a concept map like the
one below that identifies types of reactions with a general form.
As you read, add the general form of each type of reaction. For more
information on this Reading Strategy, see the **Reading and Study Skills**
in the **Skills and Reference Handbook** at the end of your textbook.

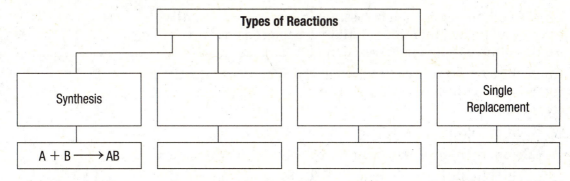

Classifying Reactions (pages 199–204)

1. Name five general types of chemical reactions. _____
   _____

2. Circle the letter of each equation that represents a synthesis reaction.

   a. $2Na + Cl_2 \longrightarrow 2NaCl$

   b. $2NaCl \longrightarrow 2Na + Cl_2$

   c. $2H_2O \longrightarrow 2H_2 + O_2$

   d. $2H_2 + O_2 \longrightarrow 2H_2O$

3. Is the following sentence true or false? A decomposition reaction is
   the opposite of a synthesis reaction. _____

4. Write the equation for the decomposition of calcium carbonate into calcium oxide
   and carbon dioxide. _____

5. Circle the letter of the correct answer. Copper reacts with silver
   nitrate in a single-replacement reaction. What are the products of
   this reaction?

   a. copper(II) nitride and silver oxide

   b. copper(II) nitrate and silver

   c. copper(II) oxide and silver nitrate

   d. copper, nitrogen, and silver oxide

© Pearson Education, Inc., publishing as Pearson Prentice Hall. All rights reserved.

6. What is a double-replacement reaction? _____

_____

7. Complete the chart by filling in the general forms of the
reactions shown.

General Forms	
Single-Replacement Reaction	**Double-Replacement Reaction**

8. Lead(II) nitrate reacts with potassium iodide to form lead(II)
iodide and potassium nitrate. Write the balanced equation
for this double-replacement reaction. _____

9. Circle the letter of the correct answer. Calcium carbonate, $CaCO_3$,
reacts with hydrochloric acid, HCl, in a double-replacement
reaction. What are the products of this reaction?

   a. calcium chloride, $CaCl_2$, and carbonic acid, H_2CO_3

   b. calcium hydride, CaH_2, chlorine, Cl_2, and carbon dioxide, CO_2

   c. calcium hydrogen carbonate, $Ca(HCO_3)_2$, and chlorine, Cl_2

   d. calcium perchlorate, $Ca(ClO_4)_2$, and methane, CH_4

10. Is the following sentence true or false? A combustion reaction is a
reaction in which a substance reacts with carbon dioxide, often
producing heat and light. _____

11. Methane, CH_4, burns in oxygen to form carbon dioxide and
water. Write the balanced equation for this reaction. _____

12. Is the following sentence true or false? The reaction that forms
water can be classified as either a synthesis reaction or a
combustion reaction. _____

Reactions as Electron Transfers (pages 204–205)

13. What is an oxidation-reduction reaction? _____

_____

14. Calcium reacts with oxygen to form calcium oxide. Which reactant
is oxidized in this reaction? _____

15. Is the following sentence true or false? When calcium reacts with
oxygen, each calcium atom gains two electrons and becomes a
calcium ion with a charge of 2–. _____

16. Is the following sentence true or false? Oxygen must be present in
order for an oxidation-reduction reaction to take place.

_____

17. The process in which an element gains electrons during a chemical
reaction is called _____.

© Pearson Education, Inc., publishing as Pearson Prentice Hall. All rights reserved.

Chapter 7   Chemical Reactions

Section 7.3 Energy Changes in Reactions
(pages 206–209)

This section discusses how chemical bonds and energy relate to chemical reactions.

Reading Strategy (page 206)

Comparing and Contrasting As you read, complete the Venn diagram below to show the differences between exothermic and endothermic reactions. For more information on this Reading Strategy, see the **Reading and Study Skills** in the **Skills and Reference Handbook** at the end of your textbook.

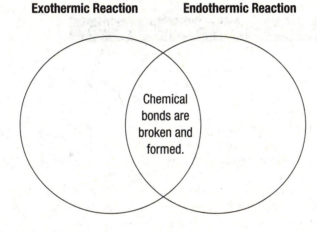

Exothermic Reaction   Endothermic Reaction

Chemical bonds are broken and formed.

Chemical Bonds and Energy (pages 206–207)

1. What is chemical energy? _____

_____

2. Chemical reactions involve the breaking of chemical bonds in the reactants and the formation of chemical bonds in the _____.

3. Is the following sentence true or false? The formation of chemical bonds absorbs energy. _____

4. What role does the spark from the igniter play in the reaction that takes place when propane is burned in a gas grill? _____

_____

5. Is the following sentence true or false? The heat and light given off by a propane stove result from the formation of new chemical bonds. _____

6. The combustion of one molecule of propane (C_3H_8) results in the formation of _____ C=O double bonds and _____ O–H single bonds.

© Pearson Education, Inc., publishing as Pearson Prentice Hall. All rights reserved.

Chapter 7   Chemical Reactions

Exothermic and Endothermic Reactions (pages 208–209)

7. During a chemical reaction, energy is either released or

_____.

8. Is the following sentence true or false? Physical and chemical changes can be either exothermic or endothermic changes.

_____

9. What is an exothermic reaction? _____

_____

10. Is the following sentence true or false? In exothermic reactions, the energy required to break the bonds in the reactants is greater than the energy released as the products form. _____

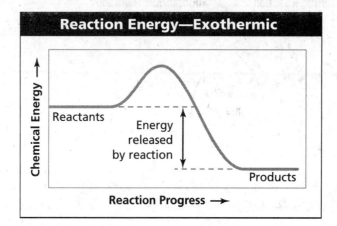

11. Circle the letter of each sentence that is correct for the graph above.

   a. The energy required to break the bonds in the reactants is greater than the energy released as the products form.

   b. The energy released as the products form is greater than the energy required to break the bonds in the reactants.

   c. The chemical energy of the reactants is greater than the chemical energy of the products.

   d. The chemical energy of the products is greater than the chemical energy of the reactants.

12. In an exothermic reaction, the difference between the chemical energy of the reactants and the chemical energy of the products equals

_____.

13. Where does the energy term appear in the equation for an endothermic reaction? _____

Conservation of Energy (page 209)

14. In an endothermic reaction, heat from the surroundings plus the chemical energy of the reactants is converted into the

_____.

© Pearson Education, Inc., publishing as Pearson Prentice Hall. All rights reserved.

Chapter 7   Chemical Reactions

Section 7.4 Reaction Rates
(pages 212–215)

This section discusses the factors that affect reaction rates.

Reading Strategy (page 212)

Building Vocabulary As you read, complete the web diagram below with key terms from this section. For more information on this Reading Strategy, see the **Reading and Study Skills** in the **Skills and Reference Handbook** at the end of your textbook.

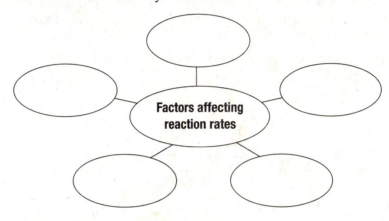

Reactions Over Time (page 212)

1. Any change that happens over time can be expressed as a(n) _____.

2. What is a reaction rate? _____

_____

Factors Affecting Reaction Rates (pages 213–215)

3. Is the following sentence true or false? One way to observe the rate of a reaction is to observe how fast products are being formed.

_____

4. Is the following sentence true or false? The rate of any reaction is a constant that does not change when the reaction conditions change.

_____

5. Generally, an increase in temperature will _____ the reaction rate.

6. Is the following sentence true or false? Storing milk in a refrigerator stops the reactions that would cause the milk to spoil.

_____

7. How does an increase in surface area affect the exposure of reactants to one another? _____

_____

© Pearson Education, Inc., publishing as Pearson Prentice Hall. All rights reserved.

Chapter 7   Chemical Reactions

8. Why does increasing the surface area of a reactant tend to increase the reaction rate? _____

   _____

9. Stirring the reactants in a reaction mixture will generally _____ the reaction rate.

10. Is the following sentence true or false? Increasing the concentration of the reactants will generally slow down a chemical reaction. _____

11. Is the following sentence true or false? A piece of material dipped in a concentrated dye solution will change color more quickly than in a dilute dye solution. _____

12. Why does an increase in pressure speed up the rate of a reaction involving gases? _____

    _____

    _____

13. What is a catalyst? _____

    _____

14. Circle the letters of the sentences that correctly identify why chemists use catalysts.

    a. to speed up a reaction

    b. to enable a reaction to occur at a higher temperature

    c. to slow down a reaction

    d. to enable a reaction to occur at a lower temperature

15. Is the following sentence true or false? Because a catalyst is quickly consumed in a reaction, it must be added to the reaction mixture over and over again to keep the reaction going. _____

16. Identify where the catalyst V_2O_5 should go in the formula shown and write it in the correct location.

    ┌──┐
    │   │
    │ $2SO_2 + O_2 \longrightarrow 2SO_3$ │
    │   │
    └──┘

17. Circle the letter of the correct answer. In the reaction represented by the equation $2H_2O_2 \longrightarrow 2H_2O + O_2$, which substance acts as a catalyst?

    a. H_2O_2 b. Pt

    c. H_2O d. O_2

18. One way that a catalyst can lower the energy barrier of a reaction is by providing a surface on which the _____ can come together.

© Pearson Education, Inc., publishing as Pearson Prentice Hall. All rights reserved.

Chapter 7   Chemical Reactions

Section 7.5 Equilibrium
(pages 216–219)

This section explains physical and chemical equilibria, and describes the factors that affect chemical equilibrium.

Reading Strategy (page 216)

Outlining As you read, make an outline of the most important ideas from this section. For more information on this Reading Strategy, see the **Reading and Study Skills** in the **Skills and Reference Handbook** at the end of your textbook.

I. Equilibrium

  A. Types of Equilibria

    1.

    2.

  B.

    1. Temperature

    2. Pressure

    3.

Types of Equilibria (pages 216–217)

1. What is equilibrium? _____

_____

_____

2. Circle the letter of the correct answer. In the system described by the equation $H_2O(l) \rightleftharpoons H_2O(g)$, at room temperature, which of the following two physical changes are in equilibrium?

  a. sublimation and condensation

  b. evaporation and melting

  c. sublimation and deposition

  d. evaporation and condensation

3. What happens when a physical change does not go to completion?

_____

_____

4. What does the single arrow imply about the reaction described in the following equation?

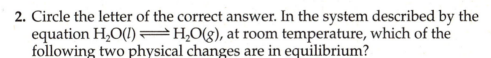
$$CH_4(g) + 2O_2(g) \longrightarrow CO_2(g) + 2H_2O(g)$$

_____

_____

© Pearson Education, Inc., publishing as Pearson Prentice Hall. All rights reserved.

Chapter 7   Chemical Reactions

5. Circle the letter of the correct answer. In the system described by the equation $2SO_2(g) + O_2(g) \rightleftharpoons 2SO_3(g)$, what two reaction types are in equilibrium?

   a. synthesis and decomposition

   b. single replacement and decomposition

   c. synthesis and combustion

   d. synthesis and double replacement

6. What happens when a chemical change does not go to completion?

   _____

   _____

Factors Affecting Chemical Equilibrium (pages 218–219)

7. Is the following sentence true or false? A change in reaction conditions does not affect a chemical equilibrium. _____

8. Circle the letter of each correct answer. The synthesis of ammonia is described by the equation $N_2(g) + 3H_2(g) \rightleftharpoons 2NH_3(g) + heat$. Which reaction is favored when the temperature is lowered?

   a. the forward reaction

   b. the reverse reaction

   c. the reaction that removes heat from the system

   d. the reaction that adds heat to the system

9. Circle the letter of each correct answer. During the synthesis of ammonia, which reaction is favored when hydrogen is added to the system?

   a. the forward reaction

   b. the reverse reaction

   c. the reaction that removes hydrogen from the system

   d. the reaction that adds hydrogen to the system

10. According to Le Châtelier's principle, how does lowering the concentration of a reaction product affect a chemical equilibrium? _____

    _____

11. Use the equation $C(s) + H_2O(g) + heat \rightleftharpoons CO(g) + H_2(g)$ to complete the table below.

An Example of Le Châtelier's Principle		
An increase in	**Shifts the equilibrium so as to**	**Favoring the**
	Remove heat	Forward reaction
Pressure	Produce fewer gas molecules	
Concentration of H_2		Reverse reaction

© Pearson Education, Inc., publishing as Pearson Prentice Hall. All rights reserved.

Name _____ Class _____ Date _____

Chapter 7   Chemical Reactions

WordWise

Answer the questions by writing the correct vocabulary term in the blanks. Use the circled letter in each term to find the hidden vocabulary word. Then, write a definition for the hidden word.

Clues

Vocabulary Terms

Describes a reaction that releases energy to its surroundings

_ _ _ _ _ _ Ⓞ _ _ _

A state in which the forward and reverse paths of a change take place at the same rate

Ⓞ _ _ _ _ _ _ _ _ _ _

A substance that affects the reaction rate without being used up in the reaction

_ Ⓞ _ _ _ _ _ _

A reaction in which a compound breaks down into two or more simpler substances

_ _ Ⓞ _ _ _ _ _ _ _ _

A reaction in which two or more substances react to form a single substance

_ _ _ Ⓞ _ _ _ _ _

The mass of one mole of a substance

_ _ _ Ⓞ _ _ _ _ _

A number that appears before a formula in a chemical equation

_ _ _ _ _ _ _ _ _ Ⓞ _

A reaction in which a substance reacts rapidly with oxygen, often producing heat and light

_ _ _ _ _ _ Ⓞ _ _ _

The substances formed as the result of a chemical change

_ _ _ _ _ _ _ Ⓞ

Hidden Term: _ _ _ _ _ _ _ _ _

Definition: _____

_____

© Pearson Education, Inc., publishing as Pearson Prentice Hall. All rights reserved.

Chapter 7   Chemical Reactions

Balancing Chemical Equations

Write a balanced equation for the reaction between potassium and water to produce hydrogen and potassium hydroxide, KOH.

**Math Skill:
Formulas and
Equations**

You may want to read more about this **Math Skill** in the **Skills and Reference Handbook** at the end of your textbook.

1. Read and Understand

What information are you given?

Reactants: K, H_2O
Products: H_2, KOH

2. Plan and Solve

Write a chemical equation with the reactants on the left side and the products on the right.

$$K + H_2O \longrightarrow H_2 + KOH$$

This equation is not balanced. The number of hydrogen atoms on the left does not equal the number of hydrogen atoms on the right. Change the coefficients of H_2O and KOH in order to balance the number of hydrogen atoms.

$$K + 2H_2O \longrightarrow H_2 + 2KOH$$

Change the coefficient of K in order to balance the number of potassium atoms.

$$2K + 2H_2O \longrightarrow H_2 + 2KOH$$

3. Look Back and Check

Is your answer reasonable?

The number of atoms on the left equals the number of atoms on the right.

Math Practice

On a separate sheet of paper, solve the following problems.

1. Magnesium burns in the presence of oxygen to form magnesium oxide, MgO. Write a balanced equation for this reaction.

2. Hydrogen peroxide, H_2O_2, decomposes to form water and oxygen. Write a balanced equation for this reaction.

3. Barium hydroxide, $Ba(OH)_2$, reacts with nitric acid, HNO_3, to form barium nitrate and water. Write a balanced equation for this reaction.

© Pearson Education, Inc., publishing as Pearson Prentice Hall. All rights reserved.

Chapter 8   Solutions, Acids, and Bases

Summary

8.1 Formation of Solutions

Every solution has two types of components:

- A solute is a substance whose particles are dissolved in a solution.
- A solvent is the substance in which the solute dissolves.

For example, seawater is a solution in which salt is the solute and water is the solvent.

Substances can dissolve in water in three ways—by dissociation, dispersion, and ionization.

- The process in which an ionic compound separates into ions as it dissolves is called dissociation. For example, sodium chloride (table salt) dissolves in water by dissociation.
- The process of dissolving by breaking into small pieces is called dispersion. For example, sugar dissolves in water by dispersion.
- The process in which neutral molecules gain or lose electrons is known as ionization. Dissolving by ionization is a chemical change. For example, hydrogen chloride gas (HCl) dissolves in water by ionization.

Three physical properties of a solution that can differ from those of its solute and solvent are conductivity, freezing point, and boiling point. A solvent may be a poor conductor of electric current. However, when a solute dissolves in the solvent, the solution may then conduct electric current. A solute can lower the freezing point of a solvent. A solute can also raise the boiling point of the solvent.

During the formation of a solution, energy is either released or absorbed. Like chemical reactions, the solution process can be described as exothermic or endothermic. In order for a solution to form, both the attractions among solute particles and the attractions among solvent particles must be broken. Breaking attractions requires energy. As the solute dissolves, new attractions form between solute and solvent particles. The formation of attractions releases energy. The difference between these energies is known as the heat of solution.

Rates of dissolving depend on the frequency and energy of collisions that occur between very small particles. During the formation of a solution, collisions occur between particles of the solute and solvent. Factors that affect the rate of dissolving include surface area, stirring, and temperature.

8.2 Solubility and Concentration

The maximum amount of a solute that dissolves in a given amount of solvent at a constant temperature is called solubility. Solubilities are usually expressed in grams of solute per 100 grams of solvent at a specified temperature.

Solutions are described as saturated, unsaturated, or supersaturated, depending on the amount of solute in solution.

- A saturated solution is one that contains as much solute as the solvent can hold at a given temperature.
- An unsaturated solution is one that has less than the maximum amount of solute that can be dissolved.
- A supersaturated solution is one that contains more solute than it can normally hold at a given temperature.

© Pearson Education, Inc., publishing as Pearson Prentice Hall. All rights reserved.

Chapter 8   Solutions, Acids, and Bases

Three factors that affect the solubility of a solute are the polarity of the solvent, temperature, and pressure.

- Solution formation is more likely to happen when the solute and solvent are both polar or both nonpolar.
- In general, the solubility of solids increases as the solvent temperature increases.
- Increasing the pressure on a gas increases its solubility in a liquid.

The concentration of a solution is the amount of solute dissolved in a specified amount of solution. Concentration can be expressed as percent by volume, percent by mass, and molarity.

8.3 Properties of Acids and Bases

An acid is a compound that produces hydronium ions (H_3O^+) when dissolved in water. Acids have certain chemical and physical properties that are similar. Some general properties of acids include sour taste, reactivity with metals, and ability to produce color changes in indicators.

- Foods that taste sour—such as lemons, grapefruits, and oranges—often contain acids.
- The reaction between an acid and a metal is an example of a single-replacement reaction.
- An indicator is any substance that changes color in the presence of an acid or a base. Blue litmus paper turns red in the presence of an acid.

A base is a compound that produces hydroxide ions (OH^-) when dissolved in water. Bases have certain physical and chemical properties that you can use to identify them. Some general properties of bases include bitter taste, slippery feel, and ability to produce color changes in indicators.

- Foods that taste bitter—such as unsweetened chocolate—often contain bases.
- Wet soap and many cleaning products that contain bases are slippery to the touch.
- Bases turn red litmus paper blue.

The reaction between an acid and a base is called neutralization. During neutralization, the negative ions in an acid combine with the positive ions in a base to produce an ionic compound called a salt. At the same time, hydronium ions from the acid combine with the hydroxide ions from the base to produce water. The neutralization reaction between an acid and a base produces a salt and water.

When an acid and a base react in water, a proton from the hydronium ion from the acid combines with the hydroxide ion from the base to form water. Acids lose, or "donate," protons. Bases "accept" protons, forming water. Acids can be defined as proton donors, and bases can be defined as proton acceptors.

8.4 Strength of Acids and Bases

One way to describe the acidity or basicity of a solution is to determine the concentration of hydronium or hydroxide ions present in solution. Another way is to describe how readily those hydronium ions or hydroxide ions formed.

Chemists use a number scale from 0 to 14 to describe the concentration of hydronium ions in a solution. The scale is known as the pH scale. The pH of a solution is a measure of its hydronium ion concentration.

- A pH of 7 indicates a neutral solution.
- Acids have a pH less than 7.
- Bases have a pH greater than 7.

© Pearson Education, Inc., publishing as Pearson Prentice Hall. All rights reserved.

Chapter 8   Solutions, Acids, and Bases

Water falls in the middle of the pH scale. If you add an acid to water, the concentration of H_3O^+ increases and the concentration of OH decreases. The lower the pH value, the greater the H_3O^+ ion concentration in solution is. If you add a base to water, the concentration of OH increases and the concentration of H_3O^+ decreases. The higher the pH value, the lower the H_3O^+ ion concentration is.

When certain acids and bases dissolve in water, the formation of ions from the solute goes almost to completion. Such acids and bases are classified as strong. When strong acids dissolve in water, they ionize almost completely. When strong bases dissolve in water, they dissociate almost completely.

Weak acids and bases ionize or dissociate only slightly in water. Weak acids and bases can be used to make buffers. A buffer is a solution that is resistant to large changes in pH.

An electrolyte is a substance that ionizes or dissociates into ions when it dissolves in water. The resulting solution can conduct electric current.

© Pearson Education, Inc., publishing as Pearson Prentice Hall. All rights reserved.

Chapter 8   Solutions, Acids, and Bases

Section 8.1 Formation of Solutions
(pages 228–234)

This section explains the parts of a solution, the processes that occur when compounds dissolve, and how the properties of a solution compare with those of its solvent and solute.

Reading Strategy (page 228)

Comparing and Contrasting Contrast dissociation and ionization by listing the ways they differ in the Venn diagram below. For more information on this reading strategy, see the **Reading and Study Skills** in the **Skills and Reference Handbook** at the end of your textbook.

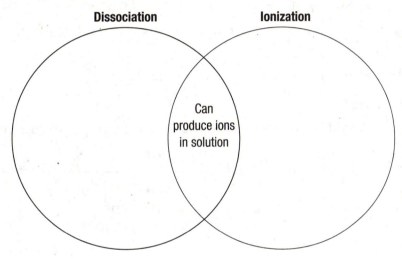

Dissociation   **Ionization**

Can produce ions in solution

Dissolving (page 229)

1. Define a solution. _____

_____

2. Circle the letter that identifies a substance whose particles are dissolved in a solution.

   a. solvent   b. solute

   c. solid   d. ion

3. Circle the letter that identifies the solvent in air.

   a. oxygen   b. carbon dioxide

   c. nitrogen   d. argon

4. The process in which an ionic compound separates into ions as it dissolves is called _____.

5. The process in which particles dissolve by breaking apart and scattering is called _____.

6. A(n) _____ is transferred from each HCl molecule to a water molecule when hydrogen chloride gas dissolves in water.

7. Is the following sentence true or false? Dissolving by ionization is a physical change. _____

© Pearson Education, Inc., publishing as Pearson Prentice Hall. All rights reserved.

Chapter 8   Solutions, Acids, and Bases

Properties of Liquid Solutions (page 231)

8. What physical properties of a solution can differ from those of its solute and solvent?

   a. _____

   b. _____

   c. _____

9. Compare the conductivities of solid sodium chloride and saltwater. _____

   _____

10. Circle the letters that identify what happens to water as it freezes.

    a. The water molecules become more organized.

    b. The water molecules become more disorganized.

    c. The water molecules ionize.

    d. The water molecules arrange themselves in a hexagonal pattern.

Heat of Solution (page 232)

11. Dissolving sodium hydroxide in water is a(n) _____ process, as it releases heat.

12. Dissolving ammonium nitrate in water is a(n) _____ process, as it absorbs heat.

13. Is the following sentence true or false? Breaking the attractions among solute particles and the attractions among solvent particles releases energy. _____

14. Describe heat of solution. _____

    _____

    _____

Factors Affecting Rates of Dissolving (page 234)

15. How are rates of dissolving similar to rates of chemical reactions?

    _____

16. Why does powdered sugar dissolve in water faster than granulated sugar? _____

    _____

17. Heating a solvent _____ the energy of its particles, making them move faster on average, and _____ the rate at which a solid solute can dissolve in the solvent.

18. Explain how stirring or shaking a mixture of powdered detergent and water can affect the rate of dissolving. _____

    _____

    _____

© Pearson Education, Inc., publishing as Pearson Prentice Hall. All rights reserved.

Chapter 8   Solutions, Acids, and Bases

Section 8.2 Solubility and Concentration
(pages 235–239)

This section explains solubility, the factors affecting solubility, and different ways of expressing the concentration of a solution.

Reading Strategy (page 235)

Previewing Before you read the section, rewrite the topic headings as *how, why,* and *what* questions. As you read, write an answer to each question. For more information on this reading strategy, see the **Reading and Study Skills** in the **Skills and Reference Handbook** at the end of your textbook.

Question	Answer
What is solubility?	
	Solvent, temperature, and pressure

Solubility (pages 235–237)

1. Define solubility. _____

   _____

2. List the following solutes in order from most soluble to least soluble in water: table salt, baking soda, table sugar.

   a. _____

   b. _____

   c. _____

3. Circle the letters that identify how solutions can be classified based on solubility.

   a. unsaturated   b. desaturated

   c. saturated   d. supersaturated

4. Describe a saturated solution. _____

   _____

5. A solution that has less than the maximum amount of solute that can be dissolved is called a(n) _____.

6. Is the following sentence true or false? It is impossible for a solution to contain more solute than the solvent can hold at a given temperature. _____

© Pearson Education, Inc., publishing as Pearson Prentice Hall. All rights reserved.

Chapter 8   Solutions, Acids, and Bases

Factors Affecting Solubility (page 237)

7. Circle the letters of factors that affect the solubility of a solute.

    a. polarity of the solvent

    b. amount of solvent

    c. pressure

    d. temperature

8. What is a common guideline for predicting solubility?
    _____

9. Describe how soap cleans grease off your hands. _____

    _____

    _____

10. Is the following statement true or false? In general, the solubility of
    solids increases as the solvent temperature increases.

    _____

11. In general, the solubility of gases decreases as the solvent
    temperature _____.

12. In general, the solubility of a gas increases as pressure
    _____.

Concentration of Solutions (pages 238–239)

13. What does the concentration of a solution refer to? _____

    _____

    _____

14. Circle the letters that identify ways to express the concentration
    of a solution.

    a. density

    b. percent by volume

    c. percent by mass

    d. molarity

15. Complete the equation.

    Percent by volume =

    _____

16. Write the equation used to calculate percent by mass.

    _____

17. Is this sentence true or false? Molarity is the number of moles of a solvent per liter
    of solution. _____

18. How many grams of NaCl are needed to make 1.00 liter of a
    3.00 M NaCl solution? _____

© Pearson Education, Inc., publishing as Pearson Prentice Hall. All rights reserved.

Chapter 8   Solutions, Acids, and Bases

Section 8.3 Properties of Acids and Bases
(pages 240–245)

This section describes the general properties of acids and bases.

Reading Strategy (page 240)

Using Prior Knowledge Before you read, write your definition of each vocabulary term in the table below. After you read, write the scientific definition of each term and compare it with your original definition. For more information on this reading strategy, see the **Reading and Study Skills** in the **Skills and Reference Handbook** at the end of your textbook.

Term	Your Definition	Scientific Definition
Acid		
Base		
Salt		

Identifying Acids (pages 240–241)

1. Define an acid. _____

_____

Match these common acids to their uses.

Acids

_____ **2.** acetic acid

_____ **3.** sulfuric acid

_____ **4.** hydrochloric acid

_____ **5.** carbonic acid

_____ **6.** nitric acid

Uses

a. Fertilizer production

b. Carbonated beverages

c. Vinegar

d. Car batteries

e. Digestive juices in stomach

7. Describe some general properties of acids. _____

_____

8. Place the following substances in the correct column in the table: lemons, vinegar, grapefruit, sour milk, tomatoes.

Foods Containing Acetic Acid	Foods Containing Citric Acid	Foods Containing Butyric Acid

© Pearson Education, Inc., publishing as Pearson Prentice Hall. All rights reserved.

Chapter 8   Solutions, Acids, and Bases

9. The reaction between an acid and a metal can be classified as a(n)

_____ .

10. Explain why an indicator is useful. _____

_____

Identifying Bases (pages 242–243)

11. Define a base. _____

_____

12. Use the following compounds to complete the chart: aluminum hydroxide, calcium hydroxide, magnesium hydroxide, and sodium hydroxide.

Common Bases		
Name	**Formula**	**Uses**
	NaOH	Drain cleaner, soap production
	Mg(OH)$_2$	Antacid, laxative
	Ca(OH)$_2$	Concrete, plaster
	Al(OH)$_3$	Deodorant, antacid

13. What can a gardener add to the soil to change the flowers of a hydrangea from pink to blue? _____

14. Circle the letter that describes how basic solutions generally taste.

   a. sweet   b. sour

   c. bitter   d. salty

15. Is the following sentence true or false? Bases turn red litmus paper blue. _____

Neutralization and Salts (page 244)

16. The reaction between an acid and a base is called _____ .

17. Describe how a salt can be produced by a chemical reaction. _____

_____

18. Write a chemical equation describing the neutralization reaction between calcium hydroxide and hydrochloric acid.

_____

Proton Donors and Acceptors (page 245)

19. Acids can be described as proton _____ ; bases can be described as proton _____ .

20. When hydrogen chloride ionizes in water, which reactant is the proton donor? Which reactant is the proton acceptor? _____

_____

© Pearson Education, Inc., publishing as Pearson Prentice Hall. All rights reserved.

Chapter 8   Solutions, Acids, and Bases

Section 8.4 Strength of Acids and Bases
(pages 246–249)

This section explains how to describe acids and bases in terms of both concentration and strength.

Reading Strategy (page 246)

Comparing and Contrasting As you read, complete the diagram by comparing and contrasting acids and bases. For more information on this reading strategy, see the **Reading and Study Skills** in the **Skills and Reference Handbook** at the end of your textbook.

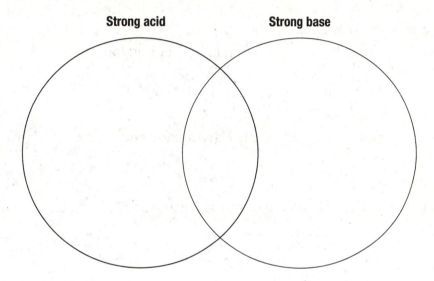

Strong acid   Strong base

The pH Scale (page 247)

1. What is the name of the number scale chemists use to describe the concentration of hydronium ions in a solution?
   _____

2. The pH scale ranges from _____ to _____.

3. Circle the letter that indicates the pH of a neutral solution.

   a. 0

   b. 3

   c. 7

   d. 12

4. Water is neutral because it contains small but equal concentrations of _____ and _____.

5. Is the following sentence true or false? The higher the pH value of a solution, the greater the H_3O^+ ion concentration is.
   _____

6. If you add acid to pure water, the concentration of H_3O^+ _____ and the concentration of OH _____.

© Pearson Education, Inc., publishing as Pearson Prentice Hall. All rights reserved.

Chapter 8   Solutions, Acids, and Bases

Strong Acids and Bases (pages 247–248)

7. What happens when strong acids and bases dissolve in water? _____

_____

8. Is the following sentence true or false? A strong acid always has a lower pH than a weak acid. _____

9. Circle the letters that identify a strong acid.

   a. HCl   b. $Ca(OH)_2$

   c. H_2O d. HNO_3

10. When dissolved in water, sodium hydroxide almost completely dissociates into _____ and _____ ions.

11. Circle the sentences that are true.

    a. Strong bases have a higher concentration of hydronium ions than pure water.

    b. Strong bases dissociate almost completely in water.

    c. Strong bases have a pH below 7.

    d. Examples of strong bases include sodium hydroxide and calcium hydroxide.

Weak Acids and Bases (page 248)

12. What happens when weak acids and bases dissolve in water? _____

_____

13. Is the following sentence true or false? A weak acid has a higher pH than a strong acid of the same concentration. _____

14. Describe the difference between concentration and strength. _____

_____

_____

15. Describe a buffer. _____

_____

Electrolytes (page 249)

16. An electrolyte is _____

_____.

17. Is the following sentence true or false? Strong acids and bases are weak electrolytes because they dissociate or ionize almost completely in water. _____

18. Is acetic acid an example of a weak electrolyte? Explain. _____

_____

© Pearson Education, Inc., publishing as Pearson Prentice Hall. All rights reserved.

Name _____ Class _____ Date _____

Chapter 8   Solutions, Acids, and Bases

WordWise

Use the clues below to identify some of the vocabulary terms from Chapter 8. Write the words on the line, putting one letter in each blank. When you finish, the words enclosed in the circle will reveal an important term.

Clues

1. A(n) _____ solution is one in which you can dissolve more solute.

2. A substance in which other materials dissolve is called a(n) _____.

3. A(n) _____ is a substance that forms ions when dissolved in water.

4. A(n) _____ is a solution containing either a weak acid and its salt or a weak base and its salt.

5. A(n) _____ is a compound that produces hydroxide ions when dissolved in water.

6. The process in which a substance breaks up into smaller particles as it dissolves is called _____.

7. The reaction between an acid and a base is called _____.

8. A(n) _____ is a compound that produces hydronium ions when dissolved in water.

9. When neutral molecules gain or lose electrons, the process is known as _____.

10. The number of moles of solute that is dissolved in 1 liter of solution is _____.

Vocabulary Terms

1. _ _ _ _ _ _ _ _ _ _
2. _ _ _ _ _ _
3. _ _ _ _ _ _ _ _ _ _
4. _ _ _ _ _ _
5. _ _ _ _ _
6. _ _ _ _ _ _ _ _ _
7. _ _ _ _ _ _ _ _ _ _ _ _
8. _ _ _ _
9. _ _ _ _ _ _ _ _
10. _ _ _ _ _ _ _

Hidden Word: _ _ _ _ _ _ _ _ _ _ _

Definition: _____

_____

© Pearson Education, Inc., publishing as Pearson Prentice Hall. All rights reserved.

Chapter 8   Solutions, Acids, and Bases

Calculating the Molarity of a Solution

Math Skill:
Calculating with
Significant Figures

You may want to read
more about this **Math
Skill** in the **Skills and
Reference Handbook**
at the end of your
textbook.

Suppose you dissolve 58.5 grams of sodium chloride into enough water to make exactly 1.00 liter of solution. What is the molarity of the solution?

1. Read and Understand

What information are you given?

   Mass of solute = 58.5 g NaCl

   Volume of solution = 1.00 L

2. Plan and Solve

What unknown are you trying to solve?

   Molarity = ?

What equation can you use?

   $$\text{Molarity} = \frac{\text{Moles of solute}}{\text{Liters of solution}}$$

Convert the mass of the solute into moles.

   $$\text{Moles of solute} = \frac{\text{Mass of NaCl}}{\text{Molar mass of NaCl}}$$

   $$= \frac{58.5 \text{ g NaCl}}{58.5 \text{ g NaCl/mol NaCl}} = 1.00 \text{ mol NaCl}$$

Solve the equation for molarity.

   $$\text{Molarity} = \frac{1.00 \text{ mol NaCl}}{1.00 \text{ L}} = 1.00 \text{ M NaCl}$$

3. Look Back and Check

Is your answer reasonable?

   A 1.00 M NaCl solution contains 1.00 mole of NaCl per liter of solution. The answer is reasonable.

Math Practice

On a separate sheet of paper, solve the following problems.

1. Suppose you had 4.0 moles of solute dissolved into 2.0 liters of solution. What is the molarity?

2. A saltwater solution containing 43.9 grams of NaCl has a total volume of 1.5 liters. What is the molarity?

3. Table sugar has a molar mass of 342 grams. How many grams of table sugar are needed to make 2.00 liters of a 0.500 M solution?

© Pearson Education, Inc., publishing as Pearson Prentice Hall. All rights reserved.

Chapter 9   Carbon Chemistry

Summary

9.1 Carbon Compounds

An organic compound contains carbon and hydrogen, often combined with a few other elements such as oxygen and nitrogen. Carbon has four valence electrons. So a carbon atom can form four single covalent bonds, or a double bond and two single bonds, or a triple bond and a single bond.

The element carbon exists in several forms with different properties. Diamond, graphite, and fullerenes are three forms of carbon.

A hydrocarbon is an organic compound that contains only the elements hydrogen and carbon. In a saturated hydrocarbon, all the bonds are single bonds. A saturated hydrocarbon contains the maximum possible number of hydrogen atoms for each carbon atom. Another name for a saturated hydrocarbon is an alkane.

Factors that determine the properties of a hydrocarbon are the number of carbon atoms and how the atoms are arranged. A hydrocarbon molecule can contain one carbon atom or thousands of carbon atoms. The carbon atoms can be arranged in a straight chain, a branched chain, or a ring.

A molecular formula shows the type and number of atoms in a molecule of a compound. A structural formula shows how those atoms are arranged. Compounds with the same molecular formula but different structural formulas are isomers.

A hydrocarbon that contains one or more double or triple bonds is an unsaturated hydrocarbon. These hydrocarbons are classified by bond type and by how their carbon atoms are arranged. There are three types of unsaturated hydrocarbons—alkenes, alkynes, and aromatic hydrocarbons.

- Alkenes are hydrocarbons that have one or more carbon-carbon double bonds.
- Alkynes are straight- or branched-chain hydrocarbons that have one or more triple bonds.
- Aromatic hydrocarbons are hydrocarbons that contain a ring structure similar to benzene.

Fossil fuels are mixtures of hydrocarbons that formed from the remains of plants or animals. Three types of fossil fuels are coal, natural gas, and petroleum.

The energy released from fossil fuels through combustion is used to heat buildings, to cook food, and for transportation.

9.2 Substituted Hydrocarbons

A hydrocarbon in which one or more hydrogen atoms have been replaced by an atom or group of atoms is a substituted hydrocarbon. The substituted atom or group of atoms is called a functional group because it determines the properties of the compound. Alcohols, organic acids, organic bases, and esters are substituted hydrocarbons.

Methanol and ethanol are alcohols. The name of an alcohol ends in –ol. The functional group in an alcohol is a hydroxyl group, OH. When a halocarbon reacts with a base, the products are an alcohol and a salt. An alcohol can also be made by reacting an alkene with water.

The functional group in organic acids is a carboxyl group, COOH. Names of organic acids end in –oic. Organic acids tend to have sharp tastes and strong odors. Vinegar is a solution of water and the organic acid called ethanoic acid.

© Pearson Education, Inc., publishing as Pearson Prentice Hall. All rights reserved.

Chapter 9   Carbon Chemistry

Amines are organic bases. The functional group in an amine is an amino group, NH_2.

Esters form when organic acids react with alcohols. The second product of the reaction is water. Esters are used in many processed foods to produce flavors such as strawberry, banana, and grape.

9.3 Polymers

A polymer is a large molecule that forms when many smaller molecules are linked together by covalent bonds. The smaller molecules that join together to form a polymer are called monomers. In some polymers, there is only one type of monomer. Other polymers have two or more kinds.

Polymers can be classified as natural polymers or synthetic polymers. Organisms produce natural polymers in their cells. Synthetic polymers are developed by chemists in research laboratories and manufactured in factories. Rubber, nylon, and polyethylene are three examples.

Almost all the large molecules produced by organisms are polymers. Four types of polymers produced in cells are starches, cellulose, nucleic acids, and proteins.

Simple sugars have the formula $C_6H_{12}O_6$. The simple sugars glucose and fructose can react to form sucrose. Glucose monomers join to form starches. Typically, a starch contains hundreds of glucose monomers. Simple sugars, slightly more complex sugars such as sucrose, and polymers built from sugar monomers are all classified as carbohydrates.

The carbohydrate cellulose is the main component of cotton and wood. Cellulose molecules contain 3000 or more glucose monomers.

Nucleic acids are large nitrogen-containing polymers found mainly in the nuclei of cells. There are two types of

nucleic acid, deoxyribonucleic acid (DNA) and ribonucleic acid (RNA). The monomers in a nucleic acid are nucleotides. The three parts of a nucleotide are a phosphate group, a sugar, and one of four organic bases. The bases in DNA are adenine, thymine, cytosine, and guanine. When two strands of DNA line up, an adenine base always pairs up with a thymine base, and a cytosine base always pairs up with a guanine base. The order of the base pairs in a strand of DNA is a code that stores information.

An amino acid is a compound that contains both carboxyl and amino functional groups in the same molecule. There are about 20 amino acids that your body needs to function. Your cells use amino acids as the monomers for constructing protein polymers. A protein is a polymer in which at least 100 amino acid monomers are linked through bonds between an amino group and a carboxyl group.

9.4 Reactions in Cells

Reactions that take place in cells follow the same rules as reactions that take place in a laboratory or classroom. Many reactions occur in solution, and catalysts are often needed. Energy is transferred, and energy is converted from one form to another. Photosynthesis and cellular respiration are two processes that allow organisms to meet their energy needs.

During photosynthesis, plants chemically combine carbon dioxide and water into carbohydrates. The process requires light and chlorophyll, a green pigment in plants. The following equation summarizes the process.

$$6H_2O + 6CO_2 + \text{Energy (light)} \longrightarrow C_6H_{12}O_6 + 6O_2$$

During photosynthesis, energy from sunlight is converted into chemical energy.

© Pearson Education, Inc., publishing as Pearson Prentice Hall. All rights reserved.

Chapter 9   Carbon Chemistry

During cellular respiration, the energy stored in the products of photosynthesis is released. The following equation summarizes the overall process.

$$C_6H_{12}O_6 + 6O_2 \longrightarrow$$
$$6H_2O + 6CO_2 + \text{Energy (heat)}$$

The relationship between photosynthesis and cellular respiration is that each process produces the reactants for the other process. Carbon dioxide and water are reactants in photosynthesis and are products of cellular respiration. Carbohydrates and oxygen are reactants in cellular respiration and are products of photosynthesis.

Enzymes and vitamins are compounds that help cells function efficiently at normal body temperature.

- Enzymes are proteins that act as catalysts for reactions in cells. Enzymes allow reactions to proceed faster at much lower temperatures than would normally happen.
- Vitamins are organic compounds that organisms need in small amounts, but cannot produce.

© Pearson Education, Inc., publishing as Pearson Prentice Hall. All rights reserved.

Chapter 9   Carbon Chemistry

Section 9.1 Carbon Compounds
(pages 262–269)

This section describes different forms of carbon that exist in nature. It also discusses saturated and unsaturated hydrocarbons. It explains the formation of fossil fuels and describes the products of their combustion.

Reading Strategy (page 262)

Previewing Before you read, use the models in Figure 2 to describe the arrangement of carbon atoms in each form of carbon. For more information on this Reading Strategy, see the **Reading and Study Skills** in the **Skills and Reference Handbook** at the end of your textbook.

Forms of Carbon	
Diamond	
Graphite	
Buckminsterfullerene	

1. The two elements that all organic compounds contain are

   _____ .

2. Circle the letter of the approximate percentage of all known compounds that are organic compounds.

   a. 10 percent   b. 30 percent

   c. 60 percent   d. 90 percent

Forms of Carbon (page 263)

3. Circle the letter of each form of carbon.

   a. soot   b. diamond

   c. fullerenes   d. graphite

4. Describe a network solid. _____

   _____

5. Circle the letter of each property of graphite.

   a. soft   b. rigid

   c. compact   d. slippery

Saturated Hydrocarbons (pages 264–265)

6. Is the following sentence true or false? A hydrocarbon is an organic compound that contains carbon, hydrogen, and oxygen. _____

7. Is the following sentence true or false? A saturated hydrocarbon contains only single bonds. _____

© Pearson Education, Inc., publishing as Pearson Prentice Hall. All rights reserved.

Chapter 9   Carbon Chemistry

8. Name the factors that determine the properties of a hydrocarbon.

a. _____   b. _____

9. Name the three ways that carbon atoms can be arranged in hydrocarbon molecules.

a. _____   b. _____   c. _____

10. Circle the letter of the correct answer. What does a structural formula show that a molecular formula does not?

a. the type of atoms in the compound

b. the number of atoms in a molecule of the compound

c. the arrangement of atoms in the compound

d. the state of the compound at room temperature

11. Describe isomers. _____

_____

Unsaturated Hydrocarbons (page 266)

12. Circle the letter of each type of unsaturated hydrocarbon.

a. alkene   b. alkane

c. alkyne   d. aromatic hydrocarbon

13. Circle the letter of the most reactive type of hydrocarbon.

a. alkanes   b. alkenes

c. alkynes   d. aromatic hydrocarbons

Fossil Fuels (page 267–268)

14. Define fossil fuels. _____

_____

15. Circle the letter of each fossil fuel.

a. coal   b. natural gas

c. ferns   d. petroleum

16. Is the following sentence true or false? In a distillation tower, compounds with lower boiling points condense first. _____

Combustion of Fossil Fuels (pages 268–269)

17. Circle the letter of each primary product of the complete combustion of fossil fuels.

a. carbon dioxide   b. carbon monoxide

c. sulfur dioxide   d. water

18. When an insufficient amount of oxygen is available for complete combustion of a fossil fuel, one product of the combustion reaction is the deadly gas _____.

19. Why is rain always slightly acidic? _____

_____

© Pearson Education, Inc., publishing as Pearson Prentice Hall. All rights reserved.

Chapter 9   Carbon Chemistry

Section 9.2 Substituted Hydrocarbons
(pages 272–274)

This section discusses organic compounds that contain atoms of elements other than carbon and hydrogen. It also explains the relationship between the properties of organic compounds and functional groups.

Reading Strategy (page 272)

Monitoring Your Understanding As you read, complete the table by connecting each functional group with the type of compound that contains the functional group. For more information on this Reading Strategy, see the **Reading and Study Skills** in the **Skills and Reference Handbook** at the end of your textbook.

Connecting Functional Groups to Types of Compounds	
Functional Group	**Type of Compound**
–OH	
–COOH	
–NH$_2$	

1. Name the two main products when methane and chlorine react.

   a. _____

   b. _____

2. To which environmental problem have researchers connected halocarbons containing chlorine and fluorine? _____

   _____

   _____

3. Describe a substituted hydrocarbon. _____

   _____

   _____

4. Is the following sentence true or false? The functional group in a substituted hydrocarbon determines the properties of the compound. _____

Alcohols (page 273)

5. Methanol and ethanol are two examples of a class of organic compounds called _____ .

6. The functional group in an alcohol is represented as –OH and is called a(n) _____ group.

7. Identify two ways a halocarbon can be produced.

   a. _____

   b. _____

© Pearson Education, Inc., publishing as Pearson Prentice Hall. All rights reserved.

Chapter 9   Carbon Chemistry

Organic Acids and Bases (pages 273–274)

8. What two physical properties do organic acids tend to have?

    a. _____

    b. _____

9. Is the following sentence true or false? Amines are organic bases. _____

10. Name three products where amines can be found.

    a. _____

    b. _____

    c. _____

11. Complete the following table.

Substituted Hydrocarbons		
Type of Compound	**Name of Functional Group**	**Formula of Functional Group**
	Hydroxyl	
Organic acid		–COOH
Organic base	Amino	

Esters (page 274)

12. What type of compound gives many flowers a pleasant odor?
    _____

13. Which two types of compounds can react and form esters?

    a. _____

    b. _____

14. Circle the letter of the other product of the reaction that forms an ester.

    a. an alcohol

    b. carbon dioxide

    c. a salt

    d. water

15. Is the following sentence true or false? Esters are used to make various fruit flavors in processed foods. _____

© Pearson Education, Inc., publishing as Pearson Prentice Hall. All rights reserved.

Chapter 9   Carbon Chemistry

Section 9.3 Polymers
(pages 275–280)

This section explains how polymers form. It also discusses examples of synthetic and natural polymers.

Reading Strategy (page 275)

Identifying Main Ideas As you read, complete the concept map to summarize two main ideas about polymers. For more information on this Reading Strategy, see the **Reading and Study Skills** in the **Skills and Reference Handbook** at the end of your textbook.

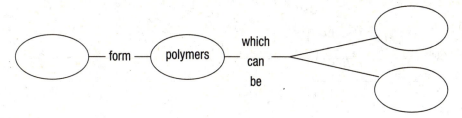

1. Describe a polymer. _____
_____

2. The smaller molecules that join together to form a polymer are called _____.

3. Is the following sentence true or false? More than one type of monomer can be present in some polymers. _____

4. Name the two general classifications of polymers.

   a. _____   b. _____

Synthetic Polymers (page 276)

5. Name three polymers that can be synthesized.

   a. _____   b. _____   c. _____

6. Is the following sentence true or false? The more carbon atoms there are in a polyethylene chain, the harder the polymer is.

   _____

Natural Polymers (pages 278–280)

7. Name four types of polymers that are produced in plant and animal cells.

   a. _____   b. _____

   c. _____   d. _____

8. Circle the letter of the molecular formula of a simple sugar.

   a. CH_2O b. $C_6H_{12}O_6$

   c. $C_{12}H_{22}O_{11}$ d. $C_{12}H_{24}O_{12}$

© Pearson Education, Inc., publishing as Pearson Prentice Hall. All rights reserved.

Name _____ Class _____ Date _____

Chapter 9   Carbon Chemistry

9. Circle the letter of the simple sugar glucose and fructose can react to form.
   a. glucose   b. fructose
   c. cellulose   d. sucrose

10. How are starches used in plants? _____
    _____

11. Simple sugars, slightly more complex sugars, and polymers built from sugar monomers are classified as _____.

12. Circle the letter of the main component of cotton and wood.
    a. cellulose   b. glucose
    c. protein   d. starch

13. Define nucleic acids. _____
    _____

14. Name the two types of nucleic acid.
    a. _____   b. _____

15. Name the three parts of a nucleotide in DNA.
    a. _____ b. _____ c. _____

16. Circle the letter of the term that best describes the structure of DNA.
    a. helix   b. double helix
    c. ring   d. chain

17. How does DNA store information? _____
    _____

18. Is the following sentence true or false? The human body can manufacture all of the essential amino acids. _____

19. Amino acids are the monomers that cells use to build the polymers known as _____.

20. Complete the following concept map about amino acids.

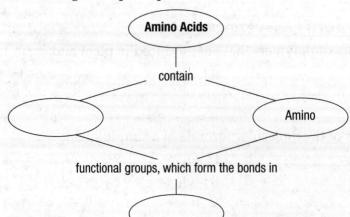

© Pearson Education, Inc., publishing as Pearson Prentice Hall. All rights reserved.

Chapter 9   Carbon Chemistry

Section 9.4 Reactions in Cells
(pages 282–284)

This section describes and compares photosynthesis and cellular respiration.
It also discusses the roles of enzymes and vitamins.

Reading Strategy (page 282)

Summarizing As you read, complete the table by recording a main
idea for each heading. For more information on this Reading Strategy,
see the **Reading and Study Skills** in the **Skills and Reference
Handbook** at the end of your textbook.

Heading	Main Idea
Photosynthesis	
Cellular Respiration	
Enzymes and Vitamins	

1. Two processes that allow organisms to meet their energy needs are
   _____ and _____.

Photosynthesis (page 282)

2. Describe what happens during photosynthesis. _____
   _____
   _____

3. Circle the letter of each requirement for photosynthesis to occur.
   a. chlorophyll   b. oxygen
   c. carbohydrates   d. light

4. Identify the energy conversion that takes place during photosynthesis. _____
   _____

5. Circle the letter of each product of photosynthesis.
   a. carbon dioxide   b. carbohydrates
   c. oxygen   d. water

6. Is the following sentence true or false? When all the reactions in
   photosynthesis are complete, energy from sunlight has been stored
   in the covalent bonds of molecules. _____

Cellular Respiration (page 283)

7. During cellular respiration, the _____ stored in the
   products of photosynthesis is released.

© Pearson Education, Inc., publishing as Pearson Prentice Hall. All rights reserved.

Chapter 9   Carbon Chemistry

8. How is cellular respiration related to photosynthesis? _____
_____

9. Is the following sentence true or false? Carbohydrates produce more energy per gram than fats do. _____

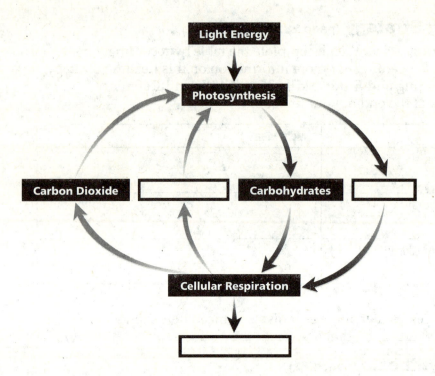

10. Complete the diagram relating photosynthesis to cellular respiration.
   a. _____   b. _____   c. _____

Enzymes and Vitamins (page 284)

11. Describe what enzymes and vitamins have in common. _____
_____

12. Define enzymes. _____
_____

13. Is the following sentence true or false? Enzymes require high temperatures in order to function. _____

14. Is the following sentence true or false? Some enzymes require a co-enzyme in order to function. _____

15. Define vitamins. _____
_____

16. Is the following sentence true or false? All vitamins dissolve in water and must be replaced daily. _____

17. Identify the property of vitamin A that allows it to build up in body tissues over time. _____

© Pearson Education, Inc., publishing as Pearson Prentice Hall. All rights reserved.

Name _____ Class _____ Date _____

WordWise

Complete the following crossword puzzle, using the clues provided below.

Clues across:

1. A hydrocarbon in which all of the bonds are single bonds

2. A compound containing carbon and hydrogen, often combined with other elements such as oxygen and nitrogen

3. A small molecule that joins with other small molecules to form a polymer

4. _____ acid: a large nitrogen-containing polymer found mainly in the nuclei of cells

5. Organic compounds that contain only carbon and hydrogen

Clues down:

6. An organic compound that organisms need in small amounts, but cannot produce

7. Organic compounds that contain both carboxyl and amino functional groups

8. Compounds with the same molecular formula but different structural formulas

9. A polymer in which at least 100 amino acid monomers are linked through bonds between an amino group and a carboxyl group

10. _____ solid: a type of solid in which all of the atoms are linked by covalent bonds

© Pearson Education, Inc., publishing as Pearson Prentice Hall. All rights reserved.

Chapter 9   Carbon Chemistry

Balancing Equations for Organic Reactions

Math Skill:
Ratios and
Proportions

You may want to read
more about this **Math
Skill** in the **Skills and
Reference Handbook**
at the end of your
textbook.

When propane, C_3H_8, combines with oxygen, the products are
carbon dioxide and water. Write a balanced equation for the
complete combustion of propane.

1. Read and Understand

What information are you given?

   Reactants = propane (C_3H_8) and oxygen (O_2)

   Products = carbon dioxide (CO_2) and water (H_2O)

2. Plan and Solve

What unknowns are you trying to determine?

   The coefficients for the equation

What equation contains the given information?

   $C_3H_8 + O_2 \longrightarrow CO_2 + H_2O$ (unbalanced equation)

*First, balance the equation for carbon. Because there are 3 carbon atoms in
C_3H_8, you need to place the coefficient 3 in front of CO_2.*

   $C_3H_8 + O_2 \longrightarrow 3CO_2 + H_2O$

*Next, balance the equation for hydrogen. Because there are 8 hydrogen
atoms in C_3H_8 and only 2 hydrogen atoms in H_2O, you need to place the
coefficient 4 in front of H_2O.*

   $C_3H_8 + O_2 \longrightarrow 3CO_2 + 4H_2O$

*Finally, balance the equation for oxygen. Because there are 6 oxygen atoms
in 3 molecules of CO_2 and 4 oxygen atoms in 4 molecules of H_2O for a
total of 10 oxygen atoms, you need to place the coefficient 5 in front of O_2.*

   $C_3H_8 + 5O_2 \longrightarrow 3CO_2 + 4H_2O$

3. Look Back and Check

Is your answer reasonable?

   Each side of the equation has 3 carbon atoms, 8 hydrogen atoms,
   and 10 oxygen atoms. The equation is balanced.

Math Practice

On a separate sheet of paper, solve the following problems.

1. Balance the equation for the reaction of benzene and hydrogen to
   form cyclohexane.

   $C_6H_6 + \underline{\hspace{1cm}} H_2 \xrightarrow{\text{Pt}} C_6H_{12}$

2. Write a balanced equation for the complete combustion of
   methane, CH_4.

3. Write a balanced equation for the combustion of glucose, $C_6H_{12}O_6$.

© Pearson Education, Inc., publishing as Pearson Prentice Hall. All rights reserved.

Chapter 10   Nuclear Chemistry

Summary

10.1 Radioactivity

Radioactivity is the process in which an unstable atomic nucleus emits charged particles and energy. Any atom containing an unstable nucleus is called a radioisotope. Common radioisotopes include uranium-238 and carbon-14.

Radioisotopes spontaneously change into other isotopes over time. When the composition of a radioisotope changes, the radioisotope is said to undergo nuclear decay. During nuclear decay, atoms of one element can change into atoms of a different element altogether.

Nuclear radiation is charged particles and energy that are given off by the nuclei of radioisotopes. Common types of nuclear radiation include alpha particles, beta particles, and gamma rays.

An alpha particle is a positively charged particle made up of two protons and two neutrons—the same as a helium nucleus. The common symbol for an alpha particle is $_2^4\text{He}$. Another symbol for an alpha particle is the Greek letter α.

Alpha decay refers to nuclear decay that releases alpha particles. Alpha particles are the least penetrating type of nuclear radiation.

A beta particle is an electron emitted by an unstable nucleus. In nuclear equations, a beta particle is written as $_{-1}^{0}\text{e}$ or β. An electron has very little mass compared with a proton. For this reason, a beta particle is assigned a mass number of 0. Beta particles are more penetrating than alpha particles.

A gamma ray is a penetrating ray of energy emitted by an unstable nucleus. Gamma radiation has no mass and no charge. Gamma rays are energy waves that travel through space at the speed of light. Gamma rays are much more penetrating than either alpha particles or beta particles.

Background radiation is nuclear radiation that occurs naturally in the environment. Radioisotopes in air, water, rocks, plants, and animals all contribute to background radiation.

10.2 Rates of Nuclear Decay

A nuclear decay rate describes how fast nuclear changes take place in a radioactive substance. Every radioisotope decays at a specific rate that can be expressed as a half-life. A half-life is the time one half of a sample of a radioisotope takes to decay. After one half-life, half of the atoms in a radioactive sample have decayed, while the other half remain unchanged.

Half-lives can vary from fractions of a second to billions of years. Unlike chemical reaction rates, nuclear decay rates are constant. Regardless of the temperature, pressure, or surface area of a uranium-238 sample, its half-life is always 4.5 billion years.

Because most materials contain at least trace amounts of radioisotopes, scientists can estimate how old they are based on rates of nuclear decay. Carbon-14 is formed in the upper atmosphere when neutrons produced by cosmic rays collide with nitrogen-14 atoms. Carbon reacts with oxygen in the atmosphere and forms carbon dioxide. As plants absorb carbon dioxide during photosynthesis, they maintain the same ratio of carbon-14 to carbon-12 as in the atmosphere. Animals absorb carbon isotopes as they eat plants. When a plant or animal dies, it can no longer absorb carbon. From this point on, the organism's carbon-14 levels decrease as the radioactive carbon decays. In radiocarbon dating, the age of an object is determined by comparing the object's carbon-14 levels with carbon-14 levels in the atmosphere.

© Pearson Education, Inc., publishing as Pearson Prentice Hall. All rights reserved.

Chapter 10   Nuclear Chemistry

10.3 Artificial Transmutation

Transmutation is the conversion of atoms of one element to atoms of another element. Nuclear decay is an example of a transmutation that occurs naturally. Scientists can perform artificial transmutations by bombarding atomic nuclei with high-energy particles such as protons, neutrons, or alpha particles.

Elements with atomic numbers greater than 92 are called transuranium elements. All transuranium elements are radioactive, and they are generally not found in nature. Scientists can create a transuranium element by the artificial transmutation of a lighter element.

In order to perform certain transmutations, scientists use devices called particle accelerators. In a particle accelerator, fast-moving charged particles are guided toward a target, where they collide with atomic nuclei.

Scientists also conduct collision experiments in order to study nuclear structure. According to the current model of the atom, protons and neutrons are made up of even smaller particles called quarks.

10.4 Fission and Fusion

The strong nuclear force is the force of attraction that binds protons and neutrons together in the nucleus. Because the strong nuclear force does not depend on charge, it acts among protons, among neutrons, and among protons and neutrons.

Electric forces in atomic nuclei depend on the number of protons. The greater the number of protons in a nucleus, the greater is the electric force that repels those protons. The strong nuclear force acts only over short ranges. As a result, the strong nuclear force felt by one proton or neutron in a large nucleus is about the same as in a small nucleus.

A nucleus becomes unstable, or radioactive, when the strong nuclear force can no longer overcome the repelling electric forces among protons. All nuclei with 83 or more protons are radioactive.

Fission is the splitting of an atomic nucleus into two smaller parts. In nuclear fission, tremendous amounts of energy can be produced from very small amounts of mass. When fission of uranium-235 is carried out, about 0.1 percent of the mass of the reactants is lost during the reaction. This "lost" mass is converted to energy. The mass-energy equation describes how mass and energy are related.

$$E = mc^2$$

In the mass-energy equation, E represents energy, m represents mass, and c represents the speed of light. The conversion of a small amount of mass releases an enormous amount of energy.

To account for the conversion of mass into energy, a modified law of conservation is used. According to the law of conservation of mass and energy, the total amount of mass and energy remains constant.

In nuclear fission, one reaction can lead to a series of reactions. During the fission of uranium-235, each reactant nucleus splits into two smaller nuclei and releases two or three neutrons. If one of these neutrons is absorbed by another uranium-235 nucleus, another fission can result. In a chain reaction, neutrons released during the splitting of an initial nucleus trigger a series of nuclear fissions. In a nuclear power plant, controlled fission of uranium-235 occurs in a vessel called a fission reactor.

Fusion is a process in which the nuclei of two atoms combine to form a larger nucleus. During fusion, a small fraction of the reactant mass is converted into energy. The sun and other stars are powered by the fusion of hydrogen into helium. Fusion requires extremely high temperatures.

© Pearson Education, Inc., publishing as Pearson Prentice Hall. All rights reserved.

Chapter 10   Nuclear Chemistry

Section 10.1 Radioactivity
(pages 292–297)

This section discusses the different types of nuclear radiation and how they affect matter.

Reading Strategy (page 292)

Previewing Before you read the section, rewrite the topic headings in the table as *how, why,* and *what* questions. As you read, write an answer to each question. For more information on this Reading Strategy, see the **Reading and Study Skills** in the **Skills and Reference Handbook** at the end of your textbook.

Exploring Radioactivity	
Question	**Answer**
What is nuclear decay?	
	Alpha, beta, gamma

Nuclear Decay (pages 292–293)

1. Describe radioactivity. _____

_____

2. A radioisotope is any atom that contains an unstable _____.

3. Describe what happens to radioisotopes during nuclear decay. _____

_____

Types of Nuclear Radiation (pages 293–296)

4. Nuclear radiation is charged particles and energy that are emitted from the _____ of radioisotopes.

5. Circle the letters that identify each common type of nuclear radiation.

   a. X-rays   b. alpha particles

   c. beta particles   d. gamma rays

6. Circle the letters that identify which groups of particles make up an alpha particle.

   a. two electrons   b. two protons

   c. two neutrons   d. four neutrons

© Pearson Education, Inc., publishing as Pearson Prentice Hall. All rights reserved.

7. How is the product isotope different from the reactant isotope in alpha decay? _____

_____

8. Circle the letters that identify each event that takes place during beta decay.

  a. A proton decomposes into a neutron and an electron.

  b. A neutron decomposes into a proton and an electron.

  c. An electron is emitted from the nucleus.

  d. A neutron is emitted from the nucleus.

9. Why are beta particles more penetrating than alpha particles?

_____

10. Is the following sentence true or false? All nuclear radiation consists of charged particles. _____

11. What is a gamma ray? _____

_____

12. How fast do gamma rays travel through space?

_____

13. Complete the following table about nuclear radiation.

Characteristics of Nuclear Radiation			
Radiation Type	Charge	Mass (amu)	Usually Stopped By
	2+		
Beta particle		$\frac{1}{1836}$	Aluminum sheet
	0		Several meters of concrete

Effects of Nuclear Radiation (pages 296–297)

14. How does nuclear radiation affect atoms? _____

_____

15. Is the following sentence true or false? One potential danger of radon gas is that prolonged exposure to it can lead to lung cancer.

_____

Detecting Nuclear Radiation (page 297)

16. Name two devices that are used to detect nuclear radiation.

  a. _____   b. _____

© Pearson Education, Inc., publishing as Pearson Prentice Hall. All rights reserved.

Chapter 10   Nuclear Chemistry

Section 10.2 Rates of Nuclear Decay
(pages 298–301)

This section discusses half-lives and explains how nuclear decay can be used to estimate the age of objects.

Reading Strategy (page 298)

Identifying Details As you read, complete the concept map below to identify details about radiocarbon dating. For more information on this Reading Strategy, see the **Reading and Study Skills** in the **Skills and Reference Handbook** at the end of your textbook.

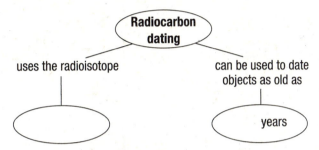

Half-life (pages 299–300)

1. A nuclear decay rate describes _____
_____.

2. Is the following sentence true or false? All radioisotopes decay at the same rate. _____

3. Describe a half-life. _____
_____

4. Circle the letter that describes a sample of a radioisotope after two half-lives.

   a. One eighth of the original sample is unchanged.

   b. One quarter of the original sample is unchanged.

   c. Half of the original sample is unchanged.

   d. Three quarters of the original sample is unchanged.

5. Circle the letter of the correct answer. Iodine-131 has a half-life of 8.07 days. What fraction of a sample of iodine-131 is left unchanged after 16.14 days?

   a. $\dfrac{1}{2}$ b. $\dfrac{1}{4}$

   c. $\dfrac{1}{8}$ d. $\dfrac{1}{16}$

6. Is the following sentence true or false? Like chemical reaction rates, nuclear decay rates vary with the conditions of reaction.

_____

© Pearson Education, Inc., publishing as Pearson Prentice Hall. All rights reserved.

Chapter 10   Nuclear Chemistry

Use the following table to answer questions 7 and 8.

Half-Lives of Selected Radioisotopes	
Isotope	**Half-life**
Radon-222	3.82 days
Iodine-131	8.07 days
Thorium-234	24.1 days
Radium-226	1620 years
Carbon-14	5730 years

7. Circle the letter that identifies which sample would be the most unchanged after 100 years.

   a. iodine-131   b. radium-226

   c. radon-222   d. thorium-234

8. Circle the letter of the correct answer. How much of a 1.00 gram sample of radium-226 is left unchanged after 4860 years?

   a. 0.500 g   b. 0.250 g

   c. 0.125 g   d. 0.050 g

Radioactive Dating (pages 300–301)

9. How is carbon-14 formed in the upper atmosphere? _____

   _____

10. Circle the letter that identifies the correct equation for the beta decay of carbon–14.

    a. $^{14}_{6}\text{C} \longrightarrow \, ^{14}_{7}\text{N} + \, ^{0}_{-1}\text{e}$ b. $^{14}_{6}\text{C} \longrightarrow \, ^{13}_{5}\text{B} + \, ^{1}_{1}\text{p}$

    c. $^{14}_{6}\text{C} \longrightarrow \, ^{14}_{5}\text{B} + \, ^{0}_{-1}\text{e}$ d. $^{14}_{6}\text{C} \longrightarrow \, ^{10}_{4}\text{Be} + \, ^{4}_{2}\text{He}$

11. Is the following sentence true or false? Plants and animals continue to absorb carbon from the atmosphere after they die. _____

12. How is the age of an object determined in radiocarbon dating? _____

    _____

13. Circle the letter of each characteristic of radiocarbon dating.

    a. Carbon-14 levels in the atmosphere can change over time.

    b. Carbon-14 levels in the atmosphere stay constant.

    c. Scientists often use objects of known age in radiocarbon dating.

    d. Objects of known age are not useful in radiocarbon dating.

14. Is the following sentence true or false? Radiocarbon dating is highly accurate in dating objects that are more than 50,000 years old. _____

© Pearson Education, Inc., publishing as Pearson Prentice Hall. All rights reserved.

Chapter 10   Nuclear Chemistry

Section 10.3 Artificial Transmutation
(pages 303–305)

This section discusses transmutations, transuranium elements,
and particle accelerators.

Reading Strategy (page 303)

Monitoring Your Understanding Preview the Key Concepts, topic
headings, vocabulary, and figures in this section. List two things you
expect to learn. After reading, state what you learned about each item
you listed. For more information on this Reading Strategy, see the
Reading and Study Skills in the **Skills and Reference Handbook** at
the end of your textbook.

Understanding Artificial Transmutation	
What I Expect to Learn	**What I Learned**

Nuclear Reactions in the Laboratory (page 303)

1. Define transmutation. _____
_____

2. An example of a transmutation that occurs naturally is _____.

3. How do scientists perform artificial transmutations? _____
_____
_____

4. Circle the letter that identifies the scientist who performed the first
   artificial transmutation.
   a. Ernest Rutherford   b. Niels Bohr
   c. Enrico Fermi   d. Lise Meitner

5. The experiment that produced the first artificial transmutation also
   provided evidence that the nucleus contains _____.

Transuranium Elements (page 304)

6. Describe a transuranium element. _____
_____

7. Is the following sentence true or false? All transuranium elements
   are radioactive. _____

© Pearson Education, Inc., publishing as Pearson Prentice Hall. All rights reserved.

Chapter 10   Nuclear Chemistry

8. Scientists can synthesize a transuranium element by the artificial transmutation of a(n) _____ element.

9. Circle the letter of the first transuranium element to be synthesized.

   a. plutonium   b. americium

   c. technetium   d. neptunium

10. Circle the letter of the element that is used as a source of radiation in smoke detectors.

   a. uranium   b. americium

   c. technetium   d. plutonium

Particle Accelerators (page 305)

11. Why are particle accelerators needed for some transmutations? _____

_____

12. Is the following sentence true or false? A particle accelerator can accelerate charged particles to speeds very close to the speed of light. _____

13. Describe a quark. _____

_____

14. Circle the letter that identifies the number of quarks in each proton or neutron.

   a. zero   b. two

   c. three   d. six

15. Complete the following concept map about alpha particles.

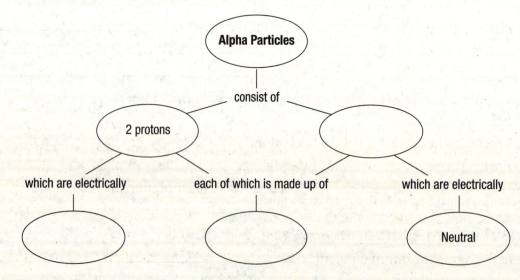

© Pearson Education, Inc., publishing as Pearson Prentice Hall. All rights reserved.

Chapter 10   Nuclear Chemistry

Section 10.4 Fission and Fusion
(pages 308–315)

*This section discusses nuclear forces and the conversion of mass into energy.
It also describes the nuclear processes of fission and fusion.*

Reading Strategy (page 308)

Comparing and Contrasting As you read, contrast fission and fusion in
the Venn diagram below by listing the ways they differ. For more
information on this Reading Strategy, see the **Reading and Study Skills**
in the **Skills and Reference Handbook** at the end of your textbook.

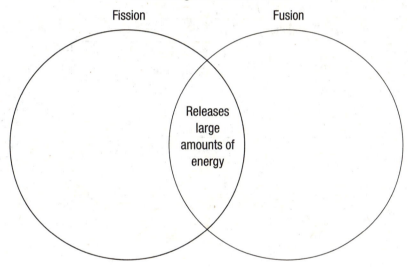

Contrasting Fission and Fusion

Fission   Fusion

Releases
large
amounts of
energy

Nuclear Forces (pages 308–309)

1. Describe the strong nuclear force. _____

   _____

2. Is the following sentence true or false? Over very short distances,
   the strong nuclear force is much greater than the electric forces
   among protons. _____

3. Electric forces in atomic nuclei depend on _____.

4. Is the following sentence true or false? The strong nuclear force on a
   proton or neutron is much greater in a large nucleus than in a small
   nucleus. _____

5. All nuclei with 83 or more protons are _____.

Fission (pages 309–313)

6. Describe fission. _____

   _____

7. Fission can produce very large amounts of energy from very small
   amounts of _____.

© Pearson Education, Inc., publishing as Pearson Prentice Hall. All rights reserved.

Chapter 10   Nuclear Chemistry

8. Circle the letter that identifies what *c* represents in Einstein's
   mass-energy equation, $E = mc^2$.

   a. the charge on a proton   b. the speed of light

   c. the charge on an electron   d. the specific heat of the material

9. Is the following sentence true or false? During nuclear reactions
   mass is not conserved, but energy is conserved.
   _____

10. Describe what can happen to a uranium-235 nucleus that absorbs
    a neutron. _____
    _____

11. Complete the following table.

Chain Reactions		
Type of Chain Reaction	Description	Example of An Application
Uncontrolled	All neutrons released during fission are free to cause other fissions.	
		Nuclear power plants

12. Describe a critical mass. _____
    _____

13. Is the following sentence true or false? Unlike power plants that
    burn fossil fuels, nuclear power plants do not emit air pollutants
    such as oxides of sulfur and nitrogen. _____

14. Describe what happens during a meltdown. _____
    _____

Fusion (page 315)

15. The state of matter in which atoms have been stripped of their
    electrons is _____.

16. Circle the letter of each main problem that scientists must face in
    designing a fusion reactor.

    a. Extremely high temperatures are necessary for a fusion reaction
       to start.

    b. The plasma that results from the reaction conditions must be
       contained.

    c. The hydrogen needed as a starting material is extremely scarce.

    d. Fusion reactions produce large quantities of radioactive waste.

© Pearson Education, Inc., publishing as Pearson Prentice Hall. All rights reserved.

Chapter 10   Nuclear Chemistry

WordWise

Write the answer to each definition using one of the scrambled words below.

abte petalric	dorataivyicit	fonius
gnostr rauncel crefo	licticar sams	lunarce tiadorian
magma yar	onisifs	pahal claptrie
pieatodorsoi	ruqak	samlap

Definition	Term
A subatomic particle theorized to be among the basic units of matter	_____
Charged particles and energy that are emitted from the nuclei of radioisotopes	_____
A positively charged particle made up of two protons and two neutrons	_____
A state of matter in which atoms have been stripped of their electrons	_____
The process in which an unstable atomic nucleus emits charged particles and energy	_____
A penetrating ray of energy emitted by an unstable nucleus	_____
The attractive force that binds protons and neutrons together in the nucleus	_____
The splitting of an atomic nucleus into two smaller parts	_____
An electron emitted by an unstable nucleus	_____
The smallest possible mass of a fissionable material that can sustain a chain reaction	_____
A process in which the nuclei of two atoms combine to form a larger nucleus	_____
Any atom containing an unstable nucleus	_____

© Pearson Education, Inc., publishing as Pearson Prentice Hall. All rights reserved.

Chapter 10   Nuclear Chemistry

Nuclear Equations for Alpha Decay

Write a balanced nuclear equation for the alpha decay of polonium-218.

Math Skill:
Formulas and
Equations

You may want to read more about this **Math Skill** in the **Skills and Reference Handbook** at the end of your textbook.

1. Read and Understand

What information are you given?

Reactant isotope = polonium-218

Radiation emitted = ^4_2He (alpha particle)

Use the periodic table to obtain the atomic number of polonium.

Reactant isotope = $^{218}_{84}Po$

2. Plan and Solve

What unknowns are you trying to calculate?

Atomic number of product isotope, $Z = ?$

Mass number of product isotope, $A = ?$

Chemical symbol of product isotope, $X = ?$

What equation contains the given information?

$$^{218}_{84}Po \longrightarrow \ ^A_ZX + \ ^4_2He$$

Write and solve equations for atomic mass and atomic number.

$218 = A + 4$ $84 = Z + 2$

$218 - 4 = A$ $84 - 2 = Z$

$214 = A$ $82 = Z$

On the periodic table, lead, Pb, has an atomic number of 82. So, X is Pb. The balanced nuclear equation is shown below.

$$^{218}_{84}Po \longrightarrow \ ^{214}_{82}Pb + \ ^4_2He$$

3. Look Back and Check

Is your answer reasonable?

The mass number on the left equals the sum of the mass numbers on the right. The atomic number on the left equals the sum of the atomic numbers on the right. The equation is balanced.

Math Practice

On separate sheet of paper, solve the following problems.

1. Write a balanced nuclear equation for the alpha decay of uranium-238.

2. Write a balanced nuclear equation for the alpha decay of thorium-230.

© Pearson Education, Inc., publishing as Pearson Prentice Hall. All rights reserved.

Chapter 11   Motion

Summary

11.1 Distance and Displacement

To describe motion accurately and completely, a frame of reference is needed. A frame of reference is a system of objects that are not moving with respect to one another.

The answer to how fast something is moving depends on the frame of reference you choose to measure the moving object's motion. Relative motion is movement in relation to a frame of reference. For example, as a train moves past a platform, people standing on the platform will see those on the train speeding by. But when the people on the train look at one another, they don't seem to be moving at all.

On a train, looking at a seat or the floor may tell you how fast you are walking relative to the train. It doesn't tell you, however, how fast you are moving relative to the ground outside. Choosing a meaningful frame of reference allows you to describe motion in a clear and relevant manner.

Distance is the length of a path between two points. When an object moves in a straight line, the distance is the length of the line connecting the object's starting point and its ending point.

The SI unit for measuring distance is the meter (m). For very large distances, it is more common to make measurements in kilometers (km). Distances that are smaller than meters are measured in centimeters (cm). One centimeter is one hundredth of a meter.

Displacement is the direction from the starting point and the length of a straight line from the starting point to the ending point. Displacement gives information both about how far away an object is from a given point and in what direction the object is from that point. For example, accurate directions give the direction from a starting point as well as the distance.

Displacement is an example of a vector. A vector is a quantity that has magnitude and direction. The magnitude can be size, length, or amount. Vector addition is the combining of vector magnitudes and directions.

Add displacements by using vector addition. When two displacements—represented by two vectors—have the same direction, you can add their magnitudes. If two displacements are in opposite directions, the magnitudes subtract from each other.

When two or more displacement vectors have different directions, they may be combined by graphing. The vector sum of two or more vectors is called the resultant vector. The resultant vector points directly from the starting point to the ending point.

11.2 Speed and Velocity

Speed is the ratio of the distance an object moves to the amount of time the object moves. The SI unit of speed is meters per second (m/s).

Two ways to describe the speed of an object are average speed and instantaneous speed. Average speed is computed for the entire time of a trip. Instantaneous speed, by contrast, is measured at a particular instant. In different situations, either one or both of these measurements may be a useful way to describe speed.

Sometimes it is useful to know how fast something moves for an entire trip. Average speed, $\bar{v}$, is the total distance traveled, d, divided by the time, t, it takes to travel that distance. This can be written as an equation:

$$\text{Average speed} = \frac{\text{Total distance}}{\text{Total time}}, \text{ or } \bar{v} = \frac{d}{t}$$

© Pearson Education, Inc., publishing as Pearson Prentice Hall. All rights reserved.

During the time an object is moving, its speed may change, but this equation tells you the average speed over the entire trip.

Sometimes, you need to know how fast you are going at a particular moment. Instantaneous speed, v, is the rate at which an object is moving at a given moment in time.

A distance-time graph is a good way to describe motion. On a line graph, slope is the change in the vertical axis value divided by the change in the horizontal axis value. The slope of a line on a distance-time graph is speed, or the change in the distance divided by the change in time.

Together, the speed and direction in which an object is moving are called velocity. Velocity is a description of both speed and direction of motion. Velocity is a vector. A change in velocity can be the result of a change in speed, a change in direction, or both.

Sometimes the motion of an object involves more than one velocity. Two or more velocities add by vector addition.

11.3 Acceleration

The rate at which velocity changes is called acceleration. Acceleration can be described as changes in speed, changes in direction, or changes in both. Acceleration is a vector.

Scientifically, acceleration applies to any change in an object's velocity. This change may be either an increase or a decrease in speed. Acceleration can be caused by positive (increasing) change in speed or by negative (decreasing) change in speed.

An example of acceleration due to change in speed is free fall, which is the movement of an object toward Earth solely because of gravity. The unit for acceleration is meters per second per second, or meters per second squared (m/s^2). Each second an object is in free fall, its velocity increases downward at a

rate of 9.8 meters per second. The change in the object's speed is 9.8 m/s^2, the acceleration due to gravity.

Acceleration isn't always the result of changes in speed. A horse on a carousel is traveling at a constant speed, but it is accelerating because its direction is constantly changing. Sometimes motion is characterized by changes in both speed and direction at the same time.

The velocity of an object moving in a straight line changes at a constant rate when the object is experiencing constant acceleration. Constant acceleration is a steady change in velocity.

You calculate acceleration for straight-line motion by dividing the change in velocity by the total time. If a is the acceleration, v_i is the initial velocity, v_f is the final velocity, and t is the total time, this equation can be written as follows.

$$\text{Acceleration} = \frac{\text{Change in velocity}}{\text{Total time}} = \frac{v_f - v_i}{t}$$

Notice in this formula that velocity is in the numerator and time is in the denominator. If the velocity increases, then the numerator is positive and thus the acceleration is also positive. If the velocity decreases, then the numerator is negative and the acceleration is also negative.

You can use a graph to calculate acceleration. The slope of a speed-time graph is acceleration. The slope is change in speed divided by change in time. Constant acceleration is represented on a speed-time graph by a straight line. A linear graph is a line graph on which the displayed data form straight-line parts.

Accelerated motion is represented by a curved line on a distance-time graph. In a nonlinear graph, a curve connects the data points that are plotted.

Instantaneous acceleration is how fast a velocity is changing at a specific instant.

© Pearson Education, Inc., publishing as Pearson Prentice Hall. All rights reserved.

Chapter 11   Motion

Section 11.1 Distance and Displacement
(pages 328–331)

This section defines distance and displacement. Methods of describing motion are presented. Vector addition and subtraction are introduced.

Reading Strategy (page 328)

Predicting Write a definition for *frame of reference* in your own words in the left column of the table. After you read the section, compare your definition to the scientific definition and explain why a frame of reference is important. For more information on this Reading Strategy, see the **Reading and Study Skills** in the **Skills and Reference Handbook** at the end of your textbook.

Frame of Reference	
Frame of reference probably means	**Frame of reference actually means**

1. What two things must you know to describe the motion of an object?
   _____

Choosing a Frame of Reference (pages 328–329)

2. Is the following sentence true or false? A frame of reference is not necessary to describe motion accurately and completely. _____

3. What is a frame of reference? _____
   _____

4. Movement in relation to a frame of reference is called _____.

5. Imagine that you are a passenger in a car. Circle the letter of the best frame of reference you could use to determine how fast the car is moving relative to the ground.
   a. the people sitting next to you in the backseat
   b. the driver of the car
   c. a van traveling in the lane next to your car
   d. a sign post on the side of the road

Measuring Distance (page 329)

6. Distance is _____.

7. Circle the letter of the SI unit best suited for measuring the length of a room in your home.
   a. kilometers   b. meters
   c. centimeters   d. millimeters

© Pearson Education, Inc., publishing as Pearson Prentice Hall. All rights reserved.

Chapter 11   Motion

Measuring Displacements (page 330)

8. Is the following sentence true or false? Five blocks south is an example of a displacement. _____

9. Compare and contrast distance and displacement. _____
_____
_____

10. What would your total displacement be if you walked from your front door, around the block, and then stopped when you reached your front door again?

   a. one block   b. two blocks

   c. the entire distance of your trip   d. zero

Combining Displacements (pages 330–331)

11. A vector is a quantity that has both _____ and _____.

12. Circle the letter of each answer that could describe the magnitude of a vector.

   a. length   b. direction

   c. amount   d. size

13. To combine two displacements that are in opposite directions, the magnitudes _____ from one another.

For questions 14 and 15, refer to the figure below.

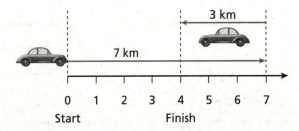

14. The magnitudes of the two displacement vectors are _____ and _____.

15. Because the two displacements are in opposite directions, the magnitude of the total displacement is _____.

16. Circle the letter that answers the question. What is the displacement of a cyclist who travels 1 mile north, then 1 mile east, and finally 1 mile south?

   a. 3 miles east   b. 1 mile north

   c. 3 miles south   d. 1 mile east

17. The vector sum of two or more other vectors is called the _____.

© Pearson Education, Inc., publishing as Pearson Prentice Hall. All rights reserved.

Chapter 11   Motion

Section 11.2 Speed and Velocity
(pages 332–337)

This section defines and compares speed and velocity. It also describes how to calculate average speed.

Reading Strategy (page 332)

Monitoring Your Understanding After you read this section, identify several things you have learned that are relevant to your life. Explain why they are relevant to you. For more information on this Reading Strategy, see the **Reading and Study Skills** in the **Skills and Reference Handbook** at the end of your textbook.

Facts About Speed and Velocity	
What Is Important	**Why It Is Important**

Speed (pages 332–334)

1. Define speed. _____
   _____

2. The SI units for speed are _____ .

3. How is instantaneous speed different from average speed? _____
   _____

4. The equation used for calculating average speed is _____ .

5. Is the following sentence true or false? You can determine how fast you were going at the midpoint of a trip by calculating average speed for the entire trip. _____

6. A student walked 1.5 km in 25 minutes, and then, realizing he was late, ran the remaining 0.5 km in 5 minutes. Calculate his average speed on the way to school.
   _____

7. What type of speed does an automobile's speedometer display?
   _____

Graphing Motion (page 334)

8. The slope of a line on a distance-time graph represents _____ .

© Pearson Education, Inc., publishing as Pearson Prentice Hall. All rights reserved.

For questions 9 through 11, refer to the graph below.

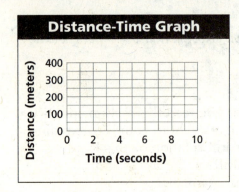

9. Draw a point on the graph that represents 200 m traveled in 4 seconds. Draw a line connecting this point with the origin (0,0). Label this as line A.

10. Draw a point on the graph that represents 100 m traveled in 10 seconds. Draw a line connecting this point with the origin (0,0). Label this as line B.

11. Calculate the average speed (slope) of lines A and B. Be sure to include units.

Velocity (page 336)

12. How do speed and velocity differ? _____

_____

13. Circle the letter of each sentence that describes a change in velocity.

    a. A moving object gains speed.

    b. A moving object changes direction.

    c. A moving object moves in a straight line at a constant speed.

    d. A moving object slows down.

14. Is the following sentence true or false? If a car travels around a gentle curve on a highway at 60 km/h, the velocity does not change. _____

Combining Velocities (page 337)

15. How do velocities combine? _____

16. A river flows at a velocity of 3 km/h relative to the riverbank. A boat moves upstream at a velocity of 15 km/h relative to the river. What is the velocity of the boat relative to the riverbank?

    a. 18 km/h downstream

    b. 15 km/h upstream

    c. 12 km/h upstream

    d. 12 km/h downstream

© Pearson Education, Inc., publishing as Pearson Prentice Hall. All rights reserved.

Chapter 11   Motion

Section 11.3 Acceleration
(pages 342–348)

This section describes the relationships among speed, velocity, and acceleration. Examples of these concepts are discussed. Sample calculations of acceleration and graphs representing accelerated motion are presented.

Reading Strategy (page 342)

Summarizing Read the section on acceleration. Then complete the concept map to organize what you know about acceleration. For more information on this Reading Strategy, see the **Reading and Study Skills** in the **Skills and Reference Handbook** at the end of your textbook.

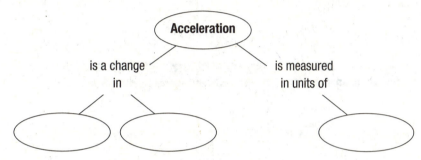

What Is Acceleration? (pages 342–345)

1. The rate at which velocity changes is called _____.

2. In terms of speed and direction, in what ways can an object accelerate? _____

   _____

3. Because acceleration is a quantity that has both magnitude and direction, it is a(n) _____.

4. Is the following sentence true or false? Acceleration is the result of increases or decreases in speed. _____

5. Ignoring air resistance, a rock in free fall will have a velocity of _____ after 4.0 seconds.

6. A horse on a carousel that is moving at a constant speed is accelerating because _____.

7. Describe constant acceleration. _____

   _____

Calculating Acceleration (pages 345–346)

8. Write the equation used to calculate the acceleration of an object.

   _____

© Pearson Education, Inc., publishing as Pearson Prentice Hall. All rights reserved.

Chapter 11   Motion

9. Is the following sentence true or false? When the final velocity is less than the initial velocity of an object, the acceleration is negative. _____

10. A skateboarder begins down a ramp at a speed of 1.0 m/s. After 3 seconds, her speed has increased to 4.0 m/s. Calculate her acceleration.

   a. 1.0 m/s^2 b. 3.0 m/s^2
   c. 5.0 m/s^2 d. 9.8 m/s^2

Graphs of Accelerated Motion (pages 346–348)

11. A speed-time graph in which the displayed data forms a straight line is an example of a(n) _____.

For questions 12 through 15, refer to the graphs below.

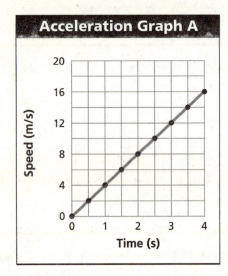

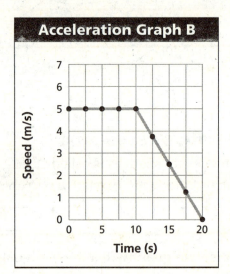

12. Graph A represents the motion of a downhill skier. How fast was the skier moving after traveling down the hill for 2.5 seconds? _____

13. In which graph does an object move at constant speed during the first 4 seconds? _____

14. Graph B represents the motion of a mountain biker. What is the biker's speed at times of 10 s and 20 s? _____

15. Determine the acceleration of the mountain biker during the 10 second to 20 second time period. Show your work.

   _____

   _____

16. The plotted data points representing acceleration in a distance-time graph form a(n) _____.

Instantaneous Acceleration (page 348)

17. The measure of how fast a velocity is changing at a specific instant is known as _____.

© Pearson Education, Inc., publishing as Pearson Prentice Hall. All rights reserved.

Chapter 11   Motion

WordWise

Complete the sentences by using one of the scrambled vocabulary words below.

vrlaeeit oinotm   mefar fo ecrneeefr   gvaeera dspee
levotciy   nerlia   centidsa
esdep   erfe lafl   aulsettrn crovet
atnicoelecar   rotcev   nnilraeon

An expression for _____ is $(v_f - v_i)/t$.

A quantity that has both magnitude and direction is called a(n)_____.

The total distance traveled divided by the total time is

_____.

A speed-time graph in which data points form a straight line is an example of a(n) _____ graph.

Common units for _____ include meters per second (m/s).

In order to accurately and completely describe the motion of an object, a(n) _____ is necessary.

You can determine _____ by measuring the length of the actual path between two points in space.

Two or more vectors combine to form a(n) _____.

Objects in _____ accelerate at 9.8 m/s².

A curve often connects data points on a(n) _____ graph.

Together, the speed and direction in which an object is moving are called _____.

Movement in relation to a frame of reference is _____.

© Pearson Education, Inc., publishing as Pearson Prentice Hall. All rights reserved.

Chapter 11 Motion

Interpreting a Distance-Time Graph

The distance-time graph below illustrates the motion of a car whose speed varied with time during a trip. Calculate the average speed of the car during the first 8 seconds of the trip. Give your answer in km/h.

Math Skill:
Line Graphs and Conversion Factors

You may want to read more about this **Math Skill** in the **Skills and Reference Handbook** at the end of your textbook.

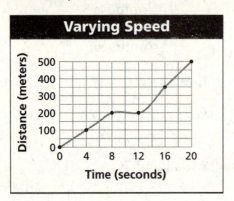

1. **Read and Understand**

   What information are you given?

   A graph of distance versus time.

2. **Plan and Solve**

   How will you determine speed for the time interval referenced in the question?

   1. To determine the distance traveled in 8 s, move your finger up from the 8 s mark on the time axis to the plotted line.

   2. Now move your finger horizontally to the left to the distance axis. Read the value from the axis. (200 m)

   3. Calculate the average speed using the formula

      Speed = Distance/Time = 200 m/8 s = 25 m/s

   4. Convert from m/s to km/h:

      (25 m/s)(3600 s/h)(1 km/1000 m) = 90 km/h

3. **Look Back and Check**

   Is your answer reasonable?

   A quick calculation from the interval of constant speed shows that the car traveled 100 meters in 4 seconds—an average speed of 25 m/s.

Math Practice

On a separate sheet of paper, solve the following problems.

1. How long did it take the car to travel a distance of 350 m? _____

2. Determine the speed of the car in km/h during the interval 0 s to 12 s.

© Pearson Education, Inc., publishing as Pearson Prentice Hall. All rights reserved.

Chapter 12   Forces and Motion

Summary

12.1 Forces

A force is a push or a pull that acts on an object. A force can cause a resting object to move, or it can accelerate a moving object by changing the object's speed or direction.

Force is measured in newtons (N). One newton is the force that causes a 1-kilogram mass to accelerate at a rate of 1 meter per second each second (m/s^2).

Forces can be combined. Forces in the same direction add together. Forces in opposite directions subtract from one another. The net force is the overall force acting on an object.

Balanced forces are forces that combine to produce a net force of zero. When the forces on an object are balanced, the net force is zero and there is no change in the object's motion.

An unbalanced force is a force that results when the net force acting on an object is not equal to zero. When an unbalanced force acts on an object, the object accelerates.

All moving objects are subject to friction. Friction is a force that opposes the motion of objects that touch as they move past each other. Friction acts at the surface where objects are in contact.

There are four main types of friction: static friction, sliding friction, rolling friction, and fluid friction.

- Static friction is the friction force that acts on objects that are not moving.
- Sliding friction is a force that opposes the motion of an object as it slides over a surface.
- Rolling friction is the friction force that acts on rolling objects.
- Fluid friction is the friction force that opposes the motion of an object through a fluid.

Gravity is a force that acts between any two masses. Gravity is an attractive force, that is, it pulls objects together.

Earth's gravity acts downward toward the center of Earth.

Both gravity and air resistance affect the motion of a falling object. Gravity causes an object to accelerate downward, whereas air resistance acts in the direction opposite to the motion and reduces acceleration. Terminal velocity is the constant velocity of a falling object when the force of air resistance equals the force of gravity.

Projectile motion is the curved path of an object in free fall after it is given an initial forward velocity (for example, a thrown ball).

12.2 Newton's First and Second Laws of Motion

The ancient Greek philosopher Aristotle incorrectly proposed that force is required to keep an object moving at constant speed. The Italian scientist Galileo Galilei concluded that moving objects not subjected to friction or any other force would continue to move indefinitely.

The English scientist Isaac Newton summarized his study of force and motion in several laws of motion. According to Newton's first law of motion, the state of motion of an object does not change as long as the net force acting on the object is zero. Thus, unless an unbalanced force acts, an object at rest remains at rest, and an object in motion remains in motion with the same speed and direction.

Newton's first law of motion is sometimes called the law of inertia. Inertia is the tendency of an object to resist change in its motion.

An unbalanced force causes an object's velocity to change. In other words, the object accelerates. The acceleration of an object also depends on its mass. Mass depends on the amount of matter the object contains.

© Pearson Education, Inc., publishing as Pearson Prentice Hall. All rights reserved.

According to Newton's second law of motion, the acceleration of an object is equal to the net force acting on it divided by the object's mass. Newton was able to put these ideas into a single formula.

Acceleration $= \frac{\text{Net force}}{\text{Mass}}$, or $a = \frac{F}{m}$

The acceleration of an object is always in the same direction as the net force. In using the formula for Newton's second law, it is helpful to realize that the units N/kg and m/s^2 are the same.

Weight (W) is the force of gravity acting on an object. An object's weight is the product of the object's mass (m) and acceleration due to gravity acting on it (g).

$$W = mg$$

12.3 Newton's Third Law of Motion and Momentum

According to Newton's third law of motion, whenever one object exerts a force on a second object, the second object exerts an equal and opposite force on the first object. The two forces are called action and reaction forces.

Momentum is the product of an object's mass and its velocity. An object with large momentum is hard to stop. The momentum for any object at rest is zero.

You can calculate momentum by multiplying an object's mass (in kilograms) and its velocity (in meters per second).

Momentum = Mass × Velocity

Momentum is measured in units of kilogram-meters per second (kg•m/s).

Under certain conditions, collisions of objects obey the law of conservation of momentum. In physics, the word *conservation* means that something has constant value. That is, conservation of momentum means that momentum does not increase or decrease.

According to the law of conservation of momentum, if no net force acts on a system, then the total momentum of the system does not change. In a closed system, the loss of momentum of one object equals the gain in momentum of another object—momentum is conserved.

12.4 Universal Forces

Electric force and magnetic force are two different aspects of the electromagnetic force. Electromagnetic force is associated with charged particles. Electric force and magnetic force are the only forces that can both attract and repel. Electric forces act between charged objects or particles such as electrons and protons. Magnetic forces act on certain metals, on the poles of magnets, and on moving charges.

Two forces, the strong nuclear force and the weak nuclear force, act within the nucleus of an atom to hold it together. These forces are strong enough to overcome the electric force of repulsion that acts among the protons.

Gravity is the weakest universal force. Gravitational force is an attractive force that acts between any two masses. Newton's law of universal gravitation states that every object in the universe attracts every other object.

The gravitational force between two objects is proportional to their masses and decreases rapidly as the distance between the masses increases. The greater the mass of the objects, the greater is the gravitational force. Gravitational force decreases with the square of the distance between objects.

Gravity keeps the moon in orbit around Earth, the planets in orbit around the sun, and the stars in orbit around their galaxies. Earth's gravitational force keeps the moon in a nearly circular orbit around Earth. A centripedal force is a center-directed force that continuously

© Pearson Education, Inc., publishing as Pearson Prentice Hall. All rights reserved.

Chapter 12   Forces and Motion

Section 12.1 Forces
(pages 356–362)

This section describes what forces are and explains how forces affect the motion of various objects.

Reading Strategy (page 356)

Relating Text and Visuals As you read about forces, look carefully at Figures 2, 3, and 5 in your textbook. Then complete the table by describing the forces and motion shown in each figure. For more information on this Reading Strategy, see the **Reading and Study Skills** in the **Skills and Reference Handbook** at the end of your textbook.

Forces and Motion		
Figure	**Is Net Force 0?**	**Effect on Motion**
2A		
2B		
3		
5A		
5B		

What is a Force? (pages 356–357)

1. A force is defined as a(n) _____ or a(n) _____ that acts on an object.

2. Is the following sentence true or false? A force can act to cause an object at rest to move or it can accelerate an object that is already moving. _____

3. How can a force change the motion of an object that is already moving?

_____

_____

4. Circle the letter of the best answer. What force causes a 1-kg mass to accelerate at a rate of 1 meter per second each second?

    a. $1 \, kg/m \bullet s^2$ b. $1 \, kg/s$

    c. $1 \, kg \bullet m$ d. 1 newton

Combining Forces (pages 357–358)

5. The overall force acting on an object after all the forces are combined is the _____.

6. How do balanced and unbalanced forces affect the motion of an object?

_____

_____

© Pearson Education, Inc., publishing as Pearson Prentice Hall. All rights reserved.

Chapter 12   Forces and Motion

Friction (pages 359–360)

7. Is the following sentence true or false? Friction is a force that helps objects that are touching move past each other more easily.

   _____

8. Circle the letters that identify types of friction.

   a. rolling   b. gravity

   c. static   d. sliding

9. The friction force that acts on objects that are at rest is

   _____.

10. Why is less force needed to keep an object moving than to start the object in motion? _____

   _____

   _____

11. Complete the table below about friction forces.

Types of Friction Forces	
Friction Force	Example
Static	
	Pushing a book along your desk
Rolling	

12. Is the following sentence true or false? Fluid friction is a force that opposes the motion of an object through a fluid such as water.

   _____

Gravity (page 361)

13. Gravity is a(n) _____ force that pulls objects together.

14. Is the following sentence true or false? Earth's gravity acts downward toward the center of Earth. _____

15. Describe how gravity and air resistance affect the motion of a falling object. _____

   _____

16. Is the following sentence true or false? Terminal velocity is the constant velocity of a falling object when the force of air resistance equals the force of gravity. _____

Projectile Motion (page 362)

17. The curved path caused by the combination of an initial forward velocity and the downward force of gravity is known as _____ motion.

© Pearson Education, Inc., publishing as Pearson Prentice Hall. All rights reserved.

Chapter 12   Forces and Motion

Section 12.2 Newton's First and Second Laws of Motion
(pages 363–369)

This section discusses how force and mass affect acceleration. The acceleration due to gravity is defined, and mass and weight are compared.

Reading Strategy (page 363)

Building Vocabulary As you read this section, write a definition in the table for each vocabulary word you encounter. Use your own words in the definitions. For more information on this Reading Strategy, see the **Reading and Study Skills** in the **Skills and Reference Handbook** at the end of your textbook.

Matter and Motion	
Vocabulary	**Definition**
Inertia	

Aristotle, Galileo, and Newton (pages 363–364)

Match each scientist with his accomplishment.

Accomplishment	Scientist
_____ **1.** Italian scientist who did experiments that helped correct misconceptions about force and motion	a. Aristotle
_____ **2.** Scientist who studied in England and introduced several laws describing force and motion	b. Galileo
_____ **3.** An ancient Greek philosopher who made many scientific discoveries through observation and logical reasoning	c. Newton

Newton's First Law of Motion (pages 364–365)

4. Is the following sentence true or false? According to Newton's first law of motion, an object's state of motion does not change as long as the net force acting on it is zero. _____

5. What is inertia? _____

© Pearson Education, Inc., publishing as Pearson Prentice Hall. All rights reserved.

Chapter 12   Forces and Motion

6. Is the following sentence true or false? The law of inertia states that an object in motion will eventually slow down and come to a complete stop if it travels far enough in the same direction. _____

Newton's Second Law of Motion (pages 365–368)

7. According to Newton's second law of motion, acceleration of an object depends upon the _____ of the object and the _____ acting on it.

Match each term with its description.

Description	Term
_____ **8.** A measure of the inertia of an object	a. mass
_____ **9.** Net force/Mass	b. net force
_____ **10.** Causes an object's velocity to change	c. acceleration

11. Is the following sentence true or false? The acceleration of an object is always in the same direction as the net force acting on the object. _____

12. Is the following sentence true or false? If the same force acts upon two objects with different masses, the acceleration will be greater for the object with greater mass. _____

Weight and Mass (pages 368–369)

13. What is weight? _____

_____

14. Write the formula used to calculate the weight of an object.

_____

15. Is the following sentence true or false? Because the weight formula shows that mass and weight are proportional, doubling the mass of an object will not affect its weight. _____

16. Complete the table below by describing the difference between mass and weight.

Mass and Weight	
Mass	**Weight**

17. On the moon, the acceleration due to gravity is only about one sixth that on Earth. Thus, an object will weigh _____ on the moon than it weighs on Earth.

© Pearson Education, Inc., publishing as Pearson Prentice Hall. All rights reserved.

Chapter 12   Forces and Motion

Section 12.3 Newton's Third Law of Motion and Momentum
(pages 372–377)

This section describes action-reaction forces and how the momentum of objects is determined.

Reading Strategy (page 372)

Summarizing As you read about momentum in this section, complete the concept map to organize what you learn. For more information on this Reading Strategy, see the **Reading and Study Skills** in the **Skills and Reference Handbook** at the end of your textbook.

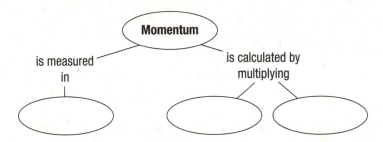

Newton's Third Law (page 373)

1. According to Newton's third law of motion, what happens whenever one object exerts a force on a second object? _____

_____

2. The equal and opposite forces described by Newton's third law are called _____ and _____ forces.

3. Circle the letters that identify each sentence that is true about action-reaction forces.

   a. Newton's second law describes action-reaction forces.

   b. Forces always exist in pairs.

   c. Action-reaction forces never cancel.

   d. All action-reaction forces produce motion.

4. Is the following statement true or false? Action-reaction forces do not cancel each other because the action force is always greater than the reaction force. _____

Momentum (pages 374–375)

5. Circle the letter of each factor that affects the momentum of a moving object.

   a. mass   b. volume   c. shape   d. velocity

6. If two identical objects are moving at different velocities, the object that is moving faster will have _____ momentum.

© Pearson Education, Inc., publishing as Pearson Prentice Hall. All rights reserved.

7. Your in-line skates are sitting in a box on a shelf in the closet. What is their momentum? _____

8. Is the following sentence true or false? An object with a small mass can have a large momentum if the object is traveling at a high speed. _____

9. Write the momentum formula, including the correct units.

_____

10. Circle the letter of the object that has the greatest momentum.

   a. a 700-gram bird flying at a velocity of 2.5 m/s

   b. a 1000-kilogram car traveling at 5 m/s

   c. a 40-kilogram shopping cart rolling along at 0.5 m/s

   d. a 300-kilogram roller coaster car traveling at 25 m/s

Conservation of Momentum (pages 376–377)

11. What does conservation of momentum mean? _____

_____

12. Is the following sentence true or false? Objects within a closed system can exert forces on one another, but other objects and forces cannot leave or enter the system. _____

13. According to the law of conservation of momentum, what happens to the total momentum of a system if no net force acts on the system?

_____

14. Is the following sentence true or false? In a closed system with two objects, the loss of momentum of one object equals the gain in momentum of the other object. _____

For questions 15 and 16, refer to the graph below.

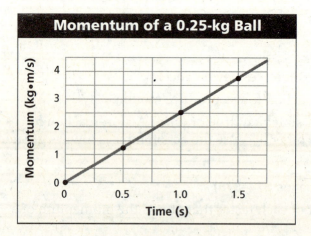

15. The momentum of the ball at one second is _____.

16. What is the speed of the ball at 0.5 seconds? Show your calculation. *Hint:* Solve the momentum formula for velocity.

© Pearson Education, Inc., publishing as Pearson Prentice Hall. All rights reserved.

Chapter 12   Forces and Motion

Section 12.4 Universal Forces
(pages 378–382)

This section defines four forces that exist throughout the universe. Each force is described and its significance is discussed.

Reading Strategy (page 378)

Comparing and Contrasting As you read this section, compare two universal forces by completing the table. For more information on this Reading Strategy, see the **Reading and Study Skills** in the **Skills and Reference Handbook** at the end of your textbook.

Universal Nuclear Forces			
Force	Acts on Which Particles?	Acts Over What Distance?	Relative Strength
Strong nuclear			
Weak nuclear			

1. What are the four universal forces?

   a. _____   b. _____

   c. _____   d. _____

Electromagnetic Forces (pages 378–379)

2. Is the following sentence true or false? Electromagnetic force is associated with charged particles. _____

3. Name the only two forces that can both attract and repel. _____

   _____

4. Objects with like charges _____ one another, and objects with opposite charges _____ one another.

5. Circle the letters of the sentences that correctly describe magnets or magnetic forces.

   a. Magnetic forces act on certain metals.

   b. Magnets have two poles, north and south.

   c. Two poles that are alike attract each other.

   d. Magnetic forces can both attract and repel.

Nuclear Forces (pages 379–380)

6. The force that holds particles in the nucleus together is the _____.

7. What evidence suggests that nuclear forces have a powerful force of attraction? _____

   _____

© Pearson Education, Inc., publishing as Pearson Prentice Hall. All rights reserved.

Chapter 12   Forces and Motion

8. Circle the letter of the best answer. Over extremely short distances, approximately how many times stronger is the strong nuclear force than the electric force of repulsion?

   a. 10   b. 100   c. 1000   d. 10,000

9. Compare and contrast the strong and weak nuclear forces. _____

   _____

   _____

   _____

Gravitational Force (pages 380–382)

10. State Newton's law of universal gravitation. _____

    _____

11. Circle the letter of each sentence that is true about gravitational force.

    a. The closer two objects are to one another, the weaker the gravitational force.

    b. The farther apart two objects are, the weaker the gravitational force.

    c. The greater the mass of an object, the stronger its gravitational force.

    d. Earth's gravitational force is stronger than the gravitational force of the sun.

12. The gravitational force of attraction between two objects depends on _____ and _____.

13. Is the following sentence true or false? Gravity is the weakest universal force, but it is the most effective force over long distances. _____

14. The sun's mass is much greater than the mass of Earth, so the sun's gravitational force is much _____ than that of Earth.

15. Why does the moon orbit Earth in a nearly circular path? _____

    _____

16. Is the following sentence true or false? The gravitational pull of the moon is the primary cause of Earth's ocean tides.

    _____

17. Is the following sentence true or false? An artificial satellite in a high orbit will slow down and lose altitude due to the pull of Earth's gravity. _____

18. List four uses of artificial satellites. _____

    _____

    _____

    _____

© Pearson Education, Inc., publishing as Pearson Prentice Hall. All rights reserved.

Name _____ Class _____ Date _____

Chapter 12   Forces and Motion

WordWise

Complete the sentences using one of the scrambled words below.

nicofirt	vtiyagr	aecmleorntcgeti corfe
ssma	raeeaclnocit	hwgeti
ten eofrc	lirnetcptae refco	swonten
lfudi tnfcriio	kewa cnuarel	teianri
mtnmoemu		

A measure of an object's inertia is its _____.

The _____ force affects all particles in a nucleus and acts only over a short range.

A sky diver experiences _____, which opposes the force of gravity.

A change in an object's speed or direction of motion is called _____.

The product of an object's mass and its velocity is

_____.

A measure of the force of gravity acting on an object is its

_____.

A center-directed _____ continuously changes the direction of an object to make it move in a circle.

A force associated with charged particles is _____.

Mass is the measure of the _____ of an object.

A force that opposes the motion of objects that touch as they move past each other is called _____.

The universal force that causes every object to attract every other object is _____.

A person's weight on Mars, measured in _____, is 0.38 times the weight on Earth.

Acceleration equals _____ divided by mass.

© Pearson Education, Inc., publishing as Pearson Prentice Hall. All rights reserved.

Name _____ Class _____ Date _____

Chapter 12 Forces and Motion

Calculating Acceleration

A car with a mass of 1300 kg accelerates as it leaves a parking lot. If the net force on the car is 3900 newtons, what is the car's *acceleration*?

Math Skill: Formulas and Equations

You may want to read more about this **Math Skill** in the **Skills and Reference Handbook** at the end of your textbook.

1. Read and Understand

What information are you given?

Mass , m = 1300 kg

Force, F = 3900 N (in the forward direction)

2. Plan and Solve

What unknown are you trying to calculate?

Acceleration, a = ?

What formula contains the given quantities and the unknown?

$$a = \frac{F}{m}$$

Replace each variable with its known value and solve.

$$a = \frac{3900 \text{ N}}{1300 \text{ kg}} = 3 \frac{\text{N}}{\text{kg}} = 3 \frac{\text{kg} \cdot \text{m/s}^2}{\text{kg}} = 3 \text{ m/s}^2$$

$a = 3$ m/s^2 in the forward direction

3. Look Back and Check

Is your answer reasonable?

Powerful sports cars can accelerate at 6 m/s^2, so a smaller acceleration of 3 m/s^2 seems reasonable.

Math Practice

On a separate sheet of paper, solve the following problems.

1. A construction worker pushes a wheelbarrow with a total mass of 50.0 kg. What is the acceleration of the wheelbarrow if the net force on it is 75 N?

2. A van with a mass of 1500 kg accelerates at a rate of 3.5 m/s^2 in the forward direction. What is the net force acting on the van? (*Hint:* Solve the acceleration formula for force.)

3. A 6.0×10^3 N force accelerates a truck entering a highway at 2.5 m/s^2. What is the mass of the truck? (*Hint:* Solve the acceleration formula for mass.)

© Pearson Education, Inc., publishing as Pearson Prentice Hall. All rights reserved.

Chapter 13   Forces in Fluids

Summary

13.1 Fluid Pressure

Pressure is the result of a force distributed over an area. To calculate pressure, divide the force by the area over which the force acts.

$$\text{Pressure} = \frac{\text{Force}}{\text{Area}}$$

In the formula, force should be in newtons (N) and area should be in square meters (m^2). The resulting unit—newtons per square meter (N/m^2)—is the SI unit of pressure, also known as a pascal (Pa).

A fluid is a substance that takes the shape of its container. Both liquids and gases are fluids. Water, oil, gasoline, air, and helium are fluids.

A fluid exerts pressure. The amount of pressure a fluid exerts depends on several factors. Water pressure increases as depth increases. The pressure in a fluid at any given depth is constant, and it is exerted equally in all directions.

Surprisingly, the shape of a container and the area of its bottom do not affect fluid pressure. For a fluid that is not moving, depth and the type of fluid are the two factors that determine the pressure the fluid exerts. Thus, the amount of fluid, measured in terms of volume or weight, does not affect pressure.

Air pressure increases with the depth of the atmosphere. Instead of referring to a certain depth of the atmosphere, however, people refer to their altitude above sea level. Air pressure decreases as the altitude increases.

The atmosphere is exerting more than 1000 newtons of force on the top of your head. Fortunately, the inside of your body also exerts pressure. The pressure inside your body balances the air pressure outside. The balanced forces cancel, resulting in a net force of zero.

13.2 Forces and Pressure in Fluids

Imagine a two-liter soda bottle completely filled with water, with its cap tightly screwed on. Note that at any given depth, equal pressure acts against any point on the inside of the bottle. Note also that the pressure increases with depth.

If you squeeze the bottle in the middle, the pressure increases equally throughout the water, not just at the point where you squeeze. The French scientist Blaise Pascal discovered this phenomenon in the 1600s. His observations led to a general principle. According to Pascal's principle, a change in pressure at any point in a fluid is transmitted equally and unchanged in all directions throughout the fluid.

Hydraulics is the science of applying Pascal's principle. A hydraulic system is a device that uses pressurized fluid acting on pistons of different sizes to change a force. In a hydraulic lift system, an input force is applied to a small piston, which pushes against the fluid sealed in the hydraulic system. The pressure produced by the small piston is transmitted through the fluid to the large piston. Thus, the pressure on both pistons is the same.

However, the pressure pushing against the large piston acts on a much larger area, which is the key to how the system works. In a hydraulic lift system, an increased output force is produced because a constant fluid pressure is exerted on the larger area of the output piston. If the large piston has eight times the area of the small piston, then the output force is eight times greater than the input force. Recall that force is equal to the product of pressure and area. Because the pressure on each piston is the same, the difference in forces is directly related to the difference in areas.

© Pearson Education, Inc., publishing as Pearson Prentice Hall. All rights reserved.

Chapter 13   Forces in Fluids

When you blow across the top of a single sheet of paper, the far end of the paper lifts upward. The Swiss scientist Daniel Bernoulli discovered the reason why the sheet of paper behaves as it does. According to Bernoulli's principle, as the speed of a fluid increases, the pressure within the fluid decreases. The air blowing across the top of the paper exerts less pressure than the stationary air underneath. Because the air below the paper is nearly motionless, it exerts a greater pressure. The difference in pressure forces the paper upward.

The ability of birds and airplanes to fly is largely explained by Bernoulli's principle. The air traveling over the top of an airplane wing moves faster than the air passing underneath. This creates a low-pressure area above the wing. The pressure difference between the top and the bottom of the wing creates an upward force known as lift. The lift created in this way is a large part of what keeps the airplane aloft. The wings of birds produce lift in much the same way as an airplane.

13.3 Buoyancy

Buoyancy is the ability of a fluid to exert an upward force on an object placed in it. Buoyancy results in the apparent loss of weight of an object in a fluid. In fact, every object in a fluid experiences buoyancy. When an object is submerged in water, the water exerts an upward force on the object, making it easier to lift. This upward force, which acts in the opposite direction of gravity, is called a buoyant force.

Because water pressure increases with depth, the forces pushing up on the bottom of a submerged object are greater than the forces from pressure pushing down on the top of the object. All other non-vertical forces cancel out one another. The result is a net upward force—the buoyant force.

The ancient Greek mathematician Archimedes is credited with an important discovery that bears his name. According to Archimedes' principle, the buoyant force on an object is equal to the weight of the fluid displaced by the object. When an object is submerged, it pushes aside—or displaces—a volume of fluid equal to its own volume.

Density and buoyancy are closely related. Recall that density is the ratio of an object's mass to its volume. If an object is less dense than the fluid it is in, it will float. If the object is more dense than the fluid it is in, it will sink. Different fluids can also float or sink in one another.

You can also determine if an object will float by analyzing the forces acting on it. The force of gravity—equal to the object's weight—acts downward on the object. The buoyant force—equal to the weight of the volume of displaced fluid—acts upward on the object. When the buoyant force is equal to the weight, an object floats or is suspended. When the buoyant force is less than the weight, the object sinks.

- An object that has the same density as the fluid it is submerged in will be suspended (it will float at any level) in the fluid. The buoyant force acting on the suspended object exactly equals the object's weight.
- When an object's weight becomes greater than the buoyant force acting on it, the object will sink.
- A heavy steel ship floats because of the shape of its hull. The hull is shaped so that it displaces a large volume of water, creating a large buoyant force. The buoyant force created by the ship's hull is large enough to counteract the ship's tremendous weight.

Objects float more easily in dense fluids. For a given displacement, the denser the fluid is, the greater the weight displaced. This greater displaced weight results in a greater buoyant force.

© Pearson Education, Inc., publishing as Pearson Prentice Hall. All rights reserved.

Chapter 13   Forces in Fluids

Section 13.1 Fluid Pressure
(pages 390–393)

This section defines pressure and describes factors that determine fluid pressure. The atmosphere as a fluid is discussed, including how air pressure changes with altitude.

Reading Strategy (page 390)

Using Prior Knowledge Before reading the section, write a common definition of the word *pressure*. After you have read the section, write the scientific definition of *pressure* and contrast it to your original definition. For more information on this Reading Strategy, see the **Reading and Study Skills** in the **Skills and Reference Handbook** at the end of your textbook.

Meanings of *Pressure*	
Common definition	
Scientific definition	

Pressure (pages 390–391)

1. Pressure is the result of a(n) _____ distributed over a(n) _____ .

2. The same force is exerted by each of the following. Which exerts the most pressure?

    a. a foot   b. a large book

    c. a fingertip   d. the tip of a ball-point pen

3. How is pressure calculated? _____
    _____

4. A wooden crate that measures 2.0 m long and 0.40 m wide rests on the floor. If the crate has a weight of 600.0 N, what pressure does it exert on the floor?

    a. 0.80 m^2 b. 480 Pa

    c. 3.0 × 10^3 N/m^2 d. 750 Pa

Pressure in Fluids (pages 391–392)

5. A substance that assumes the shape of its container is called a(n) _____ .

6. List four examples of fluids.

    a. _____   b. _____
    c. _____   d. _____

© Pearson Education, Inc., publishing as Pearson Prentice Hall. All rights reserved.

7. Circle the letter of each sentence that is true about fluid pressure.

   a. Water pressure decreases as depth decreases.

   b. Fluid pressure is exerted only at the base of the container holding the fluid.

   c. The pressure in a fluid at any given depth is constant, and it is exerted equally in all directions.

   d. The two factors that determine the pressure a fluid exerts are type of the fluid and its depth.

8. Is the following sentence true or false? The pressure at a depth of 2 feet in a large lake is greater than the pressure at the same depth in a swimming pool. _____

Air Pressure and the Atmosphere (pages 392–393)

9. Instead of referring to their depth in the atmosphere, people refer to their _____ above sea level.

For questions 10 through 13, refer to the air pressure table below.

Changes in Air Pressure with Altitude		
Altitude Above Sea Level (m)	Air Pressure (bars)	Air Pressure (kPa)
0	1.000	
200	0.9971	
400		96.68
600		94.42
800	0.9103	92.21
1000	0.8888	
1200	0.8677	87.89

10. Complete the air pressure columns in the table by converting between units of air pressure. *Hint:* 1 bar = 101.3 kPa.

11. How does air pressure change as a function of altitude?

    _____

12. Suppose a hiker is on a mountain ridge 1200 meters above sea level. Approximately what air pressure will she experience?

    _____

13. By how much does the air pressure decrease, in bars, from sea level to an altitude of 1200 meters? _____

14. Is the following sentence true or false? Air exerts a force of more than 1000 N on top of your head. _____

15. What keeps a person from being crushed by air pressure? _____

    _____

© Pearson Education, Inc., publishing as Pearson Prentice Hall. All rights reserved.

Chapter 13   Forces in Fluids

Section 13.2 Forces and Pressure in Fluids
(pages 394–397)

This section presents Pascal's and Bernoulli's principles. Examples of each principle from nature and industry are discussed.

Reading Strategy (pages 394)

Predicting Imagine two small foam balls hanging from strings at the same height with about three centimeters of space between them. Before you read the section, write a prediction about what will happen to the balls when you blow air through the space between them. Identify your reasons. After you have read the section, check the accuracy of your prediction. For more information on this Reading Strategy, see the **Reading and Study Skills** in the **Skills and Reference Handbook** at the end of your textbook.

Predicting Forces and Pressure in Fluids	
Prediction	
Reason for Prediction	

Transmitting Pressure in a Fluid (pages 394–395)

1. In a fluid-filled container, why is the pressure greater at the base of the container? _____

   _____

2. Is the following sentence true or false? If you squeeze a container filled with fluid, the pressure within the fluid increases equally throughout the fluid. _____

3. According to Pascal's principle, what happens when there is a change in pressure at any point in a fluid? _____

   _____

4. The science of applying Pascal's principle is called _____.

5. In a hydraulic lift system, an increased output force is produced because constant _____ is exerted on the larger area of the output piston.

6. Is the following sentence true or false? In a hydraulic system, the output force is greater than the input force because the pressure acting on the output piston is greater than the pressure acting on the input piston. _____

© Pearson Education, Inc., publishing as Pearson Prentice Hall. All rights reserved.

Chapter 13   Forces in Fluids

Bernoulli's Principle (pages 396–397)

7. Circle the letter of the sentence that correctly states Bernoulli's principle.

   a. As the speed of a fluid decreases, the pressure within the fluid decreases.

   b. As the speed of a fluid increases, the pressure within the fluid increases.

   c. As the speed of a fluid increases, the pressure within the fluid decreases.

   d. Fluid motion has no effect on pressure within the fluid.

8. Because the air traveling over the top of an airplane wing moves faster than the air passing underneath the wing, the pressure above the wings is _____ than the pressure below the wing.

9. What is lift, and how does it relate to an airplane's flight? _____

   _____

   _____

10. What is a spoiler on a racecar designed to do? _____

    _____

For questions 11 through 14, refer to the figure below. Place the correct letter after each phrase.

Spray Bottle with Fertilizer

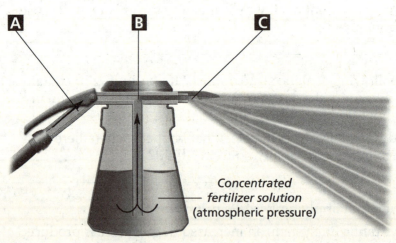

Concentrated
fertilizer solution
(atmospheric pressure)

11. Location where the water and fertilizer solution mix. _____

12. Location where water enters the sprayer at high speed. _____

13. Location where the water-fertilizer mixture exits the sprayer. _____

14. Use Bernoulli's principle to explain why the fertilizer solution moves up the tube.

    _____

    _____

    _____

© Pearson Education, Inc., publishing as Pearson Prentice Hall. All rights reserved.

Chapter 13   Forces in Fluids

Section 13.3 Buoyancy
(pages 400–404)

This section discusses buoyancy and Archimedes' principle of factors that determine whether an object will sink or float in a fluid.

Reading Strategy (page 400)

Summarizing As you read about buoyancy, write a brief summary of the text following each green heading. Your summary should include only the most important information. For more information on this Reading Strategy, see the **Reading and Study Skills** in the **Skills and Reference Handbook** at the end of your textbook.

Buoyant Force	Buoyant force is the apparent loss of weight of an object submerged in a fluid.

Buoyant Force (page 400)

1. What is buoyancy? _____

   _____

2. Circle the letter of the correct answer. In which direction does a buoyant force act?

   a. in the direction of gravity   b. perpendicular to gravity

   c. in the direction opposite of gravity   d. from above the fluid

3. Is the following sentence true or false? The greater a fluid's density, the greater its buoyant force. _____

4. Buoyancy causes an apparent _____ of weight of an object immersed in a fluid.

5. Circle the letter of each sentence that is true about buoyancy.

   a. Forces pushing up on a submerged object are greater than the forces pushing down on it.

   b. Forces acting on the sides of a submerged object cancel each other out.

   c. Gravitational forces work together with buoyant forces.

   d. The net buoyant force is non-vertical.

© Pearson Education, Inc., publishing as Pearson Prentice Hall. All rights reserved.

Chapter 13   Forces in Fluids

Archimedes' Principle (page 401)

6. According to Archimedes' principle, the weight of fluid displaced by a floating object is equal to the _____ acting on that object.

7. Is the following sentence true or false? When an object floats partially submerged in a fluid, it displaces a volume of fluid equal to its own volume. _____

Density and Buoyancy (pages 401–404)

Match each description with the correct property. Properties may be used more than once.

Description

_____ 8. This property is the ratio of an object's mass to its volume, often expressed in g/cm^3.

_____ 9. This force is equal to the force of gravity that acts on a floating object.

_____ 10. When this property is greater for an object than for the fluid it is in, the object sinks.

_____ 11. These two forces act on every object in a fluid.

_____ 12. An object will either float or be suspended when the buoyant force is equal to this.

Property

a. weight

b. buoyant force

c. density

13. Use what you know about density and buoyancy to predict whether each of the substances listed in the table will float or sink in water. The density of water is 1.0 g/cm^3.

Will It Float or Sink?		
Substance	**Density (g/cm^3)**	**Float or Sink?**
Gold	19.3	
Balsa Wood	0.15	
Ice	0.92	
Brick	1.84	
Milk	1.03	
Gasoline	0.70	

14. How is a heavy steel ship able to float?

a. Because the density of steel is 7.8 g/cm^3.

b. The ship's shape enables it to displace a large volume of water.

c. Because the density of water is 1 g/cm^3.

d. The ship's effective density is greater than that of water.

© Pearson Education, Inc., publishing as Pearson Prentice Hall. All rights reserved.

Chapter 13   Forces in Fluids

WordWise

Solve the clues to determine which vocabulary words from Chapter 13 are hidden in the puzzle. Then find and circle the terms in the puzzle. The terms may occur vertically, horizontally, or diagonally.

```
h  y  d  r  a  u  l  i  c  s  y  s  t  e  m
v  a  h  u  s  p  i  a  c  f  r  h  y  e  b
s  r  q  a  z  f  f  r  e  r  f  v  d  c  q
p  c  i  u  y  t  t  p  r  e  s  s  u  r  e
t  h  d  f  r  g  s  f  l  u  t  m  a  o  e
k  i  u  b  p  l  o  e  k  j  h  t  u  f  z
k  m  t  y  u  i  r  f  l  u  i  d  l  t  d
v  e  k  p  o  o  p  f  v  b  n  m  i  n  m
o  d  k  a  r  p  y  o  i  m  q  c  c  a  f
p  e  g  s  y  h  z  a  v  b  n  h  s  y  b
p  s  e  c  u  h  n  j  n  m  l  o  m  o  q
l  r  i  a  j  u  e  r  t  c  v  f  d  u  a
p  o  i  l  m  j  g  b  h  f  y  u  j  b  o
```

Clues	Hidden Words
Mathematician who discovered that the buoyant force on an object equals the weight of the fluid displaced by the object	_____
The result of a force distributed over an area	_____
Type of substance that assumes the shape of its container	_____
Ability of a fluid to exert an upward force on an object within it	_____
SI-unit of measure used to express pressure	_____
Upward force that keeps an aircraft aloft	_____
Device that uses pressurized fluids acting on pistons of different sizes to change a force	_____
Force that opposes the weight of an object floating in a fluid	_____

© Pearson Education, Inc., publishing as Pearson Prentice Hall. All rights reserved.

Chapter 13   Forces in Fluids

Calculating Pressure

Math Skill:
Formulas and
Equations

You may want to read
more about this **Math
Skill** in the **Skills and
Reference Handbook**
at the end of your
textbook.

Each tile on the bottom of a swimming pool has an area of
0.50 m². The water above each tile exerts a force of 11,000 N
on each tile. How much pressure does the water exert on
each tile?

1. Read and Understand

What information are you given?

Force = 11,000 N

Area = 0.50 m²

2. Plan and Solve

What formula contains the given quantities and the unknown?

$$\text{Pressure} = \frac{\text{Force}}{\text{Area}}$$

Replace each variable with its known value and solve.

$$\text{Pressure} = \frac{11,000 \text{ N}}{0.50 \text{ m}^2} = 22,000 \text{ N/m}^2 = 22,000 \text{ Pa} = 22 \text{ kPa}$$

3. Look Back and Check

Is your answer reasonable?

Because the area of each tile is a half square meter and pressure is
defined as force per square meter, the pressure exerted will be
double the magnitude of the force. Thus, an 11,000 N force will
produce 22,000 Pa of pressure on the tiles. The calculation verifies
this result.

Math Practice

On a separate sheet of paper, answer the following questions.

1. The weight of the gasoline in a 55-gallon drum creates a force of
   1456 newtons. The area of the bottom of the drum is 0.80 m². How
   much pressure does the gasoline exert on the bottom of the drum?

2. The weight of a gallon of milk is about 38 N. If you pour 3.0 gallons of
   milk into a container whose bottom has an area of 0.60 m², how much
   pressure will the milk exert on the bottom of the container?

3. A company makes garden statues by pouring concrete into a mold.
   The amount of concrete used to make a statue of a deer weighs
   3600 N. If the base of the deer statue is 0.60 meters long and
   0.40 meters wide, how much pressure will the statue exert on
   the ground? (*Hint:* Area is equal to length times width.)

© Pearson Education, Inc., publishing as Pearson Prentice Hall. All rights reserved.

Chapter 14   Work, Power, and Machines

Summary

14.1 Work and Power

Work is the product of force and distance. Work is done when a force moves an object over a distance. For example, you do work when you lift a textbook. If an object does not move, no work is done.

You can calculate work by multiplying the force exerted on the object times the distance the object moves:

$$\text{Work} = \text{Force} \times \text{Distance}$$

The joule (J) is the SI unit of work. One joule is the amount of work done when a force of 1 newton moves an object a distance of 1 meter in the direction of the force.

Power is the rate, or speed, of doing work. To do work faster, you must use more power. To increase power, you can do more work in the same time or you can do the same work in less time.

You can calculate power by dividing the amount of work done by the time needed to do the work:

$$\text{Power} = \frac{\text{Work}}{\text{Time}}$$

The watt (W) is the SI unit of power. One watt equals one joule per second.

Another unit of power is the horsepower (hp). One horsepower equals about 746 watts. The horsepower was invented by Scottish engine builder James Watt around 200 years ago. Watt defined one horsepower as the power output of a very strong horse.

14.2 Work and Machines

A machine is something that changes a force and makes work easier. Machines may change a force in three ways. They may

- increase the size of the force
- change the direction of the force
- increase the distance over which the force acts

The force you put into a machine is the input force. The distance over which the input force acts is the input distance. The work you do on the machine is the work input. The work input equals the input force times the input distance. You can increase the work input by increasing the input force, the input distance, or both.

The force a machine produces is the output force. The distance over which the output force acts is the output distance. The work the machines does is the work output. The work output equals the output force times the output distance. The only way to increase the work output is to increase the work input. You cannot get more work out of a machine than you put into it.

The moving parts of a machine must use some of the work input to overcome friction. Recall that friction acts against any moving object. Because of friction, the work output of a machine is always less than the work input.

14.3 Mechanical Advantage and Efficiency

Many machines increase the size of the input force. The number of times a machine increases the size of the input force is called its mechanical advantage. For example, a machine that increases the input force by a factor of three has a mechanical advantage of 3. There are two types of mechanical advantage: actual mechanical advantage and ideal mechanical advantage.

The actual mechanical advantage (AMA) of a machine is the ratio of output force to input force. You can calculate the actual mechanical advantage by dividing the output force by the input force:

$$\text{AMA} = \frac{\text{Output force}}{\text{Input force}}$$

© Pearson Education, Inc., publishing as Pearson Prentice Hall. All rights reserved.

Chapter 14   Work, Power, and Machines

The ideal mechanical advantage (IMA) of a machine is the mechanical advantage without friction. Friction is always present, so the actual mechanical advantage of a machine is always less than the ideal mechanical advantage. You can calculate ideal mechanical advantage by dividing input distance by output distance:

$$\text{IMA} = \frac{\text{Input distance}}{\text{Output distance}}$$

Some of the work input to any machine must be used to overcome friction. The percentage of work input that becomes work output is the efficiency of a machine. The efficiency of a machine is always less than 100 percent. The formula for calculating efficiency is

$$\text{Efficiency} = \frac{\text{Work output}}{\text{Work input}} \times 100\%$$

If the efficiency of a machine is 75 percent, then 75 percent of the work input becomes work output. The other 25 percent of work input is used to overcome friction. Reducing friction increases the efficiency of a machine. With less friction, more of the work input becomes work output.

14.4 Simple Machines

There are six different types of simple machines: lever, wheel and axle, inclined plane, wedge, screw, and pulley.

A lever is a stiff bar that can move around a fixed point. The fixed point is called the fulcrum. A seesaw is an example of a lever. To calculate the ideal mechanical advantage of a lever, you divide the input arm by the output arm. The input arm is the distance between the input force and the fulcrum. The output arm is the distance between the output force and the fulcrum. Based on the locations of the input force, the output force, and the fulcrum, levers are classified into three categories:

- First-class levers—fulcrum between input force and output force (example: seesaw)
- Second-class levers—output force between input force and fulcrum (example: wheelbarrow)
- Third-class levers—input force between fulcrum and output force (example: baseball bat)

A wheel and axle is made up of a larger outer disk attached to a smaller inner cylinder. The outer disk is the wheel, and inner cylinder is the axle. A steering wheel is an example of a wheel and axle. When you turn the large wheel, the narrow axle also turns. To calculate the mechanical advantage of a wheel and axle, you divide the radius of the disk or cylinder where the input force is applied by the radius of the disk or cylinder where the output force is produced.

An inclined plane is a slanted surface used to move an object to a different height. A wheelchair ramp is an example of an inclined plane. To calculate the ideal mechanical advantage of an inclined plane, you divide the distance along the inclined plane by its change in height. For example, a 6-meter-long ramp that gains 1 meter of height has an ideal mechanical advantage of 6.

A wedge is a V-shaped object. The two sides of the V are inclined planes that slope toward each other. An example of a wedge is a knife blade. The ideal mechanical advantage of a wedge depends on its shape. A thin wedge has a greater ideal mechanical advantage than a thick wedge of the same length.

A screw is an inclined plane wrapped around a cylinder. The turns of the inclined plane around the cylinder are called threads. The ideal mechanical advantage of a screw depends on the closeness of the threads. The closer the threads are, the greater the ideal mechanical advantage is.

© Pearson Education, Inc., publishing as Pearson Prentice Hall. All rights reserved.

Chapter 14   Work, Power, and Machines

A pulley is a simple machine that consists of a rope that fits into a groove in a wheel. It is used to help lift objects. A pulley may be fixed or movable. In a fixed pulley, the wheel is attached in a fixed location. A fixed pulley changes the direction, but not the size, of the input force. An example of a fixed pulley is the pulley at the top of a flag pole. In a movable pulley, the pulley is attached to the object being moved. A movable pulley changes both the direction and the size of the input force. A pulley system is made up of two or more individual pulleys, both fixed and movable. To calculate the ideal mechanical advantage of a pulley or pulley system, you add the number of rope sections supporting the object being lifted. A pulley system made up of several individual pulleys can have a large ideal mechanical advantage.

Most of the machines you use every day are made up of more than one simple machine. A combination of two or more simple that operate together is called a compound machine. Scissors are an example of a compound machine. Each blade of a pair of scissors is a wedge, and the two blades work together as levers. Some compound machines, such as washing machines and clocks, contain dozens of simple machines.

© Pearson Education, Inc., publishing as Pearson Prentice Hall. All rights reserved.

Chapter 14   Work, Power, and Machines

Section 14.1 Work and Power
(pages 412–416)

This section defines work and power, describes how they are related, and explains how to calculate their values.

Reading Strategy (page 412)

Relating Text and Visuals As you read, look carefully at Figures 1 and 2 and read their captions. Complete the table by describing the work shown in each figure. For more information on this Reading Strategy, see the **Reading and Study Skills** in the **Skills and Reference Handbook** at the end of your textbook.

Figure	Direction of Force	Direction of Motion	Is Work Done?
1			
2A			
2B			
2C			

What Is Work? (pages 412–413)

1. In science, work is done when a(n) _____ acts on an object in the direction the object moves.

2. Why isn't work being done on a barbell when a weight lifter is holding the barbell over his head? _____

_____

3. Describe what conditions of force and motion result in maximum work done on an object. _____

_____

4. Is the following sentence true or false? A vertical force does work on an object that is moving in a horizontal direction. _____

Calculating Work (pages 413–414)

5. In science, work that is done on an object can be described as the force acting on the object multiplied by the _____ the object moves.

6. Circle the letter of the correct form of the work equation to use when determining the distance an object moves as a result of a force applied to it.

    a. Distance = Force × Work   b. Distance = $\dfrac{\text{Force}}{\text{Work}}$

    c. Distance = $(\text{Force})^2$ d. Distance = $\dfrac{\text{Work}}{\text{Force}}$

© Pearson Education, Inc., publishing as Pearson Prentice Hall. All rights reserved.

Chapter 14   Work, Power, and Machines

7. The SI unit of work is the _____.

8. Circle the letter of the amount of work done when a 1 newton force moves an object 1 meter.

   a. 1 newton per second   b. 1 joule

   c. 1 watt   d. 1 newton per meter

What Is Power? (page 414)

9. Is the following sentence true or false? Power is the rate of doing work. _____

10. In order to do work faster, more _____ is required.

11. Circle the letter of each sentence that is true about power.

   a. Power and work are always equal.

   b. You can increase power by doing a given amount of work in a shorter period of time.

   c. When you decrease the force acting on an object, the power increases.

   d. When you do less work in a given time period, the power decreases.

Calculating Power (page 415)

12. Write a word equation describing how to calculate power. _____

_____

13. The SI unit of power is the _____.

14. Circle the letter of the expression that is equivalent to one watt.

   a. one newton per meter

   b. one joule per meter

   c. one newton per second

   d. one joule per second

15. How much work does a 100-watt light bulb do when it is lit for 30 seconds? _____

James Watt and Horsepower (page 416)

16. Circle the letter of the quantity that is approximately equal to one horsepower.

   a. 746 J   b. 746 W

   c. 7460 N/m   d. 7460 J

17. Why did James Watt use the power output of a horse to compare the power outputs of steam engines he designed? _____

_____

© Pearson Education, Inc., publishing as Pearson Prentice Hall. All rights reserved.

Chapter 14   Work, Power, and Machines

Section 14.2 Work and Machines
(pages 417–420)

This section describes how machines change forces to make work easier to do.
Input forces exerted on and output forces exerted by machines are identified
and input work and output work are discussed.

Reading Strategy (page 417)

Summarizing As you read, complete the table for each machine.
After you read, write a sentence summarizing the idea that your
table illustrates. For more information on this Reading Strategy, see
the **Reading and Study Skills** in the **Skills and Reference Handbook**
at the end of your textbook.

Machine	Increases or Decreases Input Force	Increases or Decreases Input Distance
Tire jack		
Lug wrench		
Rowing oar		
Summary: As input force decreases, the input distance increases.		

Machines Do Work (pages 417–418)

1. Describe what a machine is able to do. _____

_____

2. Is the following sentence true or false? A machine can make work
easier to do by changing the size of the force needed, the direction
of a force, or the distance over which a force acts.

_____

3. Consider the equation Work = Force × Distance. If a machine
increases the distance over which a force is exerted, the force
required to do a given amount of work _____.

4. Give an example of a machine that changes the direction of
an applied force. _____

5. When you make several trips to unload a few heavy items from a
car instead of moving them all at once, the total distance over which
you exert yourself _____.

Work Input and Work Output (pages 419–420)

6. The work done by a machine is always less than the work done on a
machine because of _____.

© Pearson Education, Inc., publishing as Pearson Prentice Hall. All rights reserved.

Chapter 14   Work, Power, and Machines

7. Circle the letter of the definition for input force.

   a. the amount of force exerted by a machine

   b. the amount of friction slowing the speed of a machine

   c. the amount of work done by a machine

   d. the amount of force exerted on a machine

8. Write a word equation that describes work input.

   _____

9. Is the following sentence true or false? Every machine uses some of its work input to overcome friction. _____

10. The force exerted by a machine is called the _____ force.

11. Circle the letter of the expression that equals the work output of a machine.

   a. $\dfrac{\text{Input distance}}{\text{Output distance}}$

   b. Output distance × Input distance

   c. $\dfrac{\text{Output distance}}{\text{friction}}$

   d. Output distance × Output force

12. Is the following sentence true or false? Output work always is less than input work. _____

For questions 13 through 15, refer to the figure below.

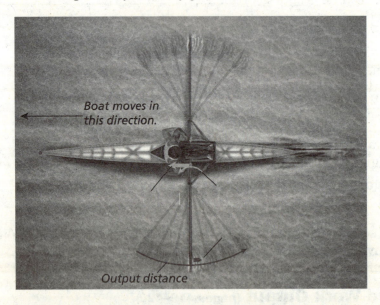

Boat moves in this direction.

Output distance

13. Which arrow represents the input force? Label it on the figure.

14. Which arrow represents the input distance? Label it on the figure.

15. Which arrow represents the output force? Label it on the figure.

16. How can you increase a machine's work output? _____

   _____

© Pearson Education, Inc., publishing as Pearson Prentice Hall. All rights reserved.

Chapter 14   Work, Power, and Machines

Section 14.3 Mechanical Advantage and Efficiency
(pages 421–426)

This section describes mechanical advantage and efficiency and how to calculate these values. Ways to maximize mechanical advantage and efficiency are discussed.

Reading Strategy (page 421)

Building Vocabulary As you read the section, write a definition in the table for each vocabulary term in your own words. For more information on this Reading Strategy, see the **Reading and Study Skills** in the **Skills and Reference Handbook** at the end of your textbook.

Mechanical Advantage	
Vocabulary	**Definition**
Mechanical advantage	

Mechanical Advantage (pages 421–423)

1. The number of times that a machine increases an input force is the _____ of the machine.

2. For a given input force, what affects the output force that a nutcracker can exert on a nut? _____
   _____

3. Mechanical advantage describes the relationship between input force and _____ force.

4. How is the actual mechanical advantage of a machine determined?
   _____

5. Greater input force is required to move an object along a ramp with a rough surface, compared to a ramp with a smooth surface, because a greater force is needed to overcome _____.

6. Is the following sentence true or false? A loading ramp with a rough surface has a greater mechanical advantage than one with a smooth surface. _____

© Pearson Education, Inc., publishing as Pearson Prentice Hall. All rights reserved.

Chapter 14 Work, Power, and Machines

7. Because friction is always present, the actual mechanical advantage of a machine is never _____ than its ideal mechanical advantage (IMA).

8. A machine's _____ is the mechanical advantage in the absence of friction.

9. What type of materials do engineers use to increase the mechanical advantage of a machine?

_____

Calculating Mechanical Advantage (pages 424–425)

10. Is the following sentence true or false? To calculate ideal mechanical advantage, divide input distance by output distance, and then divide the result by the force of friction.

_____

11. Is the following sentence true or false? An inclined plane is an example of a machine. _____

12. Calculate the IMA of a ramp for the distances given in the table.

Ideal Mechanical Advantages of Ramps		
Horizontal Distance	**Vertical Rise**	**IMA**
1.5 meters	0.5 meters	
12 meters	1.5 meters	
3.6 meters	0.3 meters	

13. Is the following sentence true or false? If the input distance of a machine is greater than the output distance, then the IMA for that machine is greater than one. _____

Efficiency (pages 425–426)

14. Why is the efficiency of a machine always less than 100 percent? _____

_____

15. Is the following sentence true or false? To calculate the efficiency of a machine, divide the work output by work input, and then multiply by 100. _____

16. What is a significant factor affecting a car's fuel efficiency?

_____

17. Calculate the efficiency of a machine with a work output of 120 J and a work input of 500 J. _____

18. Circle the letter of the work input for a machine with a work output of 240 J and an efficiency of 80 percent.

   a. 300 J   b. 200 J

   c. 320 J   d. 200 W

19. Reducing friction _____ the efficiency of a machine.

© Pearson Education, Inc., publishing as Pearson Prentice Hall. All rights reserved.

Chapter 14   Work, Power, and Machines

Section 14.4 Simple Machines
(pages 427–435)

This section presents the six types of simple machines. A discussion of how each type works and how to determine its mechanical advantage is given. Common uses of simple machines are also described.

Reading Strategy (page 427)

Summarizing After reading the section on levers, complete the concept map to organize what you know about first-class levers. On a separate sheet of paper, construct and complete similar concept maps for second- and third-class levers. For more information on this Reading Strategy, see the **Reading and Study Skills** in the **Skills and Reference Handbook** at the end of your textbook.

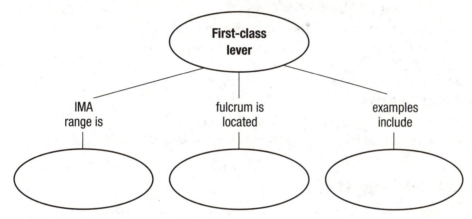

1. List the six types of simple machines.

a. _____   b. _____

c. _____   d. _____

e. _____   f. _____

Levers (pages 428–429)

2. A screwdriver used to pry the lid off a paint can is an example of a(n) _____.

3. The fixed point that a lever rotates around is called the _____.

4. To calculate the ideal mechanical advantage of any lever, divide the input arm by the _____.

5. What characteristics distinguish levers as first-class, second-class, or third-class?

_____

_____

6. Is the following sentence true or false? First-class levers always have a mechanical advantage that is greater than one.

_____

© Pearson Education, Inc., publishing as Pearson Prentice Hall. All rights reserved.

Chapter 14   Work, Power, and Machines

7. Is the following sentence true or false? All second-class levers have a mechanical advantage greater than one because the input arm is longer than the output arm. _____

Wheel and Axle (page 430)

8. Describe a wheel and axle. _____

_____

9. Circle the letter of the sentence that describes how to calculate the IMA of a wheel and axle.

   a. Multiply the area of the wheel by the area of the axle.

   b. Divide input force by output force.

   c. Divide the diameter where input force is exerted by the diameter where output force is exerted.

   d. Divide the radius of the wheel by the force exerted on it.

Inclined Planes (pages 430–431)

10. A slanted surface along which a force moves an object to a different elevation is called a(n) _____.

11. Is the following sentence true or false? The ideal mechanical advantage of an inclined plane is the distance along the incline plane divided by its change in height. _____

Wedges and Screws (page 431)

12. A thin wedge of a given length has a(n) _____ mechanical advantage than a thick wedge of the same length.

13. Screws with threads that are close together have a greater

   _____·_____.

Pulleys (pages 432–433)

14. A simple machine consisting of a rope fitted into a groove in a wheel is a(n) _____.

15. What determines the ideal mechanical advantage of a pulley or pulley system?

   _____

Compound Machines (page 435)

16. Is the following sentence true or false? A compound machine is a combination of two or more simple machines that operate together. _____

17. Circle each letter that identifies a compound machine.

   a. a car   b. a handheld screwdriver

   c. a washing machine   d. a watch

© Pearson Education, Inc., publishing as Pearson Prentice Hall. All rights reserved.

Chapter 14 Work, Power, and Machines

WordWise

Answer the question or identify the clue by writing the correct vocabulary term in the blanks. Use the circled letter(s) in each term to find the hidden vocabulary word. Then, write a definition for the hidden word.

Clues	Vocabulary Terms
$\dfrac{\text{Work output}}{\text{Work input}} \times 100\%$	_ _ _ Ⓞ _ _ _ _ _ _
A mechanical watch is an example of this.	_ _ _ _ _ Ⓞ _ _ _ _ _ _ _ _
One way to determine this is to divide output work by output force.	_ _ _ Ⓞ _ _ _ _ _ _ _ _ _ _
This is the SI unit of work.	_ _ Ⓞ _ _
On a lever, it is the distance between the fulcrum and the input force.	_ _ _ Ⓞ _ _ _ _
The IMA of this machine increases as its thickness decreases relative to its length.	_ _ Ⓞ _ _
This is exerted on a jack handle to lift a car.	Ⓞ _ _ _ _ _ _ _ _ _
This unit equals about 746 joules.	_ _ _ Ⓞ _ _ _ _ _ _
This is the distance between the output force and the fulcrum.	_ _ Ⓞ _ _ _ _ _
This SI unit of power is used to describe light bulbs.	_ Ⓞ _ _
The IMA of this machine is the distance along its surface divided by the change in height.	_ _ _ _ _ Ⓞ _ _ _ _ _ _ _
A device that can change the size of the force required to do work.	_ _ Ⓞ _ _ _ _
This quantity is equal to Work/Time.	_ _ _ Ⓞ _

Hidden words: _ _ _ _ _ _ _ _ _ _ _ _ _

Definition: _____

_____

© Pearson Education, Inc., publishing as Pearson Prentice Hall. All rights reserved.

Chapter 14   Work, Power, and Machines

Calculating Work and Power

Calculate the power of a machine that exerts a force of 800.0 N over a distance of 6.0 m in 2.0 s.

Math Skill:
Formulas and
Equations

You may want to read more about this **Math Skill** in the **Skills and Reference Handbook** at the end of your textbook.

1. Read and Understand

What information are you given?

Force = 800.0 N

Distance = 6.0 m

Time = 2.0 s

2. Plan and Solve

What variable are you trying to determine?

Power =?

What formula contains the given quantities and the unknown?

$$Power = \frac{Work}{Time} = \frac{Force \times Distance}{Time}$$

$$Power = \frac{800.0 \text{ N} \times 6.0 \text{ m}}{2.0 \text{ s}}$$

$$Power = \frac{4800 \text{ J}}{2.0 \text{ s}} = 2400 \text{ J/s} = 2400 \text{ W}$$

3. Look Back and Check

Is your answer reasonable?

Work = (2400 J/s) × 2.0 s = 4800 J

This is a reasonable answer. Substituting power and time back into the power equation yields the original value for work.

Math Practice

On a separate sheet of paper, solve the following problems.

1. Suppose 900.0 J of work are done by a light bulb in 15.0 s. What is the power of the light bulb?

2. What is the power of a machine if an output force of 500.0 N is exerted over an output distance of 8.0 m in 4.0 s?

3. The power of a machine is 6.0×10^3 J/s. This machine is scheduled for design improvements. What would its power be if the same work could be done in half the time?

© Pearson Education, Inc., publishing as Pearson Prentice Hall. All rights reserved.

Chapter 15   Energy

Summary

15.1 Energy and Its Forms

Energy is the ability to do work. Recall that work is done when a force moves an object. When work is done on an object, energy is transferred, or passed on, to that object. Therefore, work is actually a transfer of energy. Like work, energy is measured in joules (J). There are two general types of energy: kinetic energy and potential energy.

Kinetic energy is the energy of motion. All moving objects have kinetic energy. The kinetic energy of a moving object depends on the object's mass and speed. The greater the mass or speed of the object, the more kinetic energy it has. To calculate the kinetic energy of an object, you multiply half the object's mass (m) times its speed (v) squared:

$$\text{Kinetic energy} = \tfrac{1}{2}\, mv^2$$

Potential energy is energy that is stored in an object as a result of its position or shape. Two types of potential energy are gravitational potential energy and elastic potential energy. An object gains gravitational potential energy when it is raised to a greater height. The gravitational potential energy of an object depends on the object's mass (m), the force of gravity (g), and the object's height (h). The formula for gravitational potential energy is

$$\text{Potential energy} = mgh$$

An object gains elastic potential energy when it is stretched or is pressed together. For example, stretching a rubber band or pressing a spring gives the object elastic potential energy.

Energy can take several different forms. Major forms of energy are mechanical energy, thermal energy, chemical energy, electrical energy, electromagnetic energy, and nuclear energy.

- Mechanical energy is the sum of an object's potential and kinetic energy. A speeding train has mechanical energy.
- Thermal energy is the sum of the potential and kinetic energy of all the particles in an object. The faster the particles move, the higher the object's thermal energy and the warmer the object becomes. Hot molten metal contains a great deal of thermal energy.
- Chemical energy is the stored energy that holds together chemical compounds. When the compounds break down, the energy is released. A fuel such as gasoline is a rich store of chemical energy.
- Electrical energy is the transfer of electric charges. Lightning bolts are produced by electrical energy.
- Electromagnetic energy is energy that travels through space as waves. Sunlight and X-rays are examples of electromagnetic energy.
- Nuclear energy is the stored energy that holds together the nucleus of an atom. This energy can be released by breaking apart heavy nuclei. Nuclear fission is a process that splits the nucleus apart to release nuclear energy.

15.2 Energy Conversion and Conservation

Energy can be changed from one form to another. The process of changing energy from one form to another form is called energy conversion. A wind-up toy demonstrates energy conversion. When you turn the key of the toy, elastic potential energy is stored in a spring. When the spring is released, the potential energy is changed into kinetic energy, and the toy moves.

© Pearson Education, Inc., publishing as Pearson Prentice Hall. All rights reserved.

Chapter 15   Energy

When energy changes from one form to another, the total amount of energy stays the same. This supports the law of conservation of energy. The law states that energy cannot be created or destroyed. This law is one of the most important concepts in science.

A very common energy conversion is a change from gravitational potential energy to kinetic energy. This occurs whenever an object falls due to the force of gravity. Throughout the fall, the object's potential energy decreases, while its kinetic energy increases. However, the sum of the object's potential and kinetic energy remains the same because of the conservation of energy.

The change from gravitational potential energy to kinetic energy occurs when a pendulum swings downward from its highest point to its lowest point. As the pendulum swings back upward again, the kinetic energy changes back to gravitational potential energy. Another example of this type of energy conversion is a pole vault. A pole-vaulter changes kinetic energy to potential energy to propel herself into the air. Then, gravitational potential energy changes back to kinetic energy as the pole-vaulter falls back to the ground.

In the early 1900s, physicist Albert Einstein showed that energy and mass can be changed into each other. In other words, energy is released as matter is destroyed, and matter can be created from energy.

15.3 Energy Resources

Energy resources may be renewable or nonrenewable. Nonrenewable energy resources are limited in amount and take millions of years to replace. They include oil, natural gas, coal, and uranium. Several nonrenewable energy resources, including oil and coal, are known as

fossil fuels. They are called fossil fuels because they were formed underground from the remains of dead organisms. Fossil fuels are the most commonly used fuels. They are relatively cheap and widely available. However, using fossil fuels creates pollution.

Renewable energy resources can be replaced in a relatively short period of time. They include

- hydroelectric energy—energy from flowing water
- solar energy—energy from sunlight
- geothermal energy—energy from the heat beneath Earth's surface
- biomass energy—chemical energy stored in living things

These sources of energy can be changed into other, more usable forms of energy, such as electrical or thermal energy. Using renewable energy resources creates less pollution than using fossil fuels.

Fossil fuels may become scarce and expensive in the future. We can make these energy resources last longer by using them more slowly. Two ways to make fossil fuels last longer are to reduce our energy needs and to use energy more efficiently. Finding ways to use less energy or to use energy more efficiently is known as energy conservation. Examples of energy conservation include

- turning off lights when they are not being used
- carpooling or using mass transportation such as buses and subways
- using energy-efficient appliances, cars, and light bulbs

© Pearson Education, Inc., publishing as Pearson Prentice Hall. All rights reserved.

Chapter 15   Energy

Section 15.1 Energy and Its Forms
(pages 446–452)

This section describes how energy and work are related. Kinetic energy and potential energy are defined, and examples are shown for calculating these forms of energy. Examples of various types of energy are discussed.

Reading Strategy (page 446)

Building Vocabulary As you read, complete the concept map with vocabulary terms and definitions from this section. For more information on this Reading Strategy, see the **Reading and Study Skills** in the **Skills and Reference Handbook** at the end of your textbook.

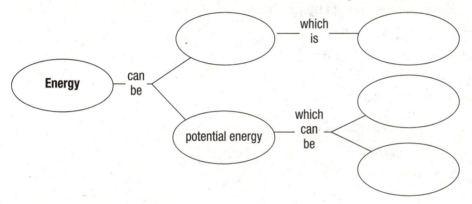

Energy and Work (page 447)

1. What is energy? _____

2. When work is done on an object, _____ is transferred to that object.

3. Circle the letter of each sentence that is true about work and energy.

    a. Energy in food is converted into muscle movement.

    b. Energy is transferred when work is done.

    c. Both work and energy are usually measured in joules.

    d. One joule equals one meter per newton.

Kinetic Energy (pages 447–448)

4. The energy of motion is called _____.

5. Is the following sentence true or false? You can determine the kinetic energy of an object if you know its mass and its volume.

    _____

6. Write the formula used to calculate an object's kinetic energy.

    _____

7. Calculate the kinetic energy of a 0.25-kg toy car traveling at a constant velocity of 2 m/s. _____

    _____

© Pearson Education, Inc., publishing as Pearson Prentice Hall. All rights reserved.

Chapter 15   Energy

Potential Energy (pages 448–450)

8. What is potential energy? _____

_____

9. Is the following sentence true or false? The work done by a rock climber going up a cliff decreases her potential energy.

_____

10. An object's gravitational potential energy depends on its _____, its _____, and the acceleration due to gravity.

11. Is the following sentence true or false? Gravitational potential energy of an object increases as its height increases.

_____

12. The potential energy of an object that is stretched or compressed is known as _____.

13. Complete the table about potential energy.

Potential Energy		
Type	**Description**	**Example**
Gravitational		
	Stretched or compressed objects	

Forms of Energy (pages 450–452)

For numbers 14 through 19, write the letter of the form of energy that best matches the description.

Descriptions

_____ **14.** Energy stored in gasoline, coal, and wood

_____ **15.** The sum of an object's potential energy and kinetic energy, excluding atomic-scale movements

_____ **16.** Produces the sun's heat and light

_____ **17.** Travels through space in the form of waves

_____ **18.** Produces lightning bolts

_____ **19.** Increases as atoms within an object move faster

Forms of Energy

a. mechanical energy

b. chemical energy

c. electrical energy

d. thermal energy

e. nuclear energy

f. electromagnetic energy

© Pearson Education, Inc., publishing as Pearson Prentice Hall. All rights reserved.

Chapter 15   Energy

Section 15.2 Energy Conversion and Conservation
(pages 453–459)

This section describes how energy is converted from one form to another. The law of conservation of energy also is presented.

Reading Strategy (page 453)

Relating Cause and Effect As you read, complete the flowchart to explain an energy conversion used by some gulls to obtain food. For more information on this Reading Strategy, see the **Reading and Study Skills** in the **Skills and Reference Handbook** at the end of your textbook.

How Gulls Use Energy Conversions

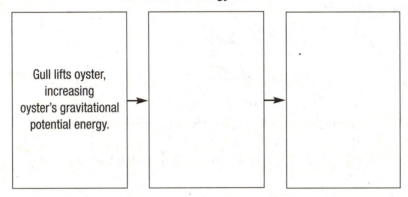

Gull lifts oyster, increasing oyster's gravitational potential energy.

Energy Conversion (page 454)

1. Is the following sentence true or false? Energy can be converted from one form to another. _____

2. When a wind-up toy is set in motion, elastic potential energy that was stored in a compressed spring is converted into the _____ of the toy's moving parts.

3. Is the following sentence true or false? The action of striking a match shows that stored chemical energy in the match can be converted into thermal energy and electromagnetic energy of the flame in a single step. _____

Conservation of Energy (page 455)

4. What does the law of conservation of energy state? _____

_____

5. Is the following sentence true or false? When an object slows down because of frictional force acting on it, an amount of energy is destroyed that is equivalent to the decrease in kinetic energy of the object. _____

6. A moving object slows down because friction causes a continual conversion of kinetic energy into _____.

© Pearson Education, Inc., publishing as Pearson Prentice Hall. All rights reserved.

Chapter 15 Energy

Energy Conversions (pages 456–458)

7. As an object falls, the gravitational potential energy of the object is converted into _____.

8. Circle the letter of each sentence that is true about pendulums.

   a. A pendulum consists of a weight suspended from a string that swings back and forth.

   b. The weight at the end of a pendulum reaches maximum kinetic energy at the highest point in the pendulum's swing.

   c. Potential energy and kinetic energy undergo constant conversion as a pendulum swings.

   d. Frictional forces enable a pendulum to continue swinging without slowing down.

9. At what point during a pole-vaulter's jump is his gravitational potential energy the greatest? _____

10. Circle the letter of the type of energy that increases as the pole bends before it propels a pole-vaulter up into the air.

    a. kinetic energy   b. mechanical energy

    c. frictional force   d. elastic potential energy

11. Is the following sentence true or false? For a mechanical change in an isolated system, the mechanical energy at the beginning equals the mechanical energy at the end of the process, as long as friction is negligible. _____

12. Tell whether the following situations illustrate *kinetic energy*, *potential energy*, or *both*.

What Type of Energy Is It?	
Situation	**Form of Energy**
A stationary wind-up toy with a compressed spring	
A descending roller coaster car	
A skier poised to take off at the top of a hill	
A car driving on a flat road	
A vibrating guitar string	

Energy and Mass (page 459)

13. What does Einstein's equation imply about mass and energy? _____

_____

14. Is the following sentence true or false? Einstein's equation, $E = mc^2$, suggests that mass and energy together are conserved.

_____

© Pearson Education, Inc., publishing as Pearson Prentice Hall. All rights reserved.

Chapter 15   Energy

Section 15.3 Energy Resources
(pages 462–466)

This section describes types of energy resources and ways to conserve them.

Reading Strategy (page 462)

Identifying Main Ideas As you read the section, write the main idea for each heading in the table. For more information on this Reading Strategy, see the **Reading and Study Skills** in the **Skills and Reference Handbook** at the end of your textbook.

Heading	Main Idea
Nonrenewable energy resources	
Renewable energy resources	
Conserving energy resources	

Nonrenewable Energy Resources (page 462)

1. What are nonrenewable energy resources? _____

   _____

2. List four examples of nonrenewable energy resources.

   a. _____   b. _____

   c. _____   d. _____

3. Circle the letter of each resource that is considered to be a fossil fuel.

   a. tree

   b. uranium

   c. oil

   d. coal

4. Is the following sentence true or false? Although fossil fuels are evenly distributed throughout Earth, they only represent ten percent of total energy consumed. _____

5. What are some advantages and disadvantages of using fossil fuels as a source of energy? _____

   _____

Renewable Energy Resources (pages 463–464)

6. An energy resource that can be replaced in a reasonably short period of time is called a(n) _____ resource.

© Pearson Education, Inc., publishing as Pearson Prentice Hall. All rights reserved.

Chapter 15   Energy

7. Circle the letter of each sentence that is true about renewable energy resources.

    a. Wind and solar energy are both renewable energy resources.

    b. Renewable energy resources are always more efficient than nonrenewable resources.

    c. Renewable energy resources can be used to generate electricity and to heat homes.

    d. Magma generates most renewable energy, either directly or indirectly.

8. Describe one energy conversion that takes place during the generation of hydroelectric power. _____
_____

9. Is the following sentence true or false? One disadvantage of hydroelectric power is that it is among the most expensive energy sources. _____

For numbers 10 through 15, match the letter of each renewable energy source to its description.

Description	Renewable Energy Sources
_____ **10.** Water pumped below ground is converted to steam.	a. hydroelectric
_____ **11.** The most likely raw material is hydrogen.	b. solar
_____ **12.** Mirrors concentrate sunlight to produce electricity.	c. geothermal
_____ **13.** Kinetic energy of moving air is converted into rotational energy of a turbine.	d. wind
_____ **14.** Energy is obtained from flowing water.	e. biomass
_____ **15.** Chemical energy stored in wood, peat, and agricultural waste can be converted into thermal energy.	f. nuclear fusion

16. Is the following sentence true or false? Hydrogen fuel cells generate electricity by combining hydrogen with oxygen.
_____

Conserving Energy Resources (page 466)

17. What are two ways that energy resources can be conserved? _____
_____

18. Name two practical ways in which people can conserve energy. _____
_____
_____

© Pearson Education, Inc., publishing as Pearson Prentice Hall. All rights reserved.

Name _____ Class _____ Date _____

Chapter 15   Energy

WordWise

Complete the sentences by using one of the scrambled vocabulary words below.

absoism reegny   ynrege vnsnoorctaie   slisfo sluef
rslao eeyngr   neegyr seonoscvri   caurnle rygnee
mrelhta eeryng   loptnieat nygeer   gyreen
mcelhaci reeyng   ctniiek yenrge   rvtnatgialoai

When an object is raised to a higher level, its _____ potential energy increases.

The motion of microscopic particles in matter partly determines the amount of _____ within it.

As a pole-vaulter springs higher into the air, her kinetic energy decreases as her gravitational potential energy increases. This is an example of _____.

Atomic fission and fusion produce _____.

When your muscles move, _____ from the cereal you ate for breakfast is converted into _____.

The _____ of a 100-kg boulder perched high on a cliff is greater than that of a 50-kg boulder at the same height.

You can recognize _____ by the changes it causes, such as motion and sound.

Formed from the remains of once-living organisms, _____ are nonrenewable energy resources.

Photovoltaic cells convert _____ into electrical energy.

Methods of _____ include ways to reduce energy needs.

When you sit around a campfire, you are enjoying energy stored in wood—a type of _____.

© Pearson Education, Inc., publishing as Pearson Prentice Hall. All rights reserved.

Chapter 15   Energy

Calculating Potential Energy

Math Skill:
Percents and
Decimals

You may want to read
more about this **Math
Skill** in the **Skills and
Reference Handbook**
at the end of your
textbook.

A 60.0-kg person is standing on the edge of a pier that
is 2.5 m above the surface of a lake. How much higher
would the pier have to be to raise the gravitational potential
energy of this person by 10 percent?

1. Read and Understand

What information are you given?

Mass of person = m = 60.0 kg

Height above lake level = h = 2.5 m

Acceleration due to gravity = g = 9.8 m/s^2

2. Plan and Solve

What variable are you trying to determine?

Gravitational potential energy = ?

What formula contains the given variables?

Gravitational potential energy (PE) = mgh

Initial PE = (60.0 kg)(9.8 m/s^2)(2.5 m) = 1500 J

Determine the 10-percent increase of PE.

(1500 J)(0.10) = 150 J

Final PE = 1500 J + 150 J = 1650 J

Rearrange the equation to determine the final height.

h = PE/mg = 1650 J/(60.0 kg)(9.8 m/s^2) = 2.8 m
The height increase for the pier would be 2.8 m − 2.5 m = 0.3 m.

3. Look Back and Check

Is your answer reasonable?

This is a reasonable answer because 0.3 m is about 10 percent of
2.5 m. A 10-percent increase in h should result in a 10-percent
increase in the gravitational PE.

Math Practice

On a separate sheet of paper, solve the following problems.

1. A 300-gram toy car and a 500-gram toy car are sitting on a shelf that
   is 2 meters higher than the floor. By what percent is the PE of the
   500-g car greater than the PE of the 300-g car?

2. An 80-kg rock climber is standing on a cliff so that his gravitational
   PE = 10,000 J. What percent increase in height is required to raise
   his PE by 3500 J?

© Pearson Education, Inc., publishing as Pearson Prentice Hall. All rights reserved.

Chapter 16   Thermal Energy and Heat

Summary

16.1 Thermal Energy and Matter

Heat is the transfer of thermal energy from one object to another because of a temperature difference. Heat flows spontaneously, or without any help, from hot objects to cold objects.

Temperature is a measure of how hot or cold an object is compared to a reference point. On the Celsius scale, the reference points are the freezing and boiling points of water. Temperature reflects the average kinetic energy of the particles in an object. As an object heats up, its particles move faster. The average kinetic energy of the particles increases, and temperature rises.

Temperature is not a direct measure of thermal energy. Recall that thermal energy is the total potential and kinetic energy of all the particles in an object. Two objects that have the same average kinetic energy of their particles will have the same temperature. However, the two objects will have different amounts of thermal energy if they have different numbers of particles. For example, a pot of tea has more thermal energy than a cup of tea at the same temperature. The average kinetic energy of particles in the cup and pot are the same, but the pot has many more particles. Therefore, the pot has more thermal energy.

Heat often affects the size of objects. When the temperature falls, many materials become smaller. This is called thermal contraction. Thermal contraction occurs because particles move more slowly and bump into each other less often when the temperature is lower. When the temperature rises, many materials become larger. This is called thermal expansion. Thermal expansion occurs because particles move faster and bump into each other more often when the temperature is higher. This causes the particles to spread farther apart. Gases expand and contract with temperature changes more than liquids or solids do. This is because the forces of attraction among gas particles are weaker.

Some materials heat up and increase in temperature more quickly than others. This is because they have a lower specific heat. Specific heat is the amount of heat needed to raise the temperature of one gram of a material by one degree Celsius. The lower a material's specific heat, the more its temperature rises when it absorbs a given amount of heat. For example, iron has a lower specific heat than plastic. If equal masses of iron and plastic absorb the same amount of heat, the iron's temperature rises more. You can calculate the amount of heat a material must absorb to produce a given change in temperature. The amount of heat absorbed by a material (Q) is the product of the mass of the material (m), the specific heat of the material (c), and the change in temperature (ΔT):

$$Q = m \times c \times \Delta T$$

Changes in thermal energy can be measured with an instrument called a calorimeter. A calorimeter uses the principle that heat flows from a hotter object to a colder object until both reach the same temperature. A heated object is placed in cool water inside the calorimeter until both object and water have the same temperature. The change in temperature of the water is measured and used to calculate the amount of heat the water has absorbed. This information can be used to calculate the specific heat of the object.

© Pearson Education, Inc., publishing as Pearson Prentice Hall. All rights reserved.

Chapter 16   Thermal Energy and Heat

16.2 Heat and Thermodynamics

Thermal energy can be transferred within a material or from one material to another. This can happen in three different ways: conduction, convection, and radiation.

Conduction is the transfer of thermal energy without the transfer of matter. Conduction occurs within a material or between materials that are touching. Nearby particles bump into each other and transfer thermal energy from particle to particle. Because the particles in gases are farther apart than the particles in liquids or solids, they bump into each other less often. As a result, conduction is slower in gases than in liquids or solids. A thermal conductor is a material that transfers thermal energy well. Aluminum is a good thermal conductor. A thermal insulator is a material that transfers thermal energy poorly. Air is a good thermal insulator.

Convection is the transfer of thermal energy by the movement of particles of a liquid or gas. The moving particles transfer thermal energy from hot areas to cold areas. This flow of moving particles is called a convection current. In a heated room, a convection current helps to keep the temperature about the same throughout the room. Convection currents also are important in nature. They cause ocean currents, weather systems, and movements of melted rock inside Earth.

Radiation is the transfer of thermal energy by waves moving through space. All objects radiate energy. As an object's temperature increases, it radiates energy at a faster rate. Heat lamps, which are used in restaurants to keep food warm, transfer heat by radiation.

Heat can be changed into other forms of energy and back into heat again. The study of changes between heat and other forms of energy is called thermodynamics.

There are several laws of thermodynamics:

- The first law of thermodynamics states that energy is conserved. For example, as an object falls and its potential energy changes to kinetic energy, the sum of potential and kinetic energy remains the same.
- The second law of thermodynamics states that thermal energy can flow from colder objects to hotter objects only if work is done on the system. For example, a refrigerator must do work to transfer heat from its cold food compartment to the warm air of the kitchen.
- The third law of thermodynamics states that absolute zero (0 kelvin) cannot be reached. Scientists cannot cool matter all the way down to absolute zero.

16.3 Using Heat

A heat engine is a device that changes heat into work. There are two main types of heat engines: external combustion engines and internal combustion engines.

- An external combustion engine burns fuel outside the engine. A steam engine is an example of an external combustion engine. Combustion outside the engine produces steam. The steam expands and moves pistons or a turbine inside the engine.
- An internal combustion engine burns fuel inside the engine. A car engine is an example of an internal combustion engine. A mixture of gasoline and air in the engine is heated. The heated gas expands and moves pistons in the engine.

© Pearson Education, Inc., publishing as Pearson Prentice Hall. All rights reserved.

Chapter 16   Thermal Energy and Heat

Heating systems are used to heat buildings. A central heating system heats many rooms from one central location. The central location of a heating system often is in the basement. Most heating systems use convection currents to distribute heat throughout the building. There are several different types of heating systems, including hot-water heating, steam heating, electric baseboard heating, and forced-air heating systems.

Refrigerators and air conditioners are cooling systems. Most cooling systems are heat pumps. A heat pump is a device that reverses the spontaneous flow of thermal energy. A heat pump causes thermal energy to move from a cold area to a hot area. A heat pump must do work in order to change the spontaneous flow of thermal energy in this way. It works by moving a fluid, called a refrigerant, through tubing. The refrigerant alternately absorbs heat and then gives it off again to cool down the inside of a refrigerator or building.

© Pearson Education, Inc., publishing as Pearson Prentice Hall. All rights reserved.

Chapter 16   Thermal Energy and Heat

Section 16.1 Thermal Energy and Matter
(pages 474–478)

This section defines heat and describes how work, temperature, and thermal energy are related to heat. Thermal expansion and contraction of materials is discussed, and uses of a calorimeter are explained.

Reading Strategy (page 474)

Previewing Before you read, preview the figures in this section and add two more questions in the table. As you read, write answers to your questions. For more information on this Reading Strategy, see the **Reading and Study Skills** in the **Skills and Reference Handbook** at the end of your textbook.

Thermal Energy and Matter	
Questions About Thermal Energy and Matter	**Answers**
Which has more thermal energy, a cup of tea or a pitcher of juice?	

Work and Heat (page 474)

1. Heat is the transfer of thermal energy from one object to another as the result of a difference in _____.

2. Circle the letter of each sentence that is true about heat.

   a. Heat is a fluid that flows between particles of matter.

   b. Heat flows spontaneously from hot objects to cold objects.

   c. Friction produces heat.

   d. The transfer of thermal energy from one object to another is heat.

Temperature (page 475)

3. What is temperature? _____

_____

4. Is the following sentence true or false? On the Celsius scale, the reference points for temperature are the freezing and boiling points of water. _____

© Pearson Education, Inc., publishing as Pearson Prentice Hall. All rights reserved.

Chapter 16   Thermal Energy and Heat

5. Circle the letter of each sentence that explains what happens when an object heats up.

   a. Its particles move faster, on average.

   b. The average kinetic energy of its particles decreases.

   c. Its mass increases.

   d. Its temperature increases.

Thermal Energy (page 475)

6. What is thermal energy? _____

   _____

7. Thermal energy depends upon the _____,
   _____, and _____ of an object.

8. Is the following sentence true or false? Two substances can be the same temperature and have different thermal energies.

   _____

Thermal Expansion and Contraction (page 476)

9. Is the following sentence true or false? Thermal contraction occurs when matter is heated, because particles of matter tend to move closer together as temperature increases. _____

10. Describe thermal expansion and contraction by completing the table below.

Thermal Expansion and Contraction			
Condition	Temperature	Space Between Particles	Volume
	Increases		
			Decreases

Specific Heat (pages 476–477)

11. The amount of heat needed to raise the temperature of one gram of material by one degree Celsius is called _____.

12. Why are you more likely to burn yourself on a metal toy than on a plastic toy if both have been sitting in the sun? _____

    _____

    _____

Measuring Heat Changes (page 478)

13. What device is used to measure changes in thermal energy?

    _____

14. Is the following sentence true or false? A calorimeter uses the principle that heat flows from a hotter object to a colder object until both reach the same temperature. _____

© Pearson Education, Inc., publishing as Pearson Prentice Hall. All rights reserved.

Chapter 16   Thermal Energy and Heat

Section 16.2 Heat and Thermodynamics
(pages 479–483)

This section discusses three kinds of thermal energy transfer and introduces the first, second, and third laws of thermodynamics.

Reading Strategy (page 479)

Build Vocabulary As you read this section, add definitions and examples to complete the table. For more information on this Reading Strategy, see the **Reading and Study Skills** in the **Skills and Reference Handbook** at the end of your textbook.

Transfer of Thermal Energy	
Definitions	**Examples**
Conduction: transfer of thermal energy with no net transfer of matter	Frying pan handle heats up
Convection:	
Radiation:	

Conduction (pages 479–480)

1. The transfer of thermal energy with no overall transfer of matter is called _____.

2. Why is conduction slower in gases than in liquids and solids? _____
_____

_____

3. Is the following sentence true or false? Conduction is faster in metals than in other solids because metals have free electrons that transfer thermal energy. _____

4. Circle the letter of each sentence that is true about conduction.

   a. Thermal energy is transferred without transfer of matter.

   b. Matter is transferred great distances during conduction.

   c. Conduction can occur between materials that are not touching.

   d. In most solids, conduction takes place as particles vibrate in place.

5. Complete the table about conduction.

Conduction		
Type of Material	**Quality of Conduction**	**Two Examples**
	Conducts thermal energy well	Copper;
Thermal insulator		Wood;

© Pearson Education, Inc., publishing as Pearson Prentice Hall. All rights reserved.

Chapter 16   Thermal Energy and Heat

Convection (pages 480–481)

6. The transfer of thermal energy when particles of a fluid move from one place to another is called _____.

7. Why is temperature higher at the bottom of an oven? _____

   _____

   _____

8. When a fluid circulates in a loop as it alternately heats up and cools down, a(n) _____ occurs.

9. Give three examples of convection currents in nature. _____

   _____

Radiation (page 481)

10. The transfer of energy by waves moving through space is called

    _____.

11. Circle the letter of each sentence that is true about radiation.

    a. Energy is transferred by waves.

    b. All objects radiate energy.

    c. The amount of energy radiated from an object decreases as its temperature increases.

    d. The farther away you are from a radiating object, the less radiation you receive.

Thermodynamics (pages 482–483)

12. Thermodynamics is the study of conversions between _____ and other forms of energy.

13. Is the following sentence true or false? Energy cannot be created or destroyed, but it can be converted into different forms.

    _____

14. Thermal energy flows spontaneously from _____ objects to _____ ones.

15. According to the second law of thermodynamics, what must happen for thermal energy to flow from a colder object to a hotter object? _____

    _____

16. Thermal energy that is not converted into work is called

    _____.

17. Is the following sentence true or false? Scientists have created a heat engine with 100 percent efficiency by reducing the temperature of the outside environment to absolute zero.

    _____

18. Is the following sentence true or false? Matter can be cooled to absolute zero. _____

© Pearson Education, Inc., publishing as Pearson Prentice Hall. All rights reserved.

Chapter 16   Thermal Energy and Heat

Section 16.3 Using Heat
(pages 486–492)

This section describes ways in which humans benefit from heat engines, heating systems, and cooling systems. It also discusses how each of these systems works.

Reading Strategy (page 486)

Sequencing As you read, complete the cycle diagram to show the sequence of events in a gasoline engine. For more information on this Reading Strategy, see the **Reading and Study Skills** in the **Skills and Reference Handbook** at the end of your textbook.

Sequence of Events in a Gasoline Engine

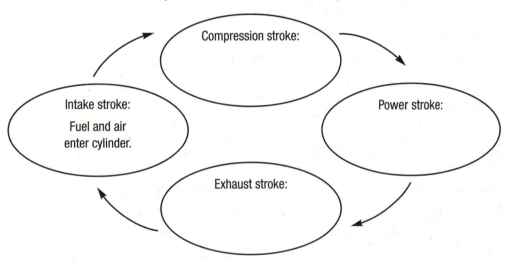

Heat Engines (pages 486–487)

1. The two main types of heat engines are the _____ and the _____.

2. A steam engine is an external combustion engine because it burns fuel _____ the engine.

3. Who developed the first practical steam engine?

    a. James Prescott Joule

    b. Thomas Newcomen

    c. James Watt

    d. Benjamin Thompson

4. How is heat converted into work in a steam engine? _____

    _____

5. A heat engine used by most cars in which fuel burns inside the engine is called a(n) _____.

6. Each upward or downward motion of a piston in an internal combustion engine is called a(n) _____.

© Pearson Education, Inc., publishing as Pearson Prentice Hall. All rights reserved.

Chapter 16   Thermal Energy and Heat

7. Is the following sentence true or false? In a typical car, the crankshaft produces a linear motion that turns the wheels. _____

8. Why is it important for an internal combustion engine to have a cooling system? _____

_____

9. Is the following sentence true or false? Gasoline engines operate very efficiently in converting fuel energy to work. _____

Heating Systems (pages 489–490)

10. What is a central heating system? _____

_____

11. List four energy sources used for central heating systems.

a. _____   b. _____

c. _____   d. _____

12. Is the following sentence true or false? In most heating systems, conduction is used to distribute most of the thermal energy. _____

Match each description with the heating system it describes.

Description	Heating System
_____ **13.** Water heated by a boiler circulates through radiators in each room, transferring thermal energy.	a. hot-water heating
_____ **14.** Fans are used to circulate warm air through ducts to the rooms in a building.	b. steam heating
_____ **15.** A hot coil heats air by conduction and radiation.	c. electric baseboard heating
_____ **16.** This system is often used in older buildings or to heat many buildings from a single location.	d. forced-air heating

Cooling Systems (pages 490–492)

17. Is the following sentence true or false? Most cooling systems, such as air conditioners and refrigerators, are heat pumps. _____

18. A fluid that vaporizes and condenses inside the tubing of a heat pump is called a(n) _____.

19. How does a heat pump reverse the normal flow of thermal energy? _____

_____

_____

© Pearson Education, Inc., publishing as Pearson Prentice Hall. All rights reserved.

Chapter 16   Thermal Energy and Heat

WordWise

Answer the questions by writing the correct vocabulary term in the blanks. Use the circled letter(s) in each term to find the hidden vocabulary word. Then, write a definition for the hidden word.

Clues	Vocabulary Terms
This flows spontaneously from hot objects to cold objects.	_ _ _ Ⓞ
Any device that converts heat into work	Ⓞ Ⓞ _ _ _ _ _ _ _ _
A heat pump does work on this so you can keep your veggies cold.	_ _ _ Ⓞ _ _ _ _ _ _ _
The Kelvin scale is used to measure this.	_ _ Ⓞ _ _ _ _ _ _
A device used to determine the specific heat of a material	_ Ⓞ Ⓞ _ _ _ _ _ _ _
The transfer of thermal energy when particles of a fluid move from place to place	_ _ _ _ _ _ _ Ⓞ _ Ⓞ
The amount of heat needed to raise the temperature of one gram of a material by one degree Celsius	Ⓞ _ _ _ _ _ _ _ _ _ _ _
The transfer of thermal energy with no overall transfer of matter	_ _ _ Ⓞ _ _ _ _
The total potential and kinetic energy of all the particles in an object	_ _ _ _ _ Ⓞ _ _ _ _ _
The transfer of energy by waves moving through space	_ Ⓞ _ _ _ Ⓞ _ Ⓞ _
According to the first law of thermodynamics, this is conserved.	_ _ _ Ⓞ _ _

Hidden words: _ _ _ _ _ _ _ _ _ _ _ _ _ _

Definition: _____

_____

© Pearson Education, Inc., publishing as Pearson Prentice Hall. All rights reserved.

Chapter 16   Thermal Energy and Heat

Calculating with Specific Heat

How much heat is required to raise the temperature of a
gold earring from 25.0°C to 30.0°C? The earring weighs
25 grams, and the specific heat of gold is 0.128 J/g•°C.

Math Skill:
Formulas and
Equations

You may want to read
more about this **Math
Skill** in the **Skills and
Reference Handbook**
at the end of your
textbook.

1. Read and Understand

What information are you given?

Specific heat = c = 0.128 J/g•°C

Mass = m = 25.0 grams

Change in Temperature = ΔT = (30.0°C − 25.0°C) = 5.0°C

2. Plan and Solve

What unknown are you trying to calculate?

Amount of heat needed = Q = ?

What formula contains the given quantities and the unknown?

Q = Mass × Specific heat × Change in Temperature

$Q = m \times c \times \Delta T$

Replace each variable with its known value.

Q = 25.0 g × 0.128 J/g•°C × 5.0°C = 16 J

3. Look Back and Check

Is your answer reasonable?

$$\frac{\text{Heat absorbed}}{(m \times c)} = 16 \text{ J}/(25.0 \text{ g} \times 0.128 \text{ J/g•°C}) = 5.0°C$$

This is a reasonable answer for the heat required to raise the
temperature of the earring.

Math Practice

On a separate sheet of paper, solve the following problems.

1. How much heat is required to raise the temperature of 25 grams
   of water from 25.0°C to 30.0°C? The specific heat of water is
   4.18 J/g•°C.

2. Determine the mass of a sample of silver if 705 J of heat are required
   to raise its temperature from 25°C to 35°C. The specific heat of silver
   is 0.235 J/g•°C.

3. An iron skillet has a mass of 500.0 g. The specific heat of iron is
   0.449 J/g•°C. The pan is heated by adding 19,082.5 J of heat. How
   much does the temperature of the pan increase?

© Pearson Education, Inc., publishing as Pearson Prentice Hall. All rights reserved.

Chapter 17   Mechanical Waves and Sound

Summary

17.1 Mechanical Waves

A mechanical wave is a movement of matter. It carries energy from place to place. Mechanical waves need matter to travel through. The matter a wave travels through is called its medium (plural, media). Solids, liquids, and gases can act as media for mechanical waves.

A mechanical wave is created when a source of energy causes a vibration in a medium. A vibration is a repeating back-and-forth motion. For example, when you shake one end of a rope up and down, you create a vibration in that end of the rope. The vibration travels through the rope as a wave. The wave carries energy from your hand to the other end of the rope.

Scientists classify mechanical waves by the way they move through a medium. There are three main types of mechanical waves:

- transverse waves,
- longitudinal waves, and
- surface waves.

In a transverse wave, the medium moves at right angles to the direction of the wave. A wave in a rope is a transverse wave. The rope moves up and down. The wave travels from one end of the rope to the other. As the wave moves through each particle in the rope, the particle moves a short distance up and down. The highest point the medium reaches is called a crest. The lowest point the medium reaches is called a trough.

In a longitudinal wave, the medium moves in the same direction as the wave. A wave in a spring toy is a longitudinal wave. When you push on one end of the spring, a few coils bunch up. This area is called a compression. Behind the compression, the coils are spread apart. This area is called a rarefaction. The compression and rarefaction travel through the spring. As the wave passes each coil in the spring, the coil moves a short distance back and forth.

A surface wave travels along the surface between two media. Ocean waves are surface waves. They travel along the surface between water and air. In a surface wave, particles of medium move up and down, like particles in a transverse wave. The particles also move back and forth, like particles in a longitudinal wave. When these two motions are combined, the particles move in circles.

17.2 Properties of Mechanical Waves

Several properties of mechanical waves help describe the waves. The properties are

- period,
- frequency,
- wavelength,
- speed, and
- amplitude.

Period is a measure of time. The period of a transverse wave is the time between one crest or trough and the next. The period of a longitudinal wave is the time between one compression or rarefaction and the next. Period is usually measured in seconds (s).

Frequency is a count, or number. The frequency of a transverse wave is the number of crests or troughs that pass a point in a given time. The frequency of a longitudinal wave is the number of compressions or rarefactions that pass a point in a give time. The unit of frequency is the hertz (Hz), or number per second. The frequency of a wave is determined by the frequency of the vibrations producing the wave.

© Pearson Education, Inc., publishing as Pearson Prentice Hall. All rights reserved.

Chapter 17   Mechanical Waves and Sound

Wavelength is a measure of distance, or length. The wavelength of a transverse wave is the distance from one crest or trough to the next. The wavelength of a longitudinal wave is the distance from one compression or rarefaction to the next. Wavelength is often measured in meters. Increasing the frequency of a wave decreases its wavelength.

Speed is a measure of how fast something is moving. You can calculate the speed of a wave by multiplying wavelength by frequency:

Speed = Wavelength × Frequency

A common unit of speed is meters per second. Two waves can have different wavelengths and frequencies and still have the same speed. Their speed will be the same as long as the product of wavelength and frequency is the same for both waves.

Amplitude is a measure of distance. The amplitude of a mechanical wave is the maximum distance the medium moves from its position at rest. For example, the amplitude of a transverse wave is the distance from the rest position to a crest or a trough. It takes more energy to produce a wave with higher crests and lower troughs. Therefore, the greater the amplitude of a wave, the greater its energy is.

17.3 Behavior of Waves

Waves meet and interact with surfaces and with other waves. Types of wave interactions include

- reflection,
- refraction,
- diffraction, and
- interference.

Reflection is the bouncing back of a wave from a surface that it cannot pass through. Reflection of a wave from a surface is like a ball bouncing off a wall. Reflection does not change the speed or frequency of a wave, but the wave can be flipped upside down.

Refraction is the bending of a wave as it enters a new medium at an angle. If the wave travels more slowly in the new medium, one side of the wave will slow down before the other side. This causes the wave to bend.

Diffraction is the bending of a wave as it moves around an obstacle or passes through a narrow opening. How much a wave bends depends on the wavelength and the size of the opening or obstacle. The bigger the wavelength compared to the size of the opening or obstacle, the more the wave bends.

The interaction of two or more waves is called interference. Two types of interference are constructive interference and destructive interference.

- In constructive interference, the crests of one wave overlap the crests of another wave. This results in a combined wave with larger amplitude.
- In destructive interference, the crests of one wave overlap the troughs of another wave. This results in a combined wave with smaller amplitude.

Sometimes a wave and its reflected wave interact to produce a standing wave. A standing wave is a wave that appears to stay in one place. It does not seem to move through the medium. A standing wave forms only if half a wavelength (or a multiple of half a wavelength) fits exactly within the length of the vibrating rope or other medium.

17.4 Sound and Hearing

Sound is carried by longitudinal waves. Properties of sound include speed, intensity, loudness, frequency, and pitch. These properties explain the behavior of sound.

- Speed is how fast sound travels. In dry air at 20°C, sound waves travel at a speed of 342 meters per second.

© Pearson Education, Inc., publishing as Pearson Prentice Hall. All rights reserved.

Chapter 17   Mechanical Waves and Sound

Sound waves travel fastest in solids, slower in liquids, and slowest in gases.

- Intensity is a measure of the energy of sound in a given area. Intensity depends on the amplitude (energy) of the sound waves and the distance from the sound source. A nearby whisper could have the same intensity as a distant shout.
- Loudness is a measure of how intense a sound seems to a listener. High-intensity sounds generally sound loud. However, loudness also depends on factors such as the sharpness of the listener's hearing.
- Frequency is the number of sound waves that occur in a given time. It depends on how fast the sound source is vibrating.
- Pitch is how high or low a sound seems to a listener. Pitch depends mostly on the frequency of the sound waves. High-frequency sounds have a high pitch. Low-frequency sounds have a low pitch.

People cannot hear sounds with very low or very high frequencies. Infrasound is sound at frequencies lower than most people can hear. Ultrasound is sound at frequencies higher than most people can hear. Ultrasound is used for sonar and ultrasound imaging. Sonar is used to find the distance of objects under water.

Ultrasound imaging is used to make maps of structures inside the body.

When a siren passes you, it may sound like it changes pitch. This is called the Doppler effect. As a source of sound approaches, an observer hears a higher frequency. This occurs because the sound waves get closer together when the sound source moves in the same direction as the sound. As the sound source moves away, the observer hears a lower frequency. This occurs because the sound waves get farther apart when the sound source moves in the opposite direction from the sound.

The ear is the organ that responds to sound. The ear has three main regions: the outer ear, the middle ear, and the inner ear.

- The outer ear gathers and focuses sound into the middle ear.
- The middle ear receives the vibrations and increases their amplitude.
- The inner ear senses the vibrations and sends signals to the brain.

Sound is recorded by changing sound waves into electronic signals. The signals are stored on tapes or disks. Sound is reproduced by changing the stored electronic signals back into sound waves. Musical instruments can make sounds of different pitches. They change pitch by changing the frequency of the sound waves.

© Pearson Education, Inc., publishing as Pearson Prentice Hall. All rights reserved.

Name _____ Class _____ Date _____

Chapter 17   Mechanical Waves and Sound

Section 17.1 Mechanical Waves
(pages 500–503)

This section explains what mechanical waves are, how they form, and how they travel. Three main types of mechanical waves—transverse, longitudinal, and surface waves—are discussed and examples are given for each type.

Reading Strategy (page 500)

Previewing As you read this section, use Figure 2 on page 501 to complete the web diagram. Then use Figures 3 and 4 to make similar diagrams for longitudinal waves and surface waves on a separate sheet of paper. For more information on this Reading Strategy, see the **Reading and Study Skills** in the **Skills and Reference Handbook** at the end of your textbook.

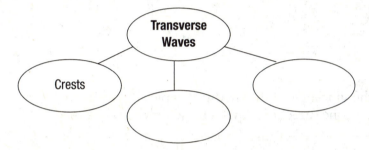

What Are Mechanical Waves? (page 500)

1. A disturbance in matter that carries energy from one place to another is called a(n) _____.

2. Is the following sentence true or false? Mechanical waves can travel through empty space. _____

3. The material through which a wave travels is called a(n) _____.

4. Is the following sentence true or false? Solids, liquids, and gases all can act as mediums for waves. _____

5. What creates a mechanical wave? _____

_____

Types of Mechanical Waves (pages 501–503)

6. Is the following sentence true or false? The three main types of mechanical waves are water waves, longitudinal waves, and surface waves. _____

7. Circle the letter of the characteristic used to classify a mechanical wave.

   a. the height of its crest

   b. the depth of its trough

   c. the way it travels through a medium

   d. the type of medium through which it travels

© Pearson Education, Inc., publishing as Pearson Prentice Hall. All rights reserved.

8. The highest point of a wave above the rest position is the
_____ and the lowest point below the rest position
is the _____.

9. What is a transverse wave? _____
_____

10. Look at the figure below. Label the missing aspects of the wave in
the rope.

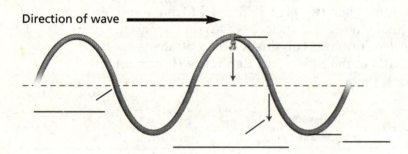

11. A wave in which the vibration of the medium is parallel to, or in
the same direction as, the direction in which the wave travels is
called a(n) _____.

12. When a longitudinal wave carries energy through a spring, the
area where the coils of a spring are closer together than they would
be in the rest position is called a(n) _____.

13. Is the following sentence true or false? A rarefaction is a region in a
longitudinal wave where particles of a medium spread out.
_____

14. Why is an ocean wave classified as a surface wave? _____
_____

15. Why do ocean waves transport objects on the surface of the water as they
approach shore? _____
_____

*Match the type of wave to each description below. The type of wave may be
used more than once.*

Description	Type of Wave
_____ **16.** P wave	a. transverse wave
_____ **17.** Direction of travel is perpendicular to vibration direction	b. longitudinal wave
_____ **18.** Rarefactions with particles that are spread out	c. surface wave
_____ **19.** A wave that travels along a boundary separating two mediums	
_____ **20.** An ocean wave	

© Pearson Education, Inc., publishing as Pearson Prentice Hall. All rights reserved.

Chapter 17   Mechanical Waves and Sound

Section 17.2 Properties of Mechanical Waves
(pages 504–507)

This section introduces measurable properties used to describe mechanical waves, including frequency, period, wavelength, speed, and amplitude.

Reading Strategy (page 504)

Build Vocabulary As you read, write a definition in your own words for each term in the table below. For more information on this Reading Strategy, see the **Reading and Study Skills** in the **Skills and Reference Handbook** at the end of your textbook.

Properties of Waves	
Vocabulary Term	**Definition**
Period	
Frequency	
Wavelength	
Amplitude	

Frequency and Period (page 504)

1. Is the following sentence true or false? A periodic motion repeats at regular time intervals. _____

2. The time required for one cycle, a complete motion that returns to its starting point, is called the _____.

3. The number of complete cycles in a given period of time is the _____ of a periodic motion.

4. Circle the letter of each sentence that is true about frequency.

   a. Frequency is measured in cycles per second, or hertz.

   b. A wave's frequency equals the frequency of the vibrating source producing it.

   c. Five cycles per minute is a frequency of five hertz.

   d. Any periodic motion has a frequency.

Wavelength (page 505)

5. The distance between a point on one wave and the same point on the next cycle of the wave is called _____.

6. How is wavelength determined for a longitudinal wave?

_____

© Pearson Education, Inc., publishing as Pearson Prentice Hall. All rights reserved.

Chapter 17   Mechanical Waves and Sound

Wave Speed (pages 505–506)

7. Write a formula you can use to determine the speed of a wave.

_____

8. Is the following sentence true or false? The speed of a wave equals its wavelength divided by its period. _____

9. What variables can cause the speed of a wave to change? _____

_____

10. Circle the letter of the sentence that tells how wavelength is related to frequency for a wave traveling at a constant speed.

    a. Wavelength is equal to frequency.

    b. Wavelength is directly proportional to frequency.

    c. Wavelength is inversely proportional to frequency.

    d. A wave with a higher frequency will have a longer wavelength.

Amplitude (page 507)

11. What is the amplitude of a wave? _____

_____

12. It takes more energy to produce a wave with higher crests and deeper troughs, so the more energy a wave has, the _____ its amplitude.

Questions 13 through 17 refer to the figure below.

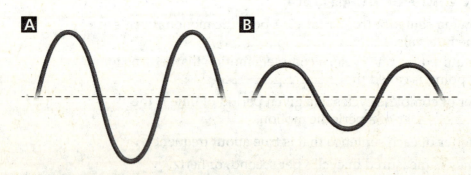

13. The type of waves shown are _____.

14. Label the rest position for waves A and B.

15. Add arrows to the figure to indicate the amplitude of each wave. Which wave has the greater amplitude? _____

16. Which wave shown has more energy? _____

17. Add an arrow to indicate one wavelength on wave B.

© Pearson Education, Inc., publishing as Pearson Prentice Hall. All rights reserved.

Chapter 17   Mechanical Waves and Sound

Section 17.3 Behavior of Waves
(pages 508–512)

This section describes different interactions that can occur when a mechanical wave encounters an obstacle, a change in medium, or another wave. These interactions include reflection, refraction, diffraction, and interference.

Reading Strategy (page 508)

Identifying Main Ideas Complete the table below. As you read, write the main idea of each topic. For more information on this Reading Strategy, see the **Reading and Study Skills** in the **Skills and Reference Handbook** at the end of your textbook.

Wave Interactions	
Topic	**Main Idea**
Reflection	
Refraction	
Diffraction	
Interference	
Standing waves	

Reflection (page 508)

1. Is the following sentence true or false? Reflection occurs when a wave bounces off a surface that it cannot pass through.

_____

2. Circle the letter of the results that occur when a wave reflects off a fixed boundary.

   a. The reflected wave will be turned upside down.

   b. The amplitude will double as it strikes the surface.

   c. The speed of the wave will decrease.

   d. The frequency of the wave will decrease.

Refraction (page 509)

3. Why does refraction occur when a wave enters a new medium at an angle? _____

_____

4. Is the following sentence true or false? Refraction always involves a change in the speed and direction of a wave. _____

© Pearson Education, Inc., publishing as Pearson Prentice Hall. All rights reserved.

Chapter 17   Mechanical Waves and Sound

Diffraction (page 510)

5. What is required in order for diffraction to occur? _____

_____

6. Is the following sentence true or false? A wave diffracts more if its wavelength is small compared to the size of an opening or obstacle. _____

Interference (pages 510–511)

7. What causes wave interference? _____

_____

8. Complete the table about interference.

Interference		
Type	**Alignment**	**Displacement Change**
Constructive	Crests align with crests; troughs align with troughs	
		Displacements combine to produce a reduced amplitude.

9. Is the following sentence true or false? Destructive interference can result in wave displacements that are above the rest position.

_____

10. How can an increased depth of a trough be considered constructive interference? _____

_____

Standing Waves (page 512)

11. At certain frequencies, interference between a wave and its reflection can produce a(n) _____.

12. Circle each letter of a sentence that is true about standing waves.

   a. A node is a point that has no displacement from the rest position.

   b. Standing waves appear to move through a medium, such as a string.

   c. Complete destructive interference occurs at antinodes.

   d. A standing wave will form for any wavelength, as long as two ends of a rope or string are stretched tightly between two points.

13. Is the following sentence true or false? If a standing wave occurs in a medium at a given frequency, another standing wave will occur if this frequency is doubled. _____

14. Give an example of a common standing wave. _____

_____

© Pearson Education, Inc., publishing as Pearson Prentice Hall. All rights reserved.

Chapter 17   Mechanical Waves and Sound

Section 17.4 Sound and Hearing
(pages 514–521)

This section discusses properties of sound waves, how they are produced, and how the ear perceives sound. A description of how music is produced and recorded also is presented.

Reading Strategy (page 514)

Using Prior Knowledge Before you read, add properties you already know about sound waves to the diagram below. Then add details about each property as you read the section. For more information on this Reading Strategy, see the **Reading and Study Skills** in the **Skills and Reference Handbook** at the end of your textbook.

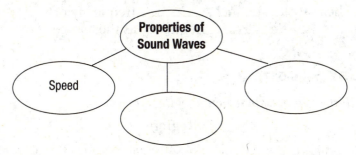

Properties of Sound Waves (pages 514–515)

1. Circle the letter of each sentence that is true about sound.

   a. Many behaviors of sound can be explained using a few properties.

   b. Sound waves are compressions and rarefactions that travel through a medium.

   c. Sound waves usually travel more slowly in solids than in gases.

   d. The speed of sound in air is about 30 meters per second.

Match each description with one or more sound properties.

Description	Property
_____ 2. This property is measured in units called decibels.	a. loudness
_____ 3. These properties are affected by the length of tubing in a musical instrument.	b. pitch
_____ 4. This property is the frequency of a sound as your ears perceive it.	c. intensity
_____ 5. These properties depend on factors such as your age and the health of your ears.	d. frequency
_____ 6. This property is a physical response to the intensity of sound.	

© Pearson Education, Inc., publishing as Pearson Prentice Hall. All rights reserved.

Chapter 17   Mechanical Waves and Sound

Ultrasound (page 516)

7. Is the following sentence true or false? Ultrasound is sound at frequencies that are lower than most people are capable of hearing.
   _____

8. Describe some applications of ultrasound. _____
   _____

The Doppler Effect (page 516)

9. Is the following sentence true or false? The Doppler effect is a change in sound frequency caused by motion of the sound source, motion of the listener, or both. _____

10. For a stationary observer, as a moving sound source approaches, the observer will first hear a(n) _____ frequency of sound and then a(n) _____ frequency as the source moves away.

Hearing and the Ear (page 517)

Match each description with the appropriate region(s) of the ear.

Description	Region
_____ **11.** Sound is gathered and focused here.	a. outer ear
_____ **12.** Nerve endings send signals to the brain.	b. middle ear
_____ **13.** The eardrum is located at the boundary between these two regions of the ear.	c. inner ear
_____ **14.** Hammer, anvil, and stirrup are located here.	
_____ **15.** Sound vibrations are amplified.	

How Sound Is Reproduced (pages 518–519)

16. How is sound recorded? _____
    _____

17. Sound is reproduced by converting _____ back into sound waves.

Music (page 521)

18. Is the following sentence true or false? Many musical instruments vary pitch by changing the frequency of standing waves.
    _____

19. Theaters are designed to prevent "dead spots" where the volume is reduced by _____ of reflected sound waves.

20. The response of a standing wave to another wave of the same frequency is called _____.

© Pearson Education, Inc., publishing as Pearson Prentice Hall. All rights reserved.

Chapter 17   Mechanical Waves and Sound

WordWise

Test your knowledge of vocabulary terms from Chapter 17 by completing this crossword puzzle.

Clues across:

1. Maximum displacement of a wave

3. The time required for one complete wave cycle

6. An apparent change in frequency of a sound source that moves relative to an observer

8. A point of no displacement in a standing wave

9. Area where particles in a medium are spread out as a longitudinal wave travels through it

10. Distance from one point to the next identical point on a wave

Clues down:

2. Type of mechanical wave whose direction of vibration is perpendicular to its direction of travel

4. A unit used to compare sound intensity levels

5. Occurs when waves overlap

6. Occurs when a wave encounters an object or opening that is close in size to its wavelength

7. Lowest point of a wave below the rest position

© Pearson Education, Inc., publishing as Pearson Prentice Hall. All rights reserved.

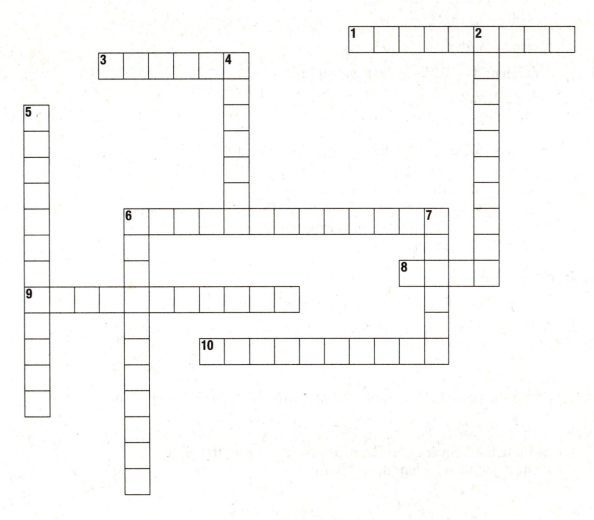

Chapter 17   Mechanical Waves and Sound

Calculating Wave Properties

A transverse wave in a rope is traveling at a speed of 3.0 m/s. The period of this mechanical wave is 0.25 s. What is the wavelength?

Math Skill: Formulas and Equations

You may want to read more about this **Math Skill** in the **Skills and Reference Handbook** at the end of your textbook.

1. Read and Understand

What information are you given?

Speed = 3.0 m/s

Period = 0.25 s

2. Plan and Solve

What unknown are you trying to calculate?

Wavelength = ?

What formula contains the given quantities and the unknown?

$$\text{Speed} = \text{Wavelength} \times \text{Frequency} = \frac{\text{Wavelength}}{\text{Period}}$$

Wavelength = Period × Speed

Replace each variable with its known value.

Speed = 3.0 m/s

Period = 0.25 s

Wavelength = 0.25 s × 3.0 m/s = 0.75 m

3. Look Back and Check

Is your answer reasonable?

$$\text{Speed} = \text{Wavelength} \times \text{Frequency} = \text{Wavelength} \times \frac{1}{\text{Period}}$$

$$\text{Speed} = 0.75 \text{ m} \times \frac{1}{0.25 \text{ s}} = 3.0 \text{ m/s}.$$

Substituting the calculated wavelength into the equation yields the original speed of 3.0 m/s.

Math Practice

On a separate sheet of paper, solve the following problems.

1. What is the speed, in m/s, of a wave on a cord if it has a wavelength of 4 m and a period of 0.5 s?

2. What is the period of a wave traveling 5 m/s if its wavelength is 20 m?

3. Calculate the frequency, in Hz, of a wave in a string traveling 1.25 m/s, with a wavelength of 0.50 m.

© Pearson Education, Inc., publishing as Pearson Prentice Hall. All rights reserved.

Chapter 18   The Electromagnetic Spectrum and Light

Summary

18.1 Electromagnetic Waves

Electromagnetic waves are transverse waves. They are made up of changing electric and magnetic fields. The fields are produced by movements of electric charges. The fields are at right angles to each other. The fields are also at right angles to the direction of the wave. Electromagnetic waves do not need a medium. They can travel through a vacuum, or empty space. The transfer of energy by electromagnetic waves is called electromagnetic radiation.

All electromagnetic waves travel at the same speed in a vacuum: 3.00×10^8 meters per second. However, electromagnetic waves may have different frequencies and wavelengths. The higher the frequency of an electromagnetic wave, the shorter its wavelength is.

Around 1800, physicist Thomas Young showed that light travels as waves. About a century later, physicist Albert Einstein suggested that light is made up of packets of energy. Scientists now call these packets of energy photons. A photon model of light helps explain the photoelectric effect. The photoelectric effect occurs when light strikes the surface of a metal, and the metal gives off electrons. Today, scientists think that light and other types of electromagnetic radiation act like both waves and particles.

Photons can also explain why a light seems dimmer when you are farther from it. Photons travel outward from a light source in all directions. The photons become more and more spread out as they move away from the light. This causes the intensity of the light to decrease. Intensity is the rate at which energy flows through an area of a given size. It determines how bright light seems. Farther from the light source, there is less energy in a given area.

Therefore, the light is less intense and not as bright.

18.2 The Electromagnetic Spectrum

All electromagnetic waves together make up the electromagnetic spectrum. In order of increasing frequency, the waves are radio waves, infrared rays, visible light, ultraviolet rays, X-rays, and gamma rays.

Radio waves have the lowest frequencies and longest wavelengths. They are used to transmit radio and television programs. At a radio station, sound waves are changed into electronic signals. The electronic signals are then coded onto radio waves. The station broadcasts the waves through the air. Your radio receives the coded radio waves. The radio decodes the radio waves and changes them back into sound waves. Radio waves also carry signals for television programs. In television, information for pictures as well as sound is coded onto the radio waves. Microwaves are the shortest-wavelength radio waves. They are used to cook and reheat food. They are also used to carry mobile phone calls.

You cannot see infrared rays. However, your skin can sense them as heat. A device called a thermograph can also sense infrared rays. A thermograph creates color-coded pictures showing which objects or organisms are warm and which are cool. The pictures are called thermograms. The pictures can be used to locate victims of disasters such as earthquakes. Infrared rays are also used in heat lamps. The lamps may be used to keep food or animals warm.

Visible light is the only part of the electromagnetic spectrum that we can see. We see each frequency of visible

© Pearson Education, Inc., publishing as Pearson Prentice Hall. All rights reserved.

light as a different color. From lowest to highest frequency, the colors of visible light are red, orange, yellow, green, blue, and violet. We use visible light to see, help keep us safe, and communicate with each other.

Ultraviolet rays help your skin produce vitamin D. However, too much ultraviolet radiation causes sunburn, wrinkles, and skin cancer. It also damages your eyes. Ultraviolet rays are used to kill germs and to help plants grow.

X-rays have high energy. They can pass through matter that visible light cannot pass through. X-rays are used to take pictures of bones and teeth. They are also used to see the contents of packages and suitcases.

Gamma rays have the highest frequency and shortest wavelength of all electromagnetic waves. They also have the most energy and the greatest ability to pass through matter. Too many gamma rays can be deadly to living things. Gamma rays are used to kill cancer cells. They are also used to make pictures of the brain and to find cracks in pipelines.

18.3 Behavior of Light

How light acts when it hits an object depends partly on the material the object is made of. Material can be transparent, translucent, or opaque.

- A transparent material allows light to pass through. You can see clearly through a transparent material. Water and clear glass are transparent.
- A translucent material allows light to pass through, but it scatters the light in all directions. You can see only the outlines of objects through a translucent material. Frosted glass and thin fabric are translucent.
- An opaque material absorbs or reflects all the light that hits it. You cannot see anything through an opaque material. Wood and metal are opaque.

When light reflects from a surface, it may form an image. An image is a copy of an object. Reflection can be regular or diffuse. Regular reflection occurs when light strikes a smooth surface and all the light reflects in the same direction. A regular image is sharp. Diffuse reflection occurs when light strikes a rough surface and the light reflects in many different directions. A diffuse image is blurry.

Light can refract, or bend. Refraction occurs when light passes at an angle from one medium into another and changes speed in the new medium. For example, refraction occurs when light passes at an angle from air into water because light travels slower in water than in air. If you place a straw in a clear glass of water, the straw appears to bend at the surface between the air and water.

Light can also be polarized by passing through a special filter called a polarizing filter. A polarizing filter reflects light waves that vibrate in certain directions. Polarizing filters are used in some sunglasses. They help reduce glare.

18.4 Color

When white light passes through a prism, it slows down. This causes the light to refract. How much the light slows down and refracts depends on its wavelength. Shorter wavelengths slow down and refract more than longer wavelengths. Violet light has the shortest wavelength and refracts the most. Red light has the longest wavelength and refracts the least. A prism separates each color of light from white light by refracting colors through different angles. This process is called *dispersion*.

Most objects reflect at least some of the light that strikes them. An object's color depends on the color of light that the object reflects. The color of light an object reflects depends, in turn, on the object's material and the color of light that strikes the object. For example, in sunlight, an apple reflects mostly red

© Pearson Education, Inc., publishing as Pearson Prentice Hall. All rights reserved.

Chapter 18   The Electromagnetic Spectrum and Light

wavelengths of light. Therefore, the apple appears red. However, in light containing only green wavelengths, the same apple absorbs all the light that hits it. No light is reflected. Therefore, in green light, the apple appears black.

Primary colors are three colors that can be combined in varying amounts to create all other possible colors. Secondary colors are colors created by combining two primary colors. The primary colors of light are red, green, and blue. All three primary colors together form white light. The secondary colors of light are cyan, yellow, and magenta.

A pigment is a material used to color paints, inks, and dyes. A pigment absorbs some colors of light and reflects other colors. The primary colors of pigments are cyan, yellow, and magenta. The secondary colors of pigments are red, green, and blue.

18.5 Sources of Light

Common light sources include incandescent, fluorescent, laser, neon, sodium-vapor, and tungsten-halogen lights. Each type of light source produces light in a different way.

- An incandescent light consists of a glass bulb containing a fine metal thread called a filament. When electrons flow through the filament, it heats up and glows.

- A fluorescent light consists of a glass tube coated on the inside with powder and filled with mercury vapor. When electrons flow through the vapor, it produces ultraviolet rays. The ultraviolet rays cause the coating of the tube to give off light.

- A laser light consists of a glass tube containing helium and neon gases. When electrons flow through the gases, atoms of the gases give off photons of light. Mirrors at both ends of the tube cause the photons to bounce back and forth. This excites other gas atoms to give off more photons. The result is a very intense light.

- A neon light consists of a glass tube containing neon or other gas. When electrons flow through the gas, it gives off colored light. Each gas produces light of a certain color.

- A sodium-vapor light consists of a glass bulb containing a small amount of sodium and a mixture of neon and argon gases. When electrons flow through the gases, they heat up. The heat causes the sodium to give off a very bright light.

- A tungsten-halogen light consists of a glass bulb containing a filament. The filament glows when electrons flow through it. The bulb also contains a halogen gas, such as bromine. The gas reduces wear on the filament. This makes the bulb lasts longer.

© Pearson Education, Inc., publishing as Pearson Prentice Hall. All rights reserved.

Chapter 18   The Electromagnetic Spectrum and Light

Section 18.1 Electromagnetic Waves
(pages 532–538)

This section describes the characteristics of electromagnetic waves.

Reading Strategy (page 532)

Comparing and Contrasting As you read about electromagnetic waves, fill in the table below. If the characteristic listed in the table describes electromagnetic waves, write E in the column for Wave Type. Write M for mechanical waves and B for both. For more information on this Reading Strategy, see the **Reading and Study Skills** in the **Skills and Reference Handbook** at the end of your textbook.

Electromagnetic and Mechanical Waves	
Travels through a vacuum	E
Travels though medium	
Fits wave model	B
Fits particle model	
Transverse wave	
Longitudinal wave	

What Are Electromagnetic Waves? (page 533)

1. What are electromagnetic waves? _____

_____

2. Electric fields are produced by electrically charged particles and by changing _____.

3. Magnetic fields are produced by magnets, by changing _____, and by vibrating charges.

4. Electromagnetic waves are produced when a(n) _____ vibrates or accelerates.

5. Circle the letter of each sentence that is true about electric and magnetic fields.

   a. An electromagnetic wave occurs when electric and magnetic fields vibrate at right angles to each other.

   b. A magnetic field is surrounded by an electric current.

   c. Changing electric and magnetic fields regenerate each other.

   d. Electromagnetic waves are produced when an electric charge vibrates.

6. Is the following sentence true or false? Electromagnetic waves need a medium to travel through. _____

7. The transfer of energy by electromagnetic waves traveling through matter or across space is called _____.

© Pearson Education, Inc., publishing as Pearson Prentice Hall. All rights reserved.

Chapter 18   The Electromagnetic Spectrum and Light

The Speed of Electromagnetic Waves (page 534)

8. As a thunderstorm approaches, you see the lightning before you hear the thunder, because light travels _____ than sound.

9. Is the following sentence true or false? All electromagnetic waves travel at the same speed through a vacuum. _____

10. Circle the letter that gives the correct speed of light in a vacuum.

   a. 3.00×10^8 kilometers per second

   b. 3.00×10^8 meters per hour

   c. 3.00×10^8 meters per second

   d. 3.00×10^8 kilometers per hour

Wavelength and Frequency (page 535)

11. Circle the letter of each sentence that is true about electromagnetic waves.

   a. Different electromagnetic waves can have different frequencies.

   b. Wavelength is directly proportional to frequency.

   c. Electromagnetic waves always travel at the speed of light.

   d. All electromagnetic waves travel at the same speed in a vacuum.

12. As the wavelengths of electromagnetic waves increase, the frequencies _____, for waves moving in a(n) _____.

Wave or Particle? (pages 536–537)

13. Electromagnetic radiation behaves sometimes like a(n) _____ and sometimes like a stream of _____.

14. Interference only occurs when two or more waves overlap, so _____ experiment showed that light behaves like a _____.

15. The emission of electrons from a metal caused by light striking the metal is called the _____ effect.

16. Blue light has a higher frequency than red light, so photons of blue light have _____ energy than photons of red light.

Intensity (page 538)

17. The closer you get to a source of light, the _____ the light appears.

18. Intensity is the _____ at which a wave's energy flows through a given unit of area.

19. As photons travel farther from the source, the _____ of light decreases.

© Pearson Education, Inc., publishing as Pearson Prentice Hall. All rights reserved.

Chapter 18   The Electromagnetic Spectrum and Light

Section 18.2 The Electromagnetic Spectrum
(pages 539–545)

This section identifies the waves in the electromagnetic spectrum and describes their uses.

Reading Strategy (page 539)

Summarizing Complete the table for the electromagnetic spectrum. List at least two uses for each kind of wave. For more information on this Reading Strategy, see the **Reading and Study Skills** in the **Skills and Reference Handbook** at the end of your textbook.

The Electromagnetic Spectrum		
Type of Waves	**Uses**	
Radio Waves	Communications	
Infrared Rays		Keeping food warm

The Waves of the Spectrum (pages 539–540)

1. Is the following sentence true or false? William Herschel determined that the temperature of colors of light was higher at the blue end and lower at the red end. _____

2. Herschel's curiosity led him to conclude there must be invisible _____ beyond the red end of the color band.

3. Is the following sentence true or false? The full range of frequencies of electromagnetic radiation is called the electromagnetic spectrum. _____

4. Name each kind of wave in the electromagnetic spectrum, from the longest to shortest wavelength.

    a. _____   b. _____

    c. _____   d. _____

    e. _____   f. _____

© Pearson Education, Inc., publishing as Pearson Prentice Hall. All rights reserved.

Chapter 18   The Electromagnetic Spectrum and Light

Radio Waves (pages 540–542)

5. Circle the letter of each way that radio waves might be used.

   a. X-ray machines   b. microwave ovens

   c. radio technology   d. television technology

6. What is the difference between amplitude modulation (AM) and frequency modulation (FM)? _____

   _____

   _____

7. How far do microwaves generally penetrate food? _____

   _____

8. How is the Doppler effect used to detect the speed of a vehicle? _____

   _____

   _____

Infrared Rays (page 543)

9. Circle the letter of each way infrared rays are used.

   a. source of light   b. to discover areas of heat differences

   c. source of heat   d. to discover areas of depth differences

10. Thermograms show variations in _____ and are used to find places where a building loses heat to the environment.

Visible Light (page 543)

11. Is the following sentence true or false? One use for visible light is to help people communicate with one another. _____

Ultraviolet Rays (page 544)

12. Ultraviolet radiation has applications in _____ and _____.

13. Is the following sentence true or false? Ultraviolet radiation helps your skin produce vitamin D. _____

X-rays (page 544)

14. Is the following sentence true or false? X-rays have higher frequencies than ultraviolet rays. _____

15. Why are X-rays helpful? _____

   _____

Gamma Rays (page 545)

16. Gamma rays have the highest _____ and therefore the most _____ and the greatest penetrating ability of all the electromagnetic waves.

17. How is gamma radiation used in medicine? _____

© Pearson Education, Inc., publishing as Pearson Prentice Hall. All rights reserved.

Chapter 18   The Electromagnetic Spectrum and Light

Section 18.3 Behavior of Light
(pages 546-549)

This section discusses the behavior of light when it strikes different types of materials.

Reading Strategy (page 546)

Monitoring Your Understanding As you read, complete the flowchart to show how different materials affect light. For more information on this Reading Strategy, see the **Reading and Study Skills** in the **Skills and Reference Handbook** at the end of your textbook.

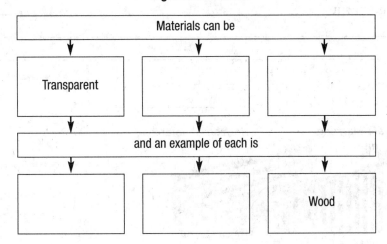

Light and Materials

Light and Materials (pages 546–547)

1. Is the following sentence true or false? Without light, nothing is visible. _____

Match each term to its definition.

Term	Definition
_____ **2.** transparent	a. Material that absorbs or reflects all of the light that strikes it
_____ **3.** opaque	b. Material that transmits light
_____ **4.** translucent	c. Material that scatters light

Interactions of Light (pages 547–549)

5. Is the following sentence true or false? Just as light can affect matter, matter can affect light. _____

6. When light strikes a new medium, it can be _____, _____, or _____.

© Pearson Education, Inc., publishing as Pearson Prentice Hall. All rights reserved.

Chapter 18   The Electromagnetic Spectrum and Light

7. When light is transmitted, it can be refracted, polarized, or
_____.

8. A copy of an object formed by reflected or refracted light waves is
known as a(n) _____.

9. When parallel light waves strike an uneven surface and reflect off
it in the same direction, _____ reflection occurs.

10. When parallel light waves strike a rough, uneven surface and
reflect in many different directions, _____
reflection occurs.

11. Light bends, or _____, when it passes at an angle
from one type of medium into another.

12. Explain why a mirage occurs. _____
_____
_____

13. Is the following sentence true or false? Light with waves that
vibrate in only one plane is polarized light. _____

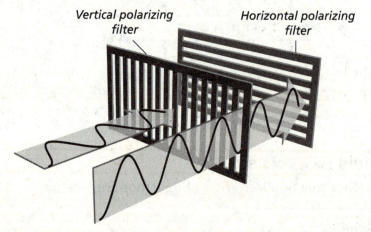

14. Refer to the drawing and complete the table on polarizing filters.

Polarizing Filters		
Direction of Light Vibration	**Filter Type**	**Action**
Horizontal wave	Vertically polarizing filter	
	Vertically polarizing filter	Light passes through.

15. How do sunglasses block glare? _____
_____

16. The effect when light is redirected as it passes through a medium
is called _____.

17. Explain why the sun looks red at sunset and sunrise. _____
_____
_____

© Pearson Education, Inc., publishing as Pearson Prentice Hall. All rights reserved.

Chapter 18   The Electromagnetic Spectrum and Light

Section 18.4 Color
(pages 550–553)

This section explains how a prism separates white light. It also discusses factors that influence the various properties of color.

Reading Strategy (page 550)

Venn Diagram As you read, label the Venn diagram for mixing primary colors of light. For more information on this Reading Strategy, see the **Reading and Study Skills** in the **Skills and Reference Handbook** at the end of your textbook.

Mixing Colors of Light

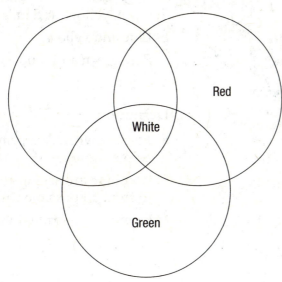

Red

White

Green

Separating White Light Into Colors (page 551)

1. What did Isaac Newton's experiments with a prism in 1666 show?

_____

_____

2. What happens when white light passes through a prism? _____

_____

3. Circle the letter of the process in which white light is separated into the colors of the rainbow.

   a. reflection   b. dispersion

   c. absorption   d. polarization

4. How does a rainbow form? _____

_____

© Pearson Education, Inc., publishing as Pearson Prentice Hall. All rights reserved.

Chapter 18   The Electromagnetic Spectrum and Light

The Colors of Objects (pages 551–552)

5. List two factors that determine the color of an object seen by reflected light.

a. _____

b. _____

6. Is the following sentence true or false? I see a red car in sunlight because the color of light reaching my eyes is mostly red light.

_____

Mixing Colors of Light (page 552)

Match the colors of light with the correct type of color.

Type of Color	Colors of Light
_____ **7.** primary colors	a. Cyan, yellow, and magenta
_____ **8.** secondary colors	b. Blue and yellow
_____ **9.** complementary colors	c. Red, green and blue

Match each color of light to its definition.

Type of Color	Definition
_____ **10.** primary colors	a. Formed when two primary colors combine
_____ **11.** secondary colors	b. Combine in varying amounts to form all possible colors
_____ **12.** complementary colors	c. Combine to form white light

Mixing Pigments (page 553)

13. What is a pigment? _____

_____

14. List four natural sources of pigments.

a. _____   b. _____

c. _____   d. _____

15. The primary colors of pigments are _____,

_____, and magenta.

Match the primary colors of pigment to the color they produce when combined.

Primary Colors	Color Produced
_____ **16.** Cyan and magenta	a. green
_____ **17.** Cyan and yellow	b. red
_____ **18.** Yellow and magenta	c. blue

19. Any two colors of pigments that combine to make black pigment are _____ colors of pigments.

© Pearson Education, Inc., publishing as Pearson Prentice Hall. All rights reserved.

Name _____ Class _____ Date _____

Chapter 18   The Electromagnetic Spectrum and Light

Section 18.5 Sources of Light
(pages 558–562)

This section discusses the major sources of light and their uses.

Reading Strategy (page 558)

Flowchart Complete the incandescent bulb flowchart. For more information on this Reading Strategy, see the **Reading and Study Skills** in the **Skills and Reference Handbook** at the end of your textbook.

Incandescent Bulb

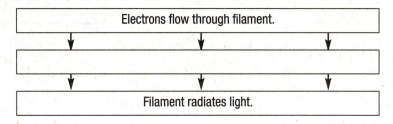

1. Objects that give off their own light are _____.

2. List six common sources of light.

   a. _____   b. _____

   c. _____   d. _____

   e. _____   f. _____

Incandescent Light (page 558)

3. The light produced when an object gets hot enough to glow is _____.

4. As electrons flow through an incandescent light bulb, the _____ heats up.

5. Is the following sentence true or false? To increase the life of the filament, incandescent light bulbs contain oxygen at very low pressure. _____

6. Most of the energy given off by incandescent bulbs is in the form of _____.

Fluorescent Light (page 559)

7. What happens in the process of fluorescence? _____

   _____

8. A solid material that can emit light by fluorescence is called a(n) _____.

9. Fluorescent bulbs emit most of their energy in the form of _____.

10. Is the following sentence true or false? Incandescent bulbs are more energy efficient than fluorescent bulbs. _____

© Pearson Education, Inc., publishing as Pearson Prentice Hall. All rights reserved.

Chapter 18   The Electromagnetic Spectrum and Light

Laser Light (page 560)

11. A laser is a device that generates _____.

12. The letters in the word *laser* stand for

     l _____

     a _____

     s _____

     e _____

     r _____.

13. What is coherent light? _____

_____

14. Why does coherent light have a relatively constant intensity? _____

_____

Neon Light (page 561)

15. How is neon light emitted? _____

_____

16. List three gases used to produce neon light.

     a. _____

     b. _____

     c. _____

17. Why do different types of neon light glow in different colors? _____

_____

_____

_____

Sodium-Vapor Light (page 562)

18. Sodium-vapor lights contain a mixture of _____
and a small amount of solid _____.

19. Explain what happens when an electric current passes through a
sodium-vapor bulb. _____

_____

_____

Tungsten-Halogen Light (page 562)

20. Explain how a tungsten-halogen light bulb works. _____

_____

_____

© Pearson Education, Inc., publishing as Pearson Prentice Hall. All rights reserved.

Name _____ Class _____ Date _____

Chapter 18   The Electromagnetic Spectrum and Light

WordWise

Complete the sentences using one of the scrambled words below.

nrcteleos	tarfes	qucreynef
treclefs	rigehh	kabcl
mefailnt	riotrafecn	ratenemypocml
yrecurm	snohpot	dairo
sifdel	culstantren	otehcern

Electromagnetic waves consist of changing electric and changing magnetic _____.

You hear thunder from a distant lightning bolt a few seconds after you see the lightning because light travels much _____ than sound.

If you know the wavelength of an electromagnetic wave in a vacuum, you can calculate its _____.

Although light behaves as a wave, the photoelectric effect shows that light also consists of bundles of energy called _____.

Antennas use _____ waves to send signals to television receivers.

Ultraviolet rays have a _____ frequency than waves of violet light.

If you can look through a material but what you see is not clear or distinct, then the material is said to be _____.

When a beam of light enters a new medium at an angle, it changes direction, and _____ occurs.

A truck appears red in the sunlight because its paint _____ mainly red light.

A color of light mixed equally with its _____ color of light yields white light.

Complementary colors of pigments combine to form _____ pigment.

An incandescent bulb produces light by using an electric current to heat a(n) _____.

Inside a fluorescent bulb, an electric current passes through _____ vapor and produces ultraviolet light.

Light that consists of a single wavelength of light with its crests and troughs lined up is called _____ light.

Neon lights emit light when _____ flow through gas in a tube.

© Pearson Education, Inc., publishing as Pearson Prentice Hall. All rights reserved.

Chapter 18   The Electromagnetic Spectrum and Light

Calculating Wavelength and Frequency

A particular AM radio station broadcasts at a frequency of 1030 MHz. What is the wavelength of the transmitted radio wave assuming it travels in a vacuum?

1. Read and Understand

What information are you given?

Speed = c = 3.00×10^8 m/s

Frequency = 1030 kHz = 1030×10^3 Hz

2. Plan and Solve

What unknown are you trying to calculate?

Wavelength = ?

What formula contains the given quantities and the unknown?

Speed = Wavelength × Frequency

$$\text{Wavelength} = \frac{\text{Speed}}{\text{Frequency}}$$

Replace each variable with its known value.

$$\text{Wavelength} = \frac{3.00 \times 10^8 \text{ m/s}}{1030 \text{ Hz} \times 10^8 \text{ Hz}}$$

$$= \frac{3.00 \times 10^8 \text{ m/s}}{1.030 \times 10^6 \text{ 1/s}} = 291 \text{ m}$$

3. Look Back and Check

Is your answer reasonable?

Radio waves have frequencies greater that 1 mm, so 291 m is a reasonable wavelength for a radio wave.

Math Practice

On a separate sheet of paper, solve the following problems.

1. In a vacuum, the wavelength of light from a laser is 630 nm (630×10^{-9} m). What is the frequency of the light?

2. If a radio wave vibrates at 80.0 MHz, what is its wavelength?

3. A radio station broadcasts at 780 kHz. The wavelength of its radio waves is 385 m. Verify that the radio wave travels at the speed of light.

Math Skill: Multiplication and Division of Exponents

You may want to read more about this **Math Skill** in the **Skills and Reference Handbook** at the end of your textbook.

© Pearson Education, Inc., publishing as Pearson Prentice Hall. All rights reserved.

Chapter 19   Optics

Summary

19.1 Mirrors

Optics includes the study of mirrors and lenses. Both mirrors and lenses form images. Recall that an image is a copy of an object. Mirrors form images by reflecting light. Reflection of light follows the law of reflection. The law states that the angle of reflection is equal to the angle of incidence. The angle of incidence is the angle at which light strikes a mirror. The angle of reflection is the angle at which light reflects from a mirror.

The images produced by mirrors may be virtual images or real images. A virtual image is a copy of an object formed at the place where the reflected light rays appear to come from. For example, light rays from your virtual image in a bathroom mirror appear to come from behind the mirror. A real image is a copy of an object formed at the place where the light rays actually meet. A real image always forms in front of the mirror. You can focus a real image on a surface such as a screen.

A plane mirror is a mirror with a flat surface. A plane mirror always produces a virtual image. The image appears to be behind the mirror. It is upright and the same size as the object. Most bathroom mirrors are plane mirrors.

Concave and convex mirrors are mirrors with curved surfaces. The surface of a concave mirror is shaped like the inside of a bowl. The surface of a convex mirror is shaped like the outside of a bowl.

Concave mirrors can form images that are real or virtual, smaller or larger than the object, and upright or upside down. The type of image formed depends on how close the object is to the mirror. Concave mirrors are used in car headlights and flashlights.

Convex mirrors can form only virtual images. The images formed by convex mirrors are always upright and smaller than the object. Convex mirrors are used in mirrors on the sides of cars. They make objects look farther away than they really are.

19.2 Lenses

Recall that light travels at a speed of 3.00×10^8 meters per second in a vacuum. Light travels slower in a medium. Media vary in how much they slow light. Air slows light very little. Some materials slow light much more. The index of refraction is a measure of how much a medium slows light compared to the speed of light in a vacuum. Air has a low index of refraction. When light enters a new medium at an angle, the change in speed causes the light to refract. How much the light refracts depends on the new material's index of refraction. The higher the index of refraction, the more light slows and refracts.

A lens is an object made of a transparent material. It has curved surfaces. The curved surfaces refract light. Lenses can be concave or convex.

A concave lens is curved inward at the center and is thickest at the outside edges. A concave lens causes light rays to spread out and form a virtual image. The image is always smaller than the object and on the same side of the lens as the object. Concave lenses are used in cameras and telescopes.

A convex lens is curved outward at the center and is thinnest at the outer edges. A convex lens causes light rays to come together at a single point. A convex lens can form either a virtual or a real image. The image may be upright or upside-down and either bigger or smaller than the object. The type of image formed depends on how close the

© Pearson Education, Inc., publishing as Pearson Prentice Hall. All rights reserved.

object is to the lens. Convex lenses are used in movie projectors and cameras.

Fiber optics are thin glass or plastic fibers that carry light rays. Light rays traveling through the fibers reflect back into the glass. This lets the fibers carry light long distances without any light escaping. To be reflected back into the fiber, light must strike the boundary between the glass and air at an angle greater than the critical angle. The critical angle is the angle of incidence that causes light to reflect along the boundary between glass and air. When the angle of light is greater than the critical angle, all of the light reflects back into the fiber. This situation is called total internal reflection. Materials with small critical angles are most likely to have total internal reflection.

19.3 Optical Instruments

Optical instruments are instruments that help you see. They include telescopes, cameras, and microscopes.

A telescope collects and focuses light from distant objects. There are two main types of telescopes: reflecting telescopes and refracting telescopes. A reflecting telescope uses mirrors and convex lenses. Light from a distant object strikes a large concave mirror and focuses to form an image. Another mirror reflects the image to the eyepiece. A convex lens in the eyepiece enlarges the image. A refracting telescope uses convex lenses. Light from a distant object passes through a convex lens, called the objective, and forms an image. A convex lens in the eyepiece enlarges the image.

A camera focuses light and records a real image of an object. Light enters a camera through an opening. The light passes through a lens, which focuses the light and forms an image. The image is recorded on film or picked up by a sensor.

A microscope focuses light to make tiny, nearby objects look bigger. A

compound microscope uses two convex lenses. One lens produces an enlarged real image. The other lens further enlarges the real image and creates the virtual image you see. Some microscopes can magnify images more than 1000 times.

19.4 The Eye and Vision

The main parts of the eye are the cornea, pupil, iris, lens, retina, and rods and cones.

- The cornea is the curved, transparent outer coating of the eye. It helps focus light entering the eye.
- The pupil is the opening that allows light to enter the eye. The iris is the colored part of the eye that contracts and expands to control the amount of light entering the eye.
- Behind the pupil is a convex lens that focuses light onto the retina, the inner surface of the back of the eye. The retina receives the image from the lens and contains cells that sense light.
- Rods and cones are the light-sensing cells in the retina. They change light into electrical signals that travel to the brain. Rods sense dim light. Cones sense colored light.

Vision problems include near-sightedness, farsightedness, and astigmatism.

- In nearsightedness, close objects are clear, but distant objects are blurry. Light rays focus in front of the retina instead of on the retina. This can occur because the cornea is too curved or the eyeball is too long.
- In farsightedness, distant objects are clear, but close objects are blurry. Light rays focus behind the retina. This can occur because the cornea is not curved enough or the eyeball is too short.
- In astigmatism, objects at any distance are blurry. Light rays focus in more than one place. This can occur because the cornea or lens is misshapen.

© Pearson Education, Inc., publishing as Pearson Prentice Hall. All rights reserved.

Chapter 19   Optics

Section 19.1 Mirrors
(pages 570–573)

This section describes the law of reflection and explains how images are formed by plane, concave, and convex mirrors. Uses of mirrors are also described.

Reading Strategy (page 570)

Comparing and Contrasting After reading this section, compare mirror types by completing the table. For more information on this Reading Strategy, see the **Reading and Study Skills** in the **Skills and Reference Handbook** at the end of your textbook.

Mirror Types		
Mirror	**Shape of Surface**	**Image (virtual, real, or both)**
Plane	Flat	Virtual
Concave		
Convex		

The Law of Reflection (pages 570–571)

1. A ray diagram shows how rays _____ when they strike mirrors and pass through lenses.

2. Is the following sentence true or false? On a ray diagram, the angle of incidence is the angle that a reflected ray makes with a line drawn perpendicular to the surface of a mirror. _____

3. Circle the letter of the sentence that best answers the following question. What does a ray diagram of the law of reflection show?

   a. The angle of incidence is greater than the angle of reflection.

   b. The angle of reflection is greater than the angle of incidence.

   c. The angle of incidence is equal to the angle of reflection.

   d. The angle of incidence increases as the angle of reflection decreases.

Plane Mirrors (page 571)

4. A mirror with a flat surface is known as a(n) _____.

5. Circle the letter of each sentence that is true about plane mirrors.

   a. Plane mirrors always produce virtual images.

   b. Plane mirrors produce right-left reversed images of objects.

   c. Light rays reflect from a mirror at an angle that is twice as large as the angle of incidence.

   d. Your image appears to be the same distance behind a mirror as you are in front of it.

© Pearson Education, Inc., publishing as Pearson Prentice Hall. All rights reserved.

6. What type of image is a copy of an object formed at the location from which the light rays appear to come?

   a. reversed image   b. virtual image

   c. real image   d. reflected image

Concave and Convex Mirrors (pages 572–573)

7. Circle the letter of the object that is most like the shape of a concave mirror.

   a. the inside of a shallow bowl   b. the bottom of a bucket

   c. the outside surface of a ball   d. a glass window pane

8. What is the focal point? _____

   _____

9. Is the following sentence true or false? A real image is a copy of an object formed at the point where light rays actually meet.

   _____

For questions 10 through 12, refer to the diagrams below.

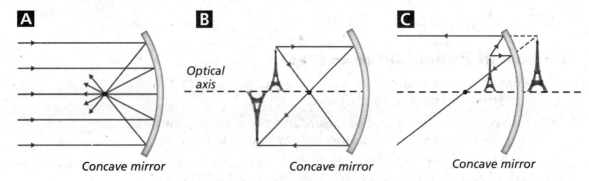

Concave mirror   Concave mirror   Concave mirror

10. Label the focal point on each diagram.

11. In B and C, label the object and image locations and identify the image as real or virtual. (*Hint:* The object is always right-side up and in front of the reflecting surface of the mirror.)

12. What determines whether a concave mirror produces a real image or a virtual image?

    a. the size of the object

    b. the shape of the object

    c. the position of the object relative to the focal point

    d. the location of the optical axis

13. A curved mirror whose outside surface is the reflecting surface is called a(n) _____ mirror.

14. Why do convex mirrors always form virtual images? _____

    _____

15. Is the following sentence true or false? The image formed by a convex lens is always upright and smaller than the object.

    _____

© Pearson Education, Inc., publishing as Pearson Prentice Hall. All rights reserved.

Chapter 19   Optics

Section 19.2 Lenses
(pages 574–578)

This section defines index of refraction and discusses how it is related to the way light behaves upon entering different materials. Image formation in concave and convex lenses are presented.

Reading Strategy (page 574)

Building Vocabulary As you read the section, define in your own words each vocabulary word listed in the table. For more information on this Reading Strategy, see the **Reading and Study Skills** in the **Skills and Reference Handbook** at the end of your textbook.

Refraction and Reflection	
Vocabulary Term	**Definition**
Index of refraction	
Critical angle	
Total internal reflection	

Index of Refraction of Light (pages 574–575)

1. Circle the letter of the sentence about the speed of light through media that is true.

   a. Once light passes from a vacuum into any medium, it speeds up.

   b. Compared to other media, air slows the speed of light only slightly.

   c. The speed of light is greater in water than in air.

   d. The speed of light in a new medium depends on the size of the new medium.

2. What determines how much a light ray bends when it passes from one medium to another? _____

   _____

3. The ratio of the speed of light in a vacuum to the speed of light in a particular material is known as the _____ of that material.

Concave and Convex Lenses (pages 576–577)

4. An object made of transparent material that has one or two curved surfaces that can refract light is called a(n) _____.

5. Two properties of a lens that affect the way it refracts light are _____ and _____.

6. A lens that is curved inward at the center and is thickest at the outside edges is called a(n) _____ lens.

© Pearson Education, Inc., publishing as Pearson Prentice Hall. All rights reserved.

Chapter 19   Optics

7. Concave lenses always cause light rays to _____.

8. Circle the letter of each sentence that is true about convex lenses.

    a. Convex lenses are diverging lenses.

    b. Fly eyes have many facets shaped like the surface of convex lenses.

    c. Convex lenses can form either real or virtual images.

    d. Convex lenses are shaped somewhat like the inside of a bowl.

9. What determines whether a convex lens will form a real image or a virtual image? _____
_____

For questions 10 and 11, refer to the diagrams below.

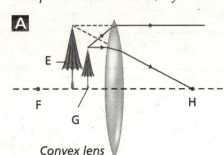
Convex lens

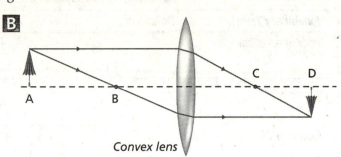
Convex lens

10. In each diagram identify the labeled items as the object, focal point, or image. Also, identify the image as virtual or real.

    A. _____   B. _____

    C. _____   D. _____

    E. _____   F. _____

    G. _____   H. _____

11. Which diagram shows the formation of a virtual image?
    _____

Total Internal Reflection (page 578)

12. Circle each letter of a sentence that is true about the critical angle.

    a. At the critical angle, light refracts along the surface between two media.

    b. All the light is reflected back into the first medium at the critical angle.

    c. Only concave lenses have critical angles.

    d. All the light is reflected back into the second, denser medium when the critical angle is exceeded.

13. Is the following sentence true or false? Materials that have small critical angles, such as the glass used in fiber optics, cause most of the light entering them to be totally internally reflected. _____

© Pearson Education, Inc., publishing as Pearson Prentice Hall. All rights reserved.

Chapter 19   Optics

Section 19.3 Optical Instruments
(pages 580–585)

This section describes optical instruments, including telescopes, cameras, and microscopes. The basic principles of image formation by these instruments are explained.

Reading Strategy (page 580)

Using Prior Knowledge Add the names and descriptions of other optical instruments you know to the diagram. Revise the diagram after you read the section. For more information on this Reading Strategy, see the **Reading and Study Skills** in the **Skills and Reference Handbook** at the end of your textbook.

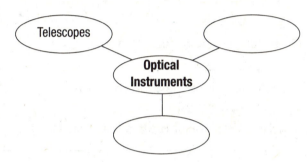

Telescopes (pages 580–581)

1. Circle the letter that best describes the amount of time it takes light from the most distant stars to reach Earth.

   a. seconds   b. hours

   c. millions of years   d. billions of years

2. An instrument that uses lenses or mirrors to collect and focus light from distant objects is called a(n) _____.

3. Complete the table about telescopes.

Telescopes		
Type	**Parts That Collect and Focus Light**	**Description of How Image Is Formed**
Reflecting telescope		
	Convex lenses	

© Pearson Education, Inc., publishing as Pearson Prentice Hall. All rights reserved.

Chapter 19   Optics

Cameras (pages 582–584)

4. Describe what a camera does. _____

_____

5. Circle the letter of each sentence that describes how cameras form or record images.

    a. An image is recorded on film or by a sensor.

    b. Light rays are focused to form virtual images.

    c. Light rays enter through an opening.

    d. Light rays are focused by the opening or lens.

6. Is the following sentence true or false? In a simple pinhole camera made from a box, an upside-down, real image is formed on the back wall of the box. _____

7. What is the purpose of the lens elements in a film camera?

_____

8. The device that controls the amount of light passing through a camera is the _____.

9. Describe what happens when you push the shutter release button on a modern film camera. _____

_____

10. How is the position of the lens of a modern film camera used to bring an object into focus? _____

_____

Microscopes (page 584)

11. An optical instrument that uses two convex lenses to magnify small objects is called a(n) _____.

12. Circle the letter that describes the path light rays follow through a compound microscope.

    a. Light rays from the objective lens pass through the object and then pass through the light source.

    b. Light rays from above pass up through the object and then pass through the objective lens.

    c. Light rays from below pass up through the object, the objective lens, and the eyepiece lens.

    d. Light rays from below pass up through the object, the concave lens, and the objective lens.

13. Is the following sentence true or false? When you look through the eyepiece of a compound microscope you see an enlarged, virtual image of the object. _____

© Pearson Education, Inc., publishing as Pearson Prentice Hall. All rights reserved.

Chapter 19   Optics

Section 19.4 The Eye and Vision
(pages 588–592)

This section describes the eye as an optical instrument. Parts of the eye and their functions are defined. Vision problems and how they can be corrected are also described.

Reading Strategy (page 588)

Outlining As you read, make an outline of the important ideas in this section. Use the green headings as the main topics and the blue headings as subtopics. For more information on this Reading Strategy, see the **Reading and Study Skills** in the **Skills and Reference Handbook** at the end of your textbook.

Section 19.4 Outline

I. The Eye and Vision

  A. Structure of the Eye

    1. _____

    2. _____

    3. _____

    4. _____

    5. _____

  B. _____

    1. _____

    2. _____

    3. _____

Structure of the Eye (pages 588–590)

Write the letter of the part of the eye that best matches each description.

Description	Part of Eye
_____ 1. Its curved surface helps to focus light entering the eye.	a. pupil
_____ 2. It focuses light onto sensor cells at the back of the eye.	b. retina
_____ 3. This opening allows light to pass through the eye.	c. cornea
_____ 4. This expands and contracts to control the amount of light entering the eye.	d. iris
_____ 5. This is the transparent outer coating of the eye.	e. lens
_____ 6. Its surface has rods and cones.	

© Pearson Education, Inc., publishing as Pearson Prentice Hall. All rights reserved.

Chapter 19   Optics

7. Is the following sentence true or false? Nerve endings called rods and cones convert light into electrical signals that are sent to the brain through the optic nerve. _____

8. Where on the retina does a blind spot occur? _____

_____

Correcting Vision Problems (pages 590–592)

For questions 9 and 10, refer to the figures below.

Problem: Nearsightedness (Eyeball is too long.)

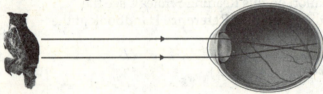

Correction:

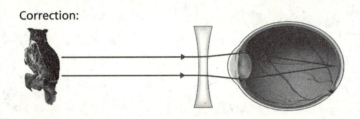

9. Circle the letter of the location where the image forms when nearsightedness occurs.

   a. on the retina   b. behind the retina

   c. before it reaches the retina   d. on the lens

10. Nearsightedness can be corrected by placing a(n) _____ lens in front of the eye.

Match each type of vision problem to its definition.

Vision Problem	Definition
_____ **11.** astigmatism	a. A condition that causes distant objects to appear blurry because the cornea is too curved or the eyeball is too long
_____ **12.** farsightedness	b. A condition that causes objects at any distance to appear blurry because the cornea or lens is misshapen
_____ **13.** nearsightedness	c. A condition that causes nearby objects to appear blurry because the cornea is not curved enough or the eyeball is too short

© Pearson Education, Inc., publishing as Pearson Prentice Hall. All rights reserved.

Chapter 19   Optics

WordWise

Use the clues below to identify vocabulary terms from Chapter 19. Write the terms below, putting one letter in each blank. When you finish, the term enclosed in the diagonal will reveal a term that is important in the study of optics.

Clues

1. Shows how the paths of light rays change when they strike mirrors or pass through lenses

2. Transparent material with one or two curved surfaces that can refract light

3. A mirror with a flat surface

4. An instrument that uses lenses or mirrors to collect and focus light from distant objects

5. Expands and contracts to control the amount of light entering the eye

6. An optical instrument that records an image of an object

7. Transparent outer layer of the eye

8. When the cornea is misshapen, this vision problem can result.

9. Type of lens that causes light rays to diverge

1. _ _ _ _ _ _ _ _ _ _

2. _ _ _ _

3. _ _ _ _ _ _ _ _ _ _ _

4. _ _ _ _ _ _ _

5. _ _ _ _

6. _ _ _ _ _ _

7. _ _ _ _ _

8. _ _ _ _ _ _ _ _ _

9. _ _ _ _ _ _ _ _ _

Hidden Word: _ _ _ _ _ _ _ _ _

Definition: _____

_____

© Pearson Education, Inc., publishing as Pearson Prentice Hall. All rights reserved.

Chapter 19   Optics

Calculating Index of Refraction

The speed of light in the mineral halite, NaCl, is approximately 1.95×10^8 m/s. Calculate the index of refraction for halite. (Recall that the speed of light in a vacuum is 3.00×10^8 m/s.)

**Math Skill:
Ratios and
Proportions**

You may want to read more about this **Math Skill** in the **Skills and Reference Handbook** at the end of your textbook.

1. Read and Understand

What information are you given?

Speed of light in halite = 1.95×10^8 m/s

Speed of light in vacuum = 3.00×10^8 m/s

2. Plan and Solve

What variable are you trying to determine?

Index of refraction = ?

What formulas contain the given variables?

$$\text{Index of refraction} = \frac{\text{Speed of light}_{vacuum}}{\text{Speed of light}_{material}} = \frac{(3.00 \times 10^8 \text{ m/s})}{(1.95 \times 10^8 \text{ m/s})} = 1.54$$

3. Look Back and Check

Is your answer reasonable?

Speed of light in vacuum = $(1.95 \times 10^8 \text{ m/s})(1.54) = 3.00 \times 10^8$ m/s

Yes, the answer is reasonable. Substituting the calculated index of refraction for halite back into the equation yields the value of the speed of light in a vacuum.

Math Practice

On a separate sheet of paper, solve the following problems.

1. The mineral uvarovite has an index of refraction of 1.86. Calculate the speed of light in this sample of uvarovite.

2. What is the index of refraction of a sample of opal, if the speed of light passing through it is 2.05×10^8 m/s?

3. Because its atomic structure varies with direction, a sample of the mineral calcite has an index of refraction of 1.486 along one direction in the crystal, while another direction has an index of refraction of 1.658. Which index represents the faster speed of light through the calcite? Explain your answer.

© Pearson Education, Inc., publishing as Pearson Prentice Hall. All rights reserved.

Chapter 20   Electricity

Summary

20.1 Electric Charge and Static Electricity

Electric charge is a trait of protons and electrons. Protons have a positive electric charge. Electrons have a negative electric charge. An atom has a net, or overall, electric charge of zero. This is because an atom has equal numbers of protons and electrons. An atom can gain or lose electrons. If an atom gains electrons, it has a net negative charge. If an atom loses electrons, it has a net positive charge. The unit of electric charge is the coulomb (C).

Like charges repel, or push, each other. Unlike charges attract, or pull, each other. Electric force is the pushing and pulling between charged objects. The electric force between two objects depends on the net charge of each object and the distance between the objects.

An electric charge has an effect on other charges in the space around it. This effect is called an electric field. An electric field exerts forces on any charged object in the field. The strength of the electric field depends on the amount of charge that produces the field and the distance from the charge.

Static electricity is the study of the behavior of electric charges, including the transfer of charges. Charges can be transferred from one object to another. This can happen in three ways: friction, induction, and contact. When you walk across a carpet, electrons are transferred from the carpet to you. You become negatively charged. This happens because of friction. As you reach for a doorknob, your negatively charged hand repels electrons in the doorknob. The end of the doorknob near your hand becomes positively charged even before you touch it. This happens because of induction. When you actually touch the doorknob, electrons rush from your hand to the doorknob. This happens because of contact. The rush of electrons

from your hand to the doorknob is called static discharge. Static discharge occurs when charges suddenly find a new pathway to follow. A lightning bolt is a huge static discharge between two clouds or between a cloud and the ground.

Although charges can be transferred, there is never any overall change in charge. This is the law of conservation of charge.

20.2 Electric Current and Ohm's Law

Electric current is a flow of electric charges. The unit of electric current is the ampere (A), which equals 1 coulomb per second. There are two types of electric current: direct current (DC) and alternating current (AC).

- Direct current always flows in the same direction. Direct current is used in flashlights and other devices that use batteries.
- Alternating current keeps changing direction. Alternating current is used in homes and schools.

An electrical conductor is a material through which charges can flow easily. Copper and silver are good electrical conductors because they have free electrons that can conduct charge. An electrical insulator is a material through which charges cannot flow easily. Wood and plastic are good electrical insulators.

As electrons flow through a wire, they collide with other electrons and with ions. This reduces the current. This opposition to the flow of charges is called resistance. The amount of resistance in a wire depends on how thick, long, and warm the wire is. A thicker wire has less resistance, because more charges can flow through it. A

© Pearson Education, Inc., publishing as Pearson Prentice Hall. All rights reserved.

longer wire has more resistance, because charges must travel farther. A warmer wire also has more resistance. This is because the wire's electrons collide more often. A material that has almost no resistance at very low temperatures is called a superconductor.

For charges to flow in a wire, the wire must be part of a closed loop. The loop also must include a source of voltage, such as a battery. Voltage is a difference in electrical potential energy. A difference in electrical potential energy causes charges to flow spontaneously, or on their own. The charges flow from a negatively charged area to a positively charged area. In a battery, one terminal is positive and the other terminal is negative. Therefore, there is a difference in electrical potential between the terminals. In a circuit, charges flow from the negative terminal through the wire to the positive terminal.

Voltage, current, and resistance are related. Georg Ohm discovered this relationship. It is called Ohm's law. According to the law, voltage (V) equals current (I) times resistance (R):

$$V = I \times R$$

This equation can also be written as

$$I = \frac{V}{R}$$

This form of the equation shows that increasing voltage increases current. It also shows that increasing resistance decreases current.

20.3 Electric Circuits

An electric circuit is a complete path through which charges can flow. Wires in a house are joined in many connected circuits. An electrician uses circuit diagrams to keep track of all the circuits in a house. Circuit diagrams use symbols to represent the different parts of a circuit. There are symbols for the source of electrical energy and for the devices

that use the energy. Circuit diagrams also show the paths through which charges can flow. In addition, switches show places where the circuit can be opened. If a switch is open, the circuit is not a complete loop, and current cannot flow. When the switch is closed, the circuit is complete, and current can flow.

There are two types of electric circuits: series circuits and parallel circuits.

- A series circuit has only one path through which current can flow. If a light bulb burns out in a series circuit, current stops flowing throughout the entire circuit.
- A parallel circuit has more than one path through which current can flow. If a light bulb burns out in a parallel circuit, current can flow through another path in the circuit.

Appliances change electrical energy to other forms of energy. For example, a toaster changes electrical energy to heat energy. Electric power is the speed at which an appliance changes electrical energy to another form of energy. Units of electric power are the watt (W) and kilowatt (kW). One kilowatt equals 1000 watts. You can calculate electric power (P) of an appliance by multiplying current (I) by voltage (V):

$$P = I \times V$$

You can also calculate the electrical energy used by an appliance. Electrical energy (E) equals power (P) multiplied by time (t):

$$E = P \times t$$

A common unit of electrical energy is the kilowatt-hour. For example, if a 6-kilowatt oven operates for 2 hours, it uses 12 kilowatt-hours of energy.

Electricity can be dangerous. It can kill people and start fires. Several things help make electrical energy safer to use. These include correct wiring, fuses, circuit breakers, insulation, and grounded plugs.

© Pearson Education, Inc., publishing as Pearson Prentice Hall. All rights reserved.

Chapter 20   Electricity

- Correct wiring can handle all the current a household needs without becoming overheated.
- Fuses and circuit breakers stop the current in a circuit if it becomes too high.
- Insulation around wires keeps the current safely inside the wires.
- Grounded plugs transfer excess current to the ground where it cannot do damage.

20.4 Electronic Devices

Electronics is the science of using electric currents to carry information. A current is encoded with a signal. It may be an analog signal or a digital signal. In an analog signal, the voltage changes continuously to code the information. In a digital signal, the current repeatedly goes on and off to code the information.

One way to control current in an electronic device is with a vacuum tube. One type of vacuum tube can increase or decrease voltage. It can also turn current on and off. Another type of vacuum tube is a cathode-ray tube. It turns electronic signals into images. Many computer monitors and televisions contain this type of vacuum tube. Vacuum tubes are too large to be used in small electronic devices.

Small electronic devices use semiconductors to control current. A semiconductor is a small piece of a solid that conducts current under certain conditions. There are two types of semiconductors: n-type and p-type. An n-type semiconductor contains weakly bound electrons that can flow. A p-type semiconductor contains positively charged holes that attract electrons. When n-type and p-type semiconductors are joined together, electrons in the n-type semiconductor are attracted to the positive holes in the p-type semiconductor. As electrons jump from hole to hole, it looks like a flow of positive charge because the locations of the holes change.

A semiconductor is an example of a solid-state component. Solid-state components are devices that use solids to control current. Most modern electronic devices have solid-state components. Three types of solid-state components are diodes, transistors, and integrated circuits.

- A diode is a solid-state component containing an n-type and a p-type semiconductor. A diode can change alternating current to direct current.
- A transistor is a solid-state component with three layers of semiconductors. A transistor can increase voltage.
- An integrated circuit consists of a thin slice of silicon. The silicon contains many solid-state components. Integrated circuits are sometimes called microchips. They are used in computers, cell phones, and pagers. Integrated circuits are tiny. They are very fast, because the current does not have far to travel.

© Pearson Education, Inc., publishing as Pearson Prentice Hall. All rights reserved.

Chapter 20   Electricity

Section 20.1 Electric Charge and Static Electricity
(pages 600–603)

This section explains how electric charge is created and how positive and negative charges affect each other. It also discusses the different ways that electric charge can be transferred.

Reading Strategy (page 600)

Identifying Main Ideas Copy the table on a separate sheet of paper. As you read, write the main ideas. For more information on this Reading Strategy, see the **Reading and Study Skills** in the **Skills and Reference Handbook** at the end of your textbook.

Characteristics of Electric Charge	
Topic	**Main Idea**
Electric Charge	An excess or shortage of electrons produces a net electric charge.
Electric Forces	
Electric Fields	
Static Electricity	

Electric Charge (pages 600–601)

1. What are the two types of electric charge?

   a. _____   b. _____

2. Is the following sentence true or false? In an atom, negatively charged electrons surround a positively charged nucleus.

   _____

3. Is the following sentence true or false? If a neutral atom gains one or more electrons, it becomes a positively charged ion.

   _____

4. What is the SI unit of electric charge? _____

Electric Forces (page 601)

5. Circle the letter of each sentence that is true about electric force.

   a. Like charges attract and opposite charges repel.

   b. Electric force is the attraction or repulsion between electrically charged objects.

   c. Electric force is inversely proportional to the amount of charge.

   d. Electric force is inversely proportional to the square of the distance between two charges.

© Pearson Education, Inc., publishing as Pearson Prentice Hall. All rights reserved.

6. Which are stronger inside an atom, electric forces or gravitational forces? _____

7. Is the following sentence true or false? Electric forces cause friction and other contact forces. _____

Electric Fields (page 602)

8. A charge's electric field is the effect the charge has on _____ in the space around it.

9. Circle the letters of the factors that the strength of an electric field depends on.

    a. the direction of the field

    b. whether the charge is positive or negative

    c. the amount of charge that produces the field

    d. the distance from the charge

10. Is the following sentence true or false? The field of a negative charge points away from the charge. _____

Static Electricity and Charging (pages 602–603)

11. Static electricity is the study of the _____.

12. Is the following sentence true or false? Charge can be transferred by friction, by contact, and by induction. _____

13. What is the law of conservation of charge? _____

_____

14. Rubbing a balloon on your hair is an example of charging by _____.

15. A charge transfer between objects that touch each other is called _____.

16. Circle the letter of each sentence that is true about charging.

    a. When you rub a balloon on your hair, your hair loses electrons and becomes positively charged.

    b. The sphere of a Van de Graaff generator transfers all of its charge to you when you touch it.

    c. Induction occurs when charge is transferred without contact between materials.

    d. Static charges cannot move.

Static Discharge (page 603)

17. Is the following sentence true or false? Static discharge occurs when a pathway through which charges can move forms suddenly. _____

18. How does lightning occur? _____

_____

_____

© Pearson Education, Inc., publishing as Pearson Prentice Hall. All rights reserved.

Chapter 20   Electricity

Section 20.2 Electric Current and Ohm's Law
(pages 604–607)

This section discusses electric current, resistance, and voltage. It also uses Ohm's Law to explain how voltage, current, and resistance are related.

Reading Strategy (page 604)

Predicting Before you read, write a prediction of what electric current is in the table below. After you read, if your prediction was incorrect or incomplete, write what electric current actually is. For more information on this Reading Strategy, see the **Reading and Study Skills** in the **Skills and Reference Handbook** at the end of your textbook.

Electric Current	
Electric Current Probably Means	**Electric Current Actually Means**

Electric Current (page 604)

1. What is electric current? _____
_____

2. Complete the following table about electric current.

Electric Current		
Type of Current	**How Charge Flows**	**Examples**
Direct		
Alternating	Two directions	

3. Electrons flow in the wire from a(n) _____ terminal to a(n) _____ terminal.

Conductors and Insulators (page 605)

4. What is an electrical conductor? _____
_____

5. What is an electrical insulator? _____
_____

6. Is the following sentence true or false? Metals are good conductors because they do not have freely moving electrons.
_____

© Pearson Education, Inc., publishing as Pearson Prentice Hall. All rights reserved.

Chapter 20   Electricity

Match each material to the category of a conductor or insulator.

Material	Category
_____ 7. Copper	a. conductor
_____ 8. Plastic	b. insulator
_____ 9. Rubber	
_____ 10. Silver	
_____ 11. Wood	

Resistance (page 605)

12. Explain why the current is reduced as electrons move through a conductor. _____

_____

_____

13. Circle the letter of each factor that affects a material's resistance.

    a. its length   b. its temperature

    c. its velocity   d. its thickness

14. What is a superconductor? _____

_____

Voltage (page 606)

Match each term to its definition.

Definition	Term
_____ 15. A device that converts chemical energy to electrical energy	a. flow of charge
	b. voltage
_____ 16. Requires a complete loop	c. battery
_____ 17. The difference in electrical potential energy between two places in an electric field	

18. Is the following sentence true or false? Three common voltage sources are batteries, solar cells, and generators. _____

Ohm's Law (page 607)

19. Is the following sentence true or false? According to Ohm's law, the voltage in a circuit equals the product of the energy and the resistance. _____

20. Doubling the voltage in a circuit doubles the current if _____ is held constant.

21. Is the following sentence true or false? Doubling the resistance in a circuit will halve the current if voltage is held constant.

_____

© Pearson Education, Inc., publishing as Pearson Prentice Hall. All rights reserved.

Chapter 20   Electricity

Section 20.3 Electric Circuits
(pages 609–613)

This section describes circuit diagrams and types of circuits. It also explains calculation of electric power and electric energy and discusses electrical safety.

Reading Strategy (page 609)

Relating Text and Visuals As you read about household circuits, complete the table by listing three things the diagram in Figure 13 helps you understand about circuits. For more information on this Reading Strategy, see the **Reading and Study Skills** in the **Skills and Reference Handbook** at the end of your textbook.

Understanding a Circuit Diagram
What Can Be Seen in the Circuit Diagram?
Wire bringing current from outside

Circuit Diagrams (pages 609–610)

1. Circuit diagrams use _____ to represent parts of a circuit, including a source of electrical energy and devices that are run by the electrical energy.

Match each symbol to what it indicates on a circuit diagram.

Symbol	What Symbol Indicates
_____ 2. +	a. The direction of current
_____ 3. −	b. A negative terminal
_____ 4. ⟶	c. A positive terminal

Series Circuits (page 610)

5. Is the following sentence true or false? In a series circuit, if one element stops functioning, then none of the elements can operate.

    _____

6. Explain why the bulbs shine less brightly when more bulbs are added to a series circuit. _____

    _____

Parallel Circuits (page 610)

7. Is the following sentence true or false? Circuits in a home are rarely wired in parallel. _____

8. If one element stops functioning in a parallel circuit, the rest of the elements _____.

© Pearson Education, Inc., publishing as Pearson Prentice Hall. All rights reserved.

Chapter 20   Electricity

Power and Energy Calculations (pages 611–612)

9. The rate at which electrical energy is converted to another form of energy is called _____.

10. The SI unit of electric power is the joule per second, or _____, which is abbreviated _____.

11. Is the following sentence true or false? Electric power is calculated by multiplying current times voltage. _____

12. Write the formula for calculating electrical energy.

_____

13. The unit of energy usually used by electric power companies is the

_____.

Electrical Safety (pages 612–613)

14. Circle the letters of what could happen if the current in a wire exceeds the circuit's safety limit.

   a. The wire could overheat.   b. The wire could get cooler.

   c. A fire could start.   d. A fuse could blow.

15. Explain how a fuse prevents current overload in a circuit. _____

_____

16. A switch that opens to prevent overloads when current in a circuit is too high is called a(n) _____.

17. Explain why touching an electrical device with wet hands is dangerous. _____

_____

18. Is the following sentence true or false? A ground-fault circuit interrupter shuts down the circuit if the current flowing through the circuit and current returning to ground are equal.

_____

19. The transfer of excess charge through a conductor to Earth is called

_____.

20. Complete the following table about equipment used to prevent electrical accidents.

Equipment to Prevent Current Overload	Equipment to Protect People from Shock	Equipment to Prevent Short Circuits
a. Circuit breaker	b. c. Grounding wire d.	e.

© Pearson Education, Inc., publishing as Pearson Prentice Hall. All rights reserved.

Chapter 20   Electricity

Section 20.4 Electronic Devices
(pages 618–622)

This section discusses how various electronic devices operate and what they are used for.

Reading Strategy (page 618)

Summarizing Copy the table on a separate sheet of paper. As you read, complete the table to summarize what you learned about solid-state components. For more information on this Reading Strategy, see the **Reading and Study Skills** in the **Skills and Reference Handbook** at the end of your textbook.

Solid–State Components		
Solid-State Component	**Description**	**Uses**
Diode		
Transistor		
Integrated Circuit		

Electronic Signals (pages 618–619)

Match each term to its definition.

Definition

_____ 1. Information sent as patterns in the controlled flow of electrons through a circuit

_____ 2. The science of using electric current to process or transmit information

_____ 3. A smoothly varying signal produced by continuously changing the voltage or current in a circuit

_____ 4. A signal that encodes information as a string of 1's and 0's

Term

a. electronics

b. analog signal

c. electronic signal

d. digital signal

5. Which type of signal is usually used by an AM radio station?

_____

6. Is the following sentence true or false? Analog signals are more reliable than digital signals. _____

© Pearson Education, Inc., publishing as Pearson Prentice Hall. All rights reserved.

Vacuum Tubes (page 619)

7. Circle the letter of each item that is true about vacuum tubes.

   a. can change alternating current to direct current

   b. never burn out

   c. can increase the strength of a signal

   d. can turn a current on or off

8. Is the following sentence true or false? An image is produced in a CRT when phosphors glow red, green, and blue in response to electron beams. _____

Semiconductors (page 621)

9. What is a semiconductor? _____

_____

10. Name the two types of semiconductors.

   a. _____   b. _____

11. Circle the letter of each sentence that is true about a p-type semiconductor.

   a. It can be made by adding a trace amount of boron to a silicon.

   b. Electrons are attracted to positively charged holes at each boron atom.

   c. As the electrons jump from hole to hole, it looks like a flow of positive charge.

   d. Boron atoms provide weakly bound electrons that can flow.

12. Is the following sentence true or false? In an n-type semiconductor, weakly bound electrons can conduct a current. _____

Solid-State Components (pages 621–622)

Match each term to its definition.

Term	Definition
_____ 13. diode	a. A solid-state component with three layers of semiconductors
_____ 14. transistor	b. A thin slice of silicon that contains many solid-state components
_____ 15. integrated circuit	c. A solid-state component that combines an n-type and p-type semiconductor

16. A chip or microchip is another name for a(n) _____.

Communications Technology (page 622)

17. Why is it useful for communication devices to use microchips? _____

_____

18. A mobile phone can store data such as phone numbers because

_____

© Pearson Education, Inc., publishing as Pearson Prentice Hall. All rights reserved.

Name _____ Class _____ Date _____

Chapter 20 Electricity

WordWise

Match each definition with the correct term in the grid and then write its number under the appropriate term. When you have filled in all the boxes, add up the numbers in each column, row, and the two diagonals.
What is surprising about the sums? _____

Definitions

1. A property that causes subatomic particles such as protons and electrons to attract or repel other matter

2. The attraction or repulsion between electrically charged objects

3. Charge transfer without contact between materials

4. Law that total charge in an isolated system is constant

5. A continuous flow of electric charge

6. Material through which charge can easily flow

7. Material through which a charge cannot easily flow

8. The opposition to the flow of charges in a material

9. A circuit in which the charge has only one path through which it can flow

10. An electric circuit with two or more paths through which charge can flow

11. A switch that opens when current in a circuit is too high

12. Information sent as patterns in the controlled flow of electrons through a circuit

13. A smoothly varying signal produced by continuously changing the voltage or current in a circuit

14. A complete path through which a charge can flow

15. A solid-state component with three layers of semiconductors

16. A thin slice of silicon that contains many solid-state components

				Diagonal = _____
integrated circuit _____	induction _____	electric force _____	analog signal _____	= _____
electric current _____	parallel circuit _____	circuit breaker _____	resistance _____	= _____
series circuit _____	electrical conductor _____	electrical insulator _____	electronic signal _____	= _____
law of conservation of charge _____	transistor _____	electric circuit _____	electric charge _____	= _____
= _____	= _____	= _____	= _____	Diagonal = _____

© Pearson Education, Inc., publishing as Pearson Prentice Hall. All rights reserved.

Chapter 20   Electricity

Power, Voltage, and Current

The power rating on an electric soldering iron is 40.0 watts. If the soldering iron is connected to a 120-volt line, how much current does it use?

Math Skill:
Formulas and
Equations

You may want to read more about this **Math Skill** in the **Skills and Reference Handbook** at the end of your textbook.

1. Read and Understand

What information are you given in the problem?
   Power = P = 40.0 watts

   Voltage = V = 120 volts

2. Plan and Solve

What unknown are you trying to calculate?
   Current = I =?

What formula contains the given quantities and the unknown?

$$P = I \times V; I = \frac{P}{V}$$

Replace each variable with its known value.

$$I = \frac{40.0 \text{ watts}}{120 \text{ volts}} = 0.33 \text{ amps}$$

3. Look Back and Check

Is your answer reasonable?

   The answer is reasonable because a soldering iron needs a relatively low current to generate heat.

Math Practice

On a separate sheet of paper, solve the following problems.

1. A steam cleaner has a power rating of 1100 watts. If the cleaner is connected to a 120-volt line, what current does it use?

2. A coffee maker uses 10.0 amps of current from a 120-volt line. How much power does it use?

3. A power mixer uses 3.0 amps of current and has a power rating of 360 watts. What voltage does this appliance require?

© Pearson Education, Inc., publishing as Pearson Prentice Hall. All rights reserved.

Chapter 21   Magnetism

Summary

21.1 Magnets and Magnetic Fields

A magnet is the source of a magnetic force. This force is exerted on other magnets, on iron or a similar metal, or on moving charges. Magnetic force acts over a distance but weakens as you move farther away from the magnet. Poles are regions of a magnet where the force is strongest. All magnets have two poles. One end of a magnet is its north pole. The other end is its south pole. If you cut a magnet in half, each half will have a north pole and a south pole. No matter how many times you cut a magnet, each piece will still have both poles. Like magnetic poles repel one another. Opposite magnetic poles attract one another.

A magnetic field surrounds a magnet. The field can exert magnetic force. A magnetic field is strongest near a magnet's poles. The field will attract or repel other magnets that enter the field. Earth is like a giant magnet. Earth's magnetic poles are close to its geographic poles. Since Earth is like a magnet, a magnetic field surrounds the planet. Earth's magnetic field is called the magnetosphere.

Electrons in atoms have tiny magnetic fields. Sometimes the magnetic fields of many electrons in a material all line up the same way. An area where this occurs is called a magnetic domain. Materials with magnetic domains can be magnetized. This means they can be turned into magnets. A material that can be magnetized is called a ferromagnetic material. Iron is an example of a ferromagnetic material. A ferromagnetic material may remain magnetized briefly or for a long time, depending on the material.

21.2 Electromagnetism

Electricity and magnetism are two parts of electromagnetic force. Both forces are due to charged particles. Recall that pushing and pulling between charged particles produces electric force. Moving charged particles produce magnetic force. This is why electrons in atoms have magnetic fields. Electrons are constantly moving around the nucleus. In the 1820s, scientist Hans Oersted discovered that moving charges create a magnetic field. You can demonstrate this by passing a current through a straight wire. The current creates a magnetic field that circles around the wire.

A coil of wire carrying current also produces a magnetic field. A coil of wire acts like a bar magnet. Each end of the coil is a pole. A coil of wire that produces a magnetic field is called a solenoid. An electromagnet is a solenoid with a rod of ferromagnetic material inside the coil. Current flowing through the coil magnetizes the rod. The rod and coil together produce a stronger magnet than the solenoid alone. In a solenoid or electromagnet, you can easily control the magnetic field by controlling the current. You can turn the magnet on and off by turning the current on and off. You can increase or decrease the current to make the magnetic field stronger or weaker. The strength of an electromagnet also depends on the number of loops of wire in the coil and the type of rod inside the coil.

Electromagnetic devices change electrical energy into mechanical energy. Such devices include galvanometers, electric motors, and loudspeakers.

- A galvanometer measures small amounts of current. Galvanometers are used in car fuel gauges.

© Pearson Education, Inc., publishing as Pearson Prentice Hall. All rights reserved.

Chapter 21   Magnetism

- An electric motor turns an axle. Electric motors are used in washing machines.
- A loudspeaker reproduces sounds. Loudspeakers are used in stereo systems.

21.3 Electrical Energy Generation and Transmission

You can produce an electric current by moving an electrical conductor relative to a magnetic field. Recall that an electrical conductor is a material, such as a metal wire, through which charge can easily flow. You can move a conductor back and forth over a magnet, or you can move a magnet back and forth over a conductor. Current will flow in the conductor whenever it moves relative to the magnet. This process is called electromagnetic induction. Scientist Michael Faraday discovered the process in the 1830s.

Power plants use generators to produce electric current. A generator produces current by turning a coil of wire in a magnetic field. There are two types of generators: AC generators and DC generators. AC generators produce alternating current. DC generators produce direct current. Most power plants today use AC generators. People can also buy small AC generators to provide electricity for their homes during power failures.

Power lines carry power from power plants to homes. The voltage is very high in the lines. The voltage must be lowered before it enters homes. A device called a transformer can decrease voltage. A transformer has two coils of wire, each with a different number of coils. Alternating current produces a changing magnetic field in one coil, called the primary coil. This changing field produces an alternating current in the other coil, called the secondary coil. There are two types of transformers: step-down and step-up.

- In a step-down transformer, the secondary coil has fewer loops than the primary coil. As a result, voltage decreases and current increases.
- In a step-up transformer, the secondary coil has more loops than the primary coil. As a result, voltage increases and current decreases.

There are six major sources of electrical energy used in the United States: coal, water, nuclear energy, wind, natural gas, and petroleum. A turbine uses the energy from one of these six sources to produce electricity. A turbine has blades like a fan. The blades turn when they are pushed by water, wind, or steam. Turning the blades of the turbine causes the coils of a generator to turn. This produces electricity. Water collected behind a dam, or blowing wind, can force the blades of a turbine to turn. Steam from water heated by burning coal or another fuel can also force the blades to turn.

© Pearson Education, Inc., publishing as Pearson Prentice Hall. All rights reserved.

Chapter 21   Magnetism

Section 21.1 Magnets and Magnetic Fields
(pages 630–633)

This section describes magnetic forces and magnetic fields. Characteristics of magnetic materials also are discussed.

Reading Strategy (page 630)

Using Prior Knowledge Before you read, copy the diagram below and add what you already know about magnets to the diagram. After you read, revise the diagram based on what you learned. For more information on this Reading Strategy, see the **Reading and Study Skills** in the **Skills and Reference Handbook** at the end of your textbook.

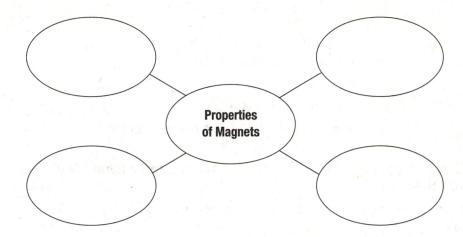

1. In the year 1600, William Gilbert published a book explaining the properties of _____.

Magnetic Forces (page 630)

2. Is the following sentence true or false? Magnetic force can be exerted on moving charges, as well as on iron or on another magnet. _____

3. What did William Gilbert discover when he used a compass to map forces around a magnetic sphere? _____

_____

4. Circle the letter of each sentence that is true about magnetic force.

   a. Two magnets that approach each other may attract or repel.

   b. Magnetic forces do not vary with distance.

   c. Opposite magnetic poles repel one another.

   d. Magnetic forces act over a distance.

© Pearson Education, Inc., publishing as Pearson Prentice Hall. All rights reserved.

Chapter 21   Magnetism

Magnetic Fields (pages 631–632)

For questions 5 and 6, refer to the figure below.

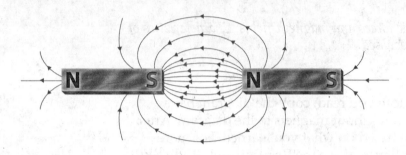

5. Where is the magnetic field the strongest? _____
_____

6. Based on this figure, what would you expect to happen when the north pole of one magnet faces the south pole of another magnet?
_____

7. Circle the letter of each sentence that is true about magnetic fields.

   a. Magnetic fields surround a magnet and can exert a magnetic force.

   b. Field lines begin near the south pole of a magnet and extend toward the north pole.

   c. Iron filings are most attracted to areas where the field is strongest.

   d. A magnetic field is strongest near the north and south poles of a magnet.

8. The area that is influenced by the magnetic field surrounding Earth is called the _____.

Magnetic Materials (pages 632–633)

Match each term with its description.

Description	Term
_____ 9. Can be magnetized because it has many domains	a. ferromagnetic material
_____ 10. Has randomly oriented domains	b. magnetic domain
_____ 11. Region that has many atoms with aligned magnetic fields	c. nonmagnetized material

12. What can cause the realignment of magnetic domains in a material?
_____
_____

© Pearson Education, Inc., publishing as Pearson Prentice Hall. All rights reserved.

Chapter 21   Magnetism

Section 21.2 Electromagnetism
(pages 635–639)

This section describes how electricity and magnetism are related. Uses of solenoids and electromagnetic devices are discussed, and a description of how these devices work is presented.

Reading Strategy (page 635)
Identifying Main Ideas Copy the table on a separate sheet of paper. As you read, write the main idea of the text that follows each topic in the table. For more information on this Reading Strategy, see the **Reading and Study Skills** in the **Skills and Reference Handbook** at the end of your textbook.

Electromagnetism	
Topic	**Main Idea**
Electricity and magnetism	
Direction of magnetic fields	
Direction of electric currents	
Solenoids and electromagnets	
Electromagnetic devices	

1. In 1820 Hans Oersted discovered a connection between electricity and _____.

Electricity and Magnetism (pages 635–636)

2. Electricity and magnetism are different aspects of a single force known as the _____ force.

3. Both aspects of the electromagnetic force are caused by

    _____.

4. Is the following sentence true or false? Moving electric charges create a magnetic field. _____

5. Is the following sentence true or false? The vibrating charges that produce an electromagnetic wave also create a magnetic field.

    _____

6. A charge moving in a magnetic field will be deflected in a direction that is _____ to both the magnetic field and to the velocity of the charge.

© Pearson Education, Inc., publishing as Pearson Prentice Hall. All rights reserved.

Solenoids and Electromagnets (pages 637–638)

7. Is the following sentence true or false? The strength of the magnetic field through the center of a coil of current-carrying wire is calculated by adding together the fields from each turn of the coil. _____

8. A coil of current-carrying wire that produces a magnetic field is called a(n) _____.

9. What is an electromagnet? _____

_____

10. Circle the letter of each sentence that is true about electromagnets.

   a. Placing an iron rod in a solenoid reduces the strength of its magnetic field.

   b. Devices that utilize electromagnets include doorbells and telephones.

   c. A magnetic field can be turned on and off with an electromagnet.

   d. An electromagnet can control the direction of a magnetic field.

11. List three factors that determine the strength of an electromagnet.

   a. _____

   b. _____

   c. _____

12. Is the following sentence true or false? Decreasing the current in the solenoid decreases the strength of an electromagnet.

_____

13. What types of solenoid cores make stronger electromagnets? _____

_____

Electromagnetic Devices (pages 638–639)

14. Electromagnetic devices change _____ energy into _____ energy.

15. Complete the following table about electromagnetic devices.

Description	Device
Uses electromagnets to convert electrical signals into sound waves	
	Electric motor
Uses an electromagnet to measure small amounts of current	

© Pearson Education, Inc., publishing as Pearson Prentice Hall. All rights reserved.

Chapter 21   Magnetism

Section 21.3 Electrical Energy Generation and Transmission
(pages 642–647)

This section describes how electricity is generated and transmitted for human use. A description of how generators and transformers function is given.

Reading Strategy (page 642)

Sequencing As you read the section, complete the flowchart to show how a step-up transformer works. Then make a similar flowchart for a step-down transformer. For more information on this Reading Strategy, see the **Reading and Study Skills** in the **Skills and Reference Handbook** at the end of your textbook.

Step-up Transformers

Current flows through smaller coil.   →   ☐   →   ☐

Generating Electric Current (pages 642–643)

1. Is the following sentence true or false? A magnetic field can be used to produce an electric current. _____

2. Circle the letter for the name of the process of generating a current by moving an electrical conductor relative to a magnetic field.

   a. electromagnetic force

   b. electromagnetic field

   c. electromagnetic induction

   d. electromagnetic conduction

3. Electrical charges can easily flow through materials known as

   _____.

4. Why is the discovery of electromagnetic induction significant? _____

   _____

5. According to Faraday's law, electric current can be induced in a conductor by _____.

6. Is the following sentence true or false? Moving a magnet relative to a coil of wire induces a current in the wire if the coil is part of a complete circuit. _____

© Pearson Education, Inc., publishing as Pearson Prentice Hall. All rights reserved.

Chapter 21   Magnetism

Generators (pages 643–644)

7. A generator converts _____ energy into _____ energy.

8. Circle the letter that best describes how most of the electrical energy used in homes and businesses is produced.

   a. with DC generators

   b. using AC generators at large power plants

   c. with small magnets moving inside coils

   d. by rotating a magnetic field around a coil of wire

9. Is the following sentence true or false? In an alternating current produced by an AC generator, the flow direction of charges switches back and forth. _____

10. Circle the letter of each sentence that is true about generators.

    a. Small generators can produce enough electricity for a small business.

    b. DC generators produce current that flows back and forth.

    c. Small generators are available for purchase by the public.

    d. Most modern power plants use DC generators.

Transformers (pages 644–645)

11. A device that increases or decreases voltage and current of two linked AC circuits is called a(n) _____ .

12. How does a transformer change voltage and current? _____
_____

13. Why are transformers necessary for home electrical service? _____
_____

14. Is the following sentence true or false? To prevent overheating wires, voltage is decreased for long-distance transmission. _____

15. How is voltage calculated in a transformer? _____
_____

16. Is the following sentence true or false? A step-down transformer decreases voltage and increases current. _____

Electrical Energy for Your Home (pages 646–647)

17. Name at least three sources used to produce electrical energy in the United States. _____
_____

18. A device with fanlike blades that can convert energy from various sources into electrical energy is called a(n) _____ .

© Pearson Education, Inc., publishing as Pearson Prentice Hall. All rights reserved.

Chapter 21   Magnetism

WordWise

Solve the clues to determine which vocabulary words from Chapter 21 are hidden in the puzzle. Then find and circle the terms in the puzzle. The terms may occur vertically, horizontally, or diagonally. Some terms may be spelled backwards.

```
f  g  d  e  l  o  p  c  i  t  e  n  g  a  m
e  a  a  t  s  o  r  m  e  v  r  p  e  a  b
r  r  q  l  z  f  f  r  e  r  e  v  g  c  t
r  c  i  u  v  t  t  c  h  n  g  n  r  r  r
o  s  d  o  m  a  i  n  i  u  e  t  a  o  a
m  o  u  b  p  l  n  b  k  t  n  u  u  f  n
a  l  t  y  o  i  r  o  o  n  e  r  m  t  s
g  e  k  p  o  u  d  s  m  a  r  b  i  n  f
n  n  k  a  t  p  p  o  i  e  a  i  c  a  o
e  o  g  o  y  h  z  a  v  b  t  n  s  y  r
t  i  e  e  h  n  j  n  m  o  e  m  o  m
i  d  i  r  j  u  e  r  t  c  r  f  r  u  e
c  t  e  z  z  w  y  n  r  p  e  r  j  b  r
```

Clues

Region where a magnetic field is strongest

Nickel is a(n) _____ material.

Current-carrying wire with a loop in it

Uses an electromagnet to measure small amounts of current

Device with fanlike blades that converts energy from various sources to electrical energy

Area influenced by Earth's magnetic field

Converts mechanical energy into electrical energy

Aligned magnetic fields

Step-down or step-up

Hidden Words

_____

_____

_____

_____

_____

_____

_____

_____

_____

© Pearson Education, Inc., publishing as Pearson Prentice Hall. All rights reserved.

Chapter 21   Magnetism

Calculating Voltage

A step-down transformer has a primary coil with 500 turns of wire, and a secondary coil with 50 turns. If the input voltage is 120 V, what is the output voltage?

Math Skill:
Ratios and Proportions

You may want to read more about this **Math Skill** in the **Skills and Reference Handbook** at the end of your textbook.

1. Read and Understand

What information are you given?

Input Voltage = 120 V

Primary Coil: 500 turns

Secondary Coil: 50 turns

2. Plan and Solve

What unknown are you trying to calculate?

Output Voltage = ?

What formula contains the given quantities and the unknown?

$$\frac{\text{Secondary Coil turns}}{\text{Primary Coil turns}} = \frac{\text{Output Voltage}}{\text{Input Voltage}}$$

Replace each variable with its known value.

$$\frac{50 \text{ turns}}{500 \text{ turns}} = \frac{\text{Output Voltage}}{120 \text{ V}}$$

$$\text{Output Voltage} = \frac{50 \text{ turns}}{500 \text{ turns}} \times 120 \text{ V} = 12 \text{ V}$$

3. Look Back and Check

Is your answer reasonable?

The ratio of secondary to primary turns is 1 : 10. 12 V is one tenth of 120 V, so the answer is reasonable.

Math Practice

On a separate sheet of paper, solve the following problems.

1. What is the ratio of turns for the secondary to primary coils in a step-down transformer, if the input voltage from a substation is 7200 V, and the output voltage to a home is 240 V?

2. The input voltage from a generating plant to a transformer is 11,000 V. If the output voltage from the transformer to high-voltage transmission lines is 240,000 V, what is the ratio of secondary to primary turns in this step-up transformer?

3. A step-down transformer has 200 turns of wire in its primary coil. How many turns are in the secondary coil if the input voltage = 120 V, and the output voltage = 6 V?

© Pearson Education, Inc., publishing as Pearson Prentice Hall. All rights reserved.

Summary

22.1 Earth's Structure

Geology is the study of planet Earth. Geologists are scientists who study Earth. They study what Earth is made of and the forces that change Earth's surface. Two types of forces change Earth's surface: constructive forces and destructive forces. Constructive forces build up Earth's surface. Destructive forces slowly wear away Earth's surface. These forces have been at work for billions of years. They are still changing Earth's surface today.

Earth consists of three main layers: the crust, the mantle, and the core. The layers differ in the materials they are made of. The layers also differ in density, temperature, and pressure.

The crust is the outer layer of Earth. It is thin and rocky. It consists mainly of silicates. Silicates are compounds containing silicon and oxygen. There are two types of crust: continental crust and oceanic crust.

- Continental crust makes up the continents. It consists mainly of less-dense rocks such as granite. It is relatively thick.
- Oceanic crust makes up the ocean floors. It consists mainly of more-dense rocks such as basalt. It is relatively thin.

The mantle is the layer below the crust. It is a very thick layer. The mantle consists of hot, solid rock. As you go deeper in the mantle, temperature and pressure increase. Like the crust, the mantle consists mainly of silicates. However, the mantle is denser than the crust. The mantle has three layers: the lithosphere, the asthenosphere, and the mesophere.

- The lithosphere is the top layer of the mantle. It contains rock that is rigid, or stiff.

- The asthenosphere lies just below the lithosphere. It contains rock that is soft and can flow slowly.
- The mesophere is the bottom layer of the mantle. It contains rock that is rigid.

The core is the layer below the mantle. It is a large sphere at the center of Earth. It consists mostly of iron. The core is extremely hot and under great pressure. The core is divided into two parts: the outer core and the inner core.

- The outer core contains liquid rock that flows. The iron in the flowing rock produces an electric current and creates Earth's magnetic field.
- The inner core is solid, even though it is extremely hot. It is under so much pressure that its particles are squeezed together in solid form.

22.2 Minerals

Most of Earth consists of rocks, and rocks consist of minerals. Minerals are inorganic solids. Inorganic means not made from living things. Minerals are also naturally occurring. This means that humans do not make them. In addition, minerals have a crystal structure. Recall that crystals are solids with their atoms arranged in a regular pattern. Minerals are also unique substances. Each mineral has its own chemical composition. There are thousands of different minerals. However, only a few minerals are common. Examples of minerals are quartz, sulfur, talc, diamond, mica, and halite.

Each mineral has a set of properties that help identify it. The properties are crystal structure, color, streak, luster, density, hardness, fracture, and cleavage.

- Crystal structure refers to the shape of a mineral's crystals. For example,

© Pearson Education, Inc., publishing as Pearson Prentice Hall. All rights reserved.

quartz crystals are shaped like prisms. Other minerals have crystals shaped like cubes or sheets.

- Color refers to the color of the mineral itself. Some minerals have a characteristic color. For example, sulfur is always yellow. Other minerals may not always be the same color. For example, quartz can be white or violet.
- Streak is the color of a mineral's powder. You can see a mineral's streak by scraping the mineral against a certain type of plate. The powder left on the plate is the streak. The color of a mineral's streak may be different from the color of the mineral itself.
- Luster refers to how shiny a mineral is. It depends on how the mineral's surface reflects light. Minerals can have a metallic, silky, greasy, pearly, glassy, or earthy luster.
- Density is the amount of mass in a given volume of a material. The density of a mineral depends on what elements the mineral contains. For example, quartz consists of silicon and oxygen. Both of these elements have relatively low atomic masses. As a result, quartz is relatively low in density.
- Hardness measures how difficult a mineral is to scratch. A hard mineral can scratch a softer mineral, but a soft mineral cannot scratch a harder mineral. Diamond is the hardest mineral. It can scratch all other minerals. Talc is the softest mineral. It cannot scratch any other minerals.
- Fracture refers to how a mineral breaks. Quartz breaks into pieces with evenly curved surfaces. Some minerals break into pieces with jagged surfaces.
- Cleavage is a mineral's tendency to split apart along regular, well-defined planes. For example, mica splits into sheets, and halite splits into cubes.

22.3 Rocks and the Rock Cycle

Rocks are classified into three major groups based on how they form. The three groups are igneous, sedimentary, and metamorphic rocks.

Igneous rocks form from magma. Magma is a mixture of melted rock and gases. It forms underground. Lava is magma that flows out of volcanoes onto Earth's surface. When magma or lava cools and hardens, it forms igneous rock. If magma hardens underground, the igneous rock is called intrusive rock. Granite is an example of intrusive igneous rock. If lava hardens at Earth's surface, the igneous rock is called extrusive rock. Basalt is an example of extrusive igneous rock. Magma cools slowly underground. When magma cools slowly, it forms large crystals. As a result, intrusive rocks have large crystals. At Earth's surface, lava cools more quickly and forms small crystals. Therefore, extrusive rocks have small crystals.

Sedimentary rocks form from sediment. Sediment is small pieces of solid material from rocks or living things. Sediment settles to the bottom of oceans and lakes. As the sediment piles up, it puts pressure on the lower layers. Gradually, the pressure turns the sediment into rock. There are three types of sedimentary rocks: clastic, chemical, and organic.

- Clastic rocks form from broken pieces of other rocks. The pieces may be large or small. Sandstone is an example of clastic rock.
- Chemical rocks form from dissolved minerals. When the water evaporates, the minerals are left behind. Tufa is an example of chemical rock.
- Organic rocks form from the shells and bones of dead animals. The shells and bones sink to the bottom of oceans and lakes. They are pressed together over time. Limestone is an example of organic rock.

© Pearson Education, Inc., publishing as Pearson Prentice Hall. All rights reserved.

Chapter 22   Earth's Interior

Metamorphic rocks form from other rocks. High temperature and pressure gradually change the original rocks into new kinds of rocks. The original rocks can be any kind of rocks, including metamorphic rocks.

The rock cycle is a series of repeating processes in which rocks change from one type to another. Forces within Earth and at Earth's surface cause rocks to change form. For example, magma at Earth's surface hardens to form igneous rock. The igneous rock is gradually broken down into sediment. The sediment becomes part of sedimentary rock. The sedimentary rock is pushed deep underground. Heat and pressure change the sedimentary rock into metamorphic rock. The metamorphic rock later melts to form magma, and the rock cycle begins again.

22.4 Plate Tectonics

Plate tectonics is a scientific theory. The theory states that pieces of lithosphere move slowly on top of the asthenosphere. The pieces of lithosphere are called plates. The theory of plate tectonics explains the formation and movement of Earth's plates.

At one time, all the land surface of Earth formed a single supercontinent. Later, the supercontinent broke into pieces that moved apart. The continents are still moving. Continental drift is the process in which continents move slowly across Earth's surface.

The mid-ocean ridge is a chain of underwater mountains. It reaches into all of Earth's oceans, forming the world's longest mountain chain. There is a huge crack in the crust all along the mid-ocean ridge. On each side of the crack, pieces of ocean floor move slowly apart. This is called sea-floor spreading. As pieces of ocean floor move apart, magma from the mantle pushes up through the crack. The magma forms new crust. As the new crust moves away from the crack, it cools

and hardens. It also becomes denser. Gravity eventually causes the denser crust to sink back into the mantle. This is called subduction. It occurs in regions called subduction zones. Sea-floor spreading and subduction occur together in a continuous cycle. Sea-floor spreading creates new oceanic crust at the mid-ocean ridge. Subduction destroys old oceanic crust at subduction zones.

According to the theory of plate tectonics, continental drift and sea-floor spreading are caused by convection currents in Earth's mantle. Hot melted rock from the mantle rises at the mid-ocean ridge. The rock cools and spreads out to form lithosphere. Pieces of lithosphere later sink back into the mantle at subduction zones. Through these movements, heat flows from Earth's hot inside toward the cooler surface.

There are about 12 major plates. Most major plates contain both continental and oceanic crust. The edges of plates meet at plate boundaries. Most mountains form along plate boundaries. There are three types of plate boundaries: divergent, convergent, and transform boundaries. At each type of boundary, plates move in a different way.

- At a divergent boundary, plates move away from each other. Magma rises and forms new rock at the gap between divergent plates. The magma may form mountains, such as the mid-ocean ridge.

- At a convergent boundary, plates move toward each other. When the plates come together, the denser plate may slide under the other plate and sink into the mantle. Alternatively, the edges of the two plates may buckle and fold to form mountains.

- At a transform boundary, plates slide past each other in opposite directions. Rock is not created or destroyed at a transform boundary.

© Pearson Education, Inc., publishing as Pearson Prentice Hall. All rights reserved.

Chapter 22   Earth's Interior

22.5 Earthquakes

An earthquake is a movement of Earth's lithosphere. It occurs when rocks suddenly shift and release stored energy. The energy released during an earthquake is carried by waves. Earthquake waves are called seismic waves. Seismic waves can cause thousands of deaths and billions of dollars in damage.

The movement of plates explains why earthquakes occur. As plates move, they cause stress in the crust. Stress is a force that squeezes rocks together, stretches them apart, or pushes them in different directions. Stress in the crust causes faults and folds. A fault is a break in a mass of rock along which movement can occur. A fold is a bend in layers of rock. Both faults and folds tend to form along plate boundaries.

When stress builds up along a fault, an earthquake may occur. Earthquakes occur because stress forces have become greater than the rock can bear and the rock suddenly shifts. The place beneath Earth's surface where an earthquake begins is called the focus. The place on Earth's surface directly above the focus is called the epicenter. After an earthquake occurs, seismic waves move out in all directions from the focus. Earthquakes produce three main types of seismic waves: P waves, S waves, and surface waves.

- P waves are longitudinal waves. They push and pull the ground like a spring. P waves are the fastest seismic waves. They can travel through both solids and liquids.
- S waves are transverse waves. They shake the ground up and down or back and forth. S waves can travel only through solids and not through liquids.
- Surface waves are seismic waves that reach Earth's surface. Surface waves are slower than P and S waves. However, surface waves move the ground more and cause greater damage than P and S waves.

Scientists can find the epicenter and strength of an earthquake using seismographs. A seismograph is a device that detects and records seismic waves. Information from several seismographs in different places is needed to determine where an earthquake occurred. The strength of an earthquake is measured on a scale. The most useful scale for geologists is the moment magnitude scale. This scale measures the amount of energy released by an earthquake.

Every day, earthquakes occur all around the world. Most earthquakes occur along plate boundaries because this is where many faults are found. Scientists have used data on earthquakes to learn more about the inside of Earth. For example, scientists know that Earth's outer core is liquid because S waves cannot pass through it.

22.6 Volcanoes

A volcano is a mountain that forms when magma reaches Earth's surface. The process begins deep inside Earth. Rock in the mantle melts and forms magma. The magma rises up toward the crust. The magma rises because it is less dense than the solid rock around it. Before the magma breaks through the crust, it may collect in a space underground called a magma chamber. The magma may rise to the surface through a narrow, vertical channel called a pipe. When the volcano erupts, the magma finally breaks through the surface. A vent is an opening in the ground where magma escapes to the surface. There may be more than one vent. The central vent may have a bowl-shaped pit called a crater.

Some volcanoes erupt with an explosion. Other volcanoes erupt quietly. How a volcano erupts depends on how easily the magma flows. Thin magma flows easily. It causes quiet eruptions. Thick magma resists flowing. It can clog

© Pearson Education, Inc., publishing as Pearson Prentice Hall. All rights reserved.

Chapter 22   Earth's Interior

a volcanic pipe so that great pressure builds up inside the volcano. When the volcano finally erupts, it explodes.

Most volcanoes occur along plate boundaries or at hot spots in the crust. At a convergent boundary, a plate sinking into the mantle causes melting. Magma forms and rises to the surface. At a divergent boundary, magma rises to fill the gap between two separating plates. A hot spot is a region where hot rock extends from deep within the mantle all the way to the surface.

There are three major types of volcanoes: shield volcanoes, cinder cones, and composite volcanoes.

- A shield volcano is a wide, flat volcano. It is produced by a quiet eruption of thin magma. Because the magma is thin, it travels a long way before it hardens.
- A cinder cone is a small volcano with steep sides. It is produced by the eruption of ash and cinders instead of magma.

- A composite volcano is a tall volcano with steep sides. It is produced by repeated explosive eruptions of thick magma and ash.

Sometimes magma does not reach the surface. Instead it cools and hardens in the crust to form intrusive igneous rock. A batholith is a large mass of intrusive igneous rock that has been forced up to Earth's surface. Batholiths often form mountain ranges. Magma also may harden in the cracks between layers of rock. If the cracks run in the same direction as the rock layers, the formation is called a sill. If the cracks run at right angles to the direction of the rock layers, the formation is called a dike. In addition, magma may harden in the pipe of a volcano. This forms a structure called a volcanic neck.

Lava sometimes erupts from many long, thin cracks in the crust. This lava may spread out over a huge area before hardening. After many years, layers of hardened lava may form a high flat area called a lava plateau.

© Pearson Education, Inc., publishing as Pearson Prentice Hall. All rights reserved.

Section 22.1 Earth's Structure
(pages 660–663)

This section explains what geologists study. It describes the main layers of Earth.

Reading Strategy (page 660)

Building Vocabulary Copy the table on a separate sheet of paper and add more rows as needed. As you read the section, define each vocabulary term in your own words. For more information on this Reading Strategy, see the **Reading and Study Skills** in the **Skills and Reference Handbook** at the end of your textbook.

Earth's Structure	
Vocabulary Term	**Definition**
Geologist	
Uniformitarianism	
Crust	

The Science of Geology (pages 660–661)

1. The study of planet Earth, including its composition and structure is called _____.

2. Is the following sentence true or false? People who study Earth and the processes that have shaped Earth over time are called geologists.
_____

3. What is uniformitarianism? _____
_____
_____

A Cross Section of Earth (pages 661–663)

4. Circle the letters of the major layers of Earth's interior.

   a. crust

   b. atmosphere

   c. mantle

   d. core

5. Scientists divide Earth's interior into the crust, mantle, and core based on the _____.

6. Much of the Earth's crust is made up of _____.

© Pearson Education, Inc., publishing as Pearson Prentice Hall. All rights reserved.

Name _____ Class _____ Date _____

Chapter 22   Earth's Interior

Match each type of crust to its characteristics. Each type of crust will have more than one characteristic.

Crust	Characteristic
_____ **7.** oceanic crust	a. Averages about 7 kilometers thick
_____ **8.** continental crust	b. Consists mainly of less-dense rocks
	c. Averages 40 kilometers in thickness
	d. Composed mostly of dense rocks
	e. Makes up the ocean floor
	f. Makes up the continents

9. The layer of Earth called the _____ is found directly below the crust.

10. Circle the letters of each sentence that is true about Earth's mantle.

  a. It is the thickest layer of Earth.

  b. It is divided into layers based on the physical properties of rock.

  c. It is less dense than the crust.

  d. It is made mainly of silicates.

11. The lithosphere includes the uppermost part of Earth's mantle and Earth's _____.

12. Is the following sentence true or false? Rock flows slowly in the asthenosphere. _____

13. The stronger, lower part of the mantle is called the _____.

14. The sphere of metal inside Earth is called the _____.

15. Is the following sentence true or false? The outer core of Earth is liquid. _____

16. Label the main layers of Earth's interior in the diagram below.

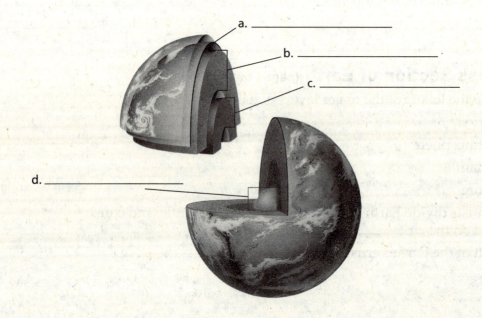

a. _____

b. _____

c. _____

d. _____

© Pearson Education, Inc., publishing as Pearson Prentice Hall. All rights reserved.

Chapter 22   Earth's Interior

Section 22.2 Minerals
(pages 664–669)

This section describes minerals and rocks found on Earth and their different properties.

Reading Strategy (page 664)

Outlining Copy the outline on a separate sheet of paper and add more lines as needed. Before you read, make an outline of this section. Use the green headings as main topics and the blue headings as subtopics. As you read, add supporting details. For more information on this Reading Strategy, see the **Reading and Study Skills** in the **Skills and Reference Handbook** at the end of your textbook.

Minerals

I. Minerals and Rocks

II. The Properties of Minerals

    A. Crystal Structure

    B. _____

    C. _____

    D. _____

Minerals and Rocks (page 665)

1. A solid combination of minerals or mineral materials is a(n)

   _____.

2. Is the following sentence true or false? A mineral is a naturally occurring, inorganic solid with a crystal structure and a characteristic chemical composition. _____

3. A material is called _____ if it is not produced from a living thing.

4. Circle the letters of sentences that are true about minerals.

   a. Within each mineral, chemical composition is nearly constant.

   b. Minerals are organic.

   c. There are about 4000 known minerals.

   d. Minerals are the building blocks of rocks.

The Properties of Minerals (pages 666–669)

5. Is the following sentence true or false? Minerals such as sulfur can sometimes be identified by color. _____

6. What could cause two samples of the same mineral to have different colors?

   _____

   _____

7. Is the following sentence true or false? The color of a mineral's streak is not always the same color as the mineral. _____

© Pearson Education, Inc., publishing as Pearson Prentice Hall. All rights reserved.

Chapter 22   Earth's Interior

8. How is a mineral's streak found? _____
_____

9. The density of a mineral depends on its _____

10. Is the following sentence true or false? The hardness of a mineral is the way in which its surface reflects light. _____

11. To determine the hardness of a mineral, geologists use _____ tests.

12. Is the following sentence true or false? The fracture of a mineral is how it breaks. _____

13. A type of fracture in which a mineral splits evenly is called _____.

14. Complete the table about the properties by which minerals can be identified.

Minerals and Properties	
Property	**Description**
Crystal Structure	
	The color of a mineral's powder
Luster	
	A mineral's mass divided by its volume
Hardness	
	How a mineral breaks
Cleavage	

Match each mineral to its property.

Mineral	**Property**
_____ 15. calcite	a. Gives off visible light under an ultraviolet light
_____ 16. Iceland spar	b. Becomes electrically charged when heated
_____ 17. magnetite	c. Refracts light into two separate rays
_____ 18. tourmaline	d. Is attracted by a magnet
_____ 19. fluorite	e. Easily dissolved by acids

© Pearson Education, Inc., publishing as Pearson Prentice Hall. All rights reserved.

Chapter 22   Earth's Interior

Section 22.3 Rocks and the Rock Cycle
(pages 670–675)

This section describes how rocks are classified. It also explains how rocks change form in the rock cycle.

Reading Strategy (page 670)

Comparing and Contrasting After you read, compare groups of rocks by completing the table. For more information on this Reading Strategy, see the **Reading and Study Skills** in the **Skills and Reference Handbook** at the end of your textbook.

Groups of Rocks		
Rock Group	**Formed by**	**Example**
Igneous		
		Sandstone
	Heat and pressure	

Classifying Rocks (page 670)

1. Circle the letters of the major groups into which rocks are classified.

   a. sedimentary   b. igneous

   c. calcite   d. metamorphic

2. Scientists divide rocks into groups based on _____.

Igneous Rock (page 671)

3. A rock that forms from magma is called a(n) _____.

4. A mixture of molten rock and gases that forms underground is called _____.

5. What is lava? _____

6. Is the following sentence true or false? Igneous rock is formed when molten material cools and solidifies either inside Earth or at the surface. _____

Match each type of igneous rock to its characteristics. Each type of rock will have more than one characteristic.

Igneous Rock

_____ 7. intrusive rock

_____ 8. extrusive rock

Characteristic

a. Forms underground

b. Forms at Earth's surface

c. Has a fine-grained texture

d. Has a coarse-grained texture

e. Cools quickly

f. Cools slowly

© Pearson Education, Inc., publishing as Pearson Prentice Hall. All rights reserved.

Chapter 22   Earth's Interior

Sedimentary Rock (pages 672–673)

9. The process of _____ breaks down rock at Earth's surface.

10. When sediment is squeezed and cemented together, _____ rocks are formed.

11. Circle the groups into which geologists classify sedimentary rocks.

   a. clastic rocks

   b. foliated rocks

   c. organic rocks

   d. chemical rocks

12. Sedimentary rocks formed from broken fragments of other rocks are called _____ rocks.

13. Is the following sentence true or false? Clastic rocks are classified mainly based on the number of fragments they have.

   _____

14. Minerals that precipitate out of solution form _____.

Metamorphic Rock (page 674)

15. Circle the ways a rock can be transformed into a metamorphic rock.

   a. by heat

   b. by precipitation

   c. by pressure

   d. by chemical reaction

16. Where do most metamorphic rocks form? _____

   _____

17. Is the following sentence true or false? Metamorphism can change the mineral content and texture of a rock. _____

18. Metamorphic rocks with crystals arranged in parallel bands or layers are called _____ rocks.

The Rock Cycle (pages 674-675)

19. Circle the letters of the sentences that are true about the rock cycle.

   a. A metamorphic rock that melts and cools to form a new rock becomes an igneous rock.

   b. Forces within Earth and at the surface cause rocks to change form in the rock cycle.

   c. In the rock cycle, rocks may wear away, undergo metamorphism, or melt and form new igneous rock.

   d. The rock cycle is a series of processes in which rocks change from one type to another continuously.

© Pearson Education, Inc., publishing as Pearson Prentice Hall. All rights reserved.

Chapter 22   Earth's Interior

Section 22.4 Plate Tectonics
(pages 676–683)

This section describes the theory of plate tectonics. It also examines sea-floor spreading, plate boundaries, and mountain building.

Reading Strategy (page 676)

Previewing Before you read this section, rewrite the headings as how, why, and what questions about plate tectonics. As you read, write answers to the questions. For more information on this Reading Strategy, see the **Reading and Study Skills** in the **Skills and Reference Handbook** at the end of your textbook.

Plate Tectonics
Questions on Plate Tectonics
What is the hypothesis of continental drift?

1. Is the following sentence true or false? According to the theory of plate tectonics, Earth's plates move about quickly on top of the crust. _____

2. What does the theory of plate tectonics explain about Earth's plates?

_____

Continental Drift (page 677)

3. Explain Alfred Wegener's hypothesis about the continents. _____

_____

4. The process by which the continents move slowly across Earth's surface is called _____.

Sea-floor Spreading (pages 678–679)

5. The world's longest mountain chain is the underwater chain called the _____.

6. Is the following sentence true or false? The theory of sea-floor spreading explains why rocks of the ocean floor are youngest near the mid-ocean ridge. _____

7. Is the following sentence true or false? Old oceanic plates sink into the mantle at mid-ocean ridges in a process called subduction. _____

8. A depression in the ocean floor where subduction takes place is called a(n) _____.

© Pearson Education, Inc., publishing as Pearson Prentice Hall. All rights reserved.

9. Circle the letter that completes the sentence. Sea-floor spreading
   _____ new oceanic crust at mid-ocean ridges.

   a. creates   b. destroys

10. The process called _____ destroys old oceanic crust
    at subduction zones.

The Theory of Plate Tectonics (pages 679–680)

11. Is the following sentence true or false? The concept of sea-floor
    spreading supports the theory of plate tectonics by providing a
    way for the pieces of Earth's crust to move. _____

12. Heat from Earth's interior causes convection currents in Earth's
    _____.

13. Circle the sentences that are true about the theory of
    plate tectonics.

    a. The ocean floor sinks back into the mantle at subduction zones.

    b. The heat that drives convection currents comes from solar energy.

    c. Hot rock rises at mid-ocean ridges, cools and spreads out as
       ocean sea floor.

    d. Plate motions are the surface portion of mantle convection.

14. Describe the two sources of the heat in Earth's mantle.

    a. _____

    b. _____

Plate Boundaries (pages 681–682)

15. Identify each type of plate boundary.

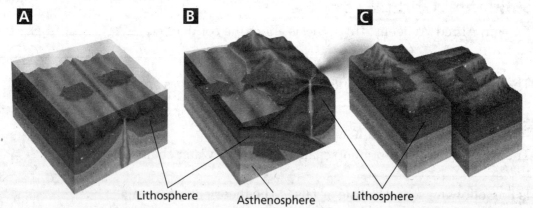

Lithosphere   Asthenosphere   Lithosphere

a. _____   b. _____   c. _____

Mountain Building (page 683)

16. Is the following sentence true or false? Most mountains form along
    plate boundaries. _____

17. Describe how the Himalayan Mountains were formed. _____
    _____

© Pearson Education, Inc., publishing as Pearson Prentice Hall. All rights reserved.

Chapter 22   Earth's Interior

Section 22.5 Earthquakes
(pages 684–689)

This section explains what earthquakes are, what causes them, and their effects.

Reading Strategy (page 684)

Building Vocabulary Copy the table on a separate sheet of paper and add more rows as needed. As you read, define each term for this section in your own words. For more information on this Reading Strategy, see the **Reading and Study Skills** in the **Skills and Reference Handbook** at the end of your textbook.

Earthquake Terms	
Vocabulary Terms	**Definitions**
Earthquake	
Seismic waves	
Stress	

1. An earthquake releases _____ energy that is carried by vibrations called _____.

Stress in Earth's Crust (page 685)

2. Name three ways that stress can affect rocks.

    a. _____

    b. _____

    c. _____

3. Is the following sentence true or false? Stress from moving tectonic plates produces faults and folds in Earth's crust. _____

Match each result of stress to its characteristics. Each result will have more than one characteristic.

Result of Stress	Characteristic
_____ 4. fault	a. A bend in layers of rock
_____ 5. fold	b. Many occur along plate boundaries
	c. A break in a mass of rock where movement happens
	d. Forms where rocks are squeezed but do not break

6. Is the following sentence true or false? Rocks tend to fold instead of break under low temperature or pressure. _____

© Pearson Education, Inc., publishing as Pearson Prentice Hall. All rights reserved.

Chapter 22   Earth's Interior

Earthquakes and Seismic Waves (pages 686–687)

7. Why do earthquakes occur? _____

_____

8. Is the following sentence true or false? The location underground where an earthquake begins is called the focus.

_____

9. The location on Earth's surface directly above the focus of an earthquake is called the _____.

10. Circle the sentences that are true about the physics of earthquakes.

    a. Stress builds in areas where rocks along fault lines snag and remain locked.

    b. In an earthquake, rocks break and grind past each other, releasing energy.

    c. Potential energy is transformed into kinetic energy in the form of seismic waves.

    d. Potential energy increases as rocks break and move.

Match each type of seismic wave to its characteristic.

Seismic Waves	Characteristic
_____ **11.** P waves	a. Transverse waves that cannot travel through liquids
_____ **12.** S waves	b. Slowest moving type of wave that develops when seismic waves reach Earth's surface
_____ **13.** surface waves	c. Longitudinal waves similar to sound waves that cause particles in the material to vibrate in the direction of the waves' motion

14. Typically, the first seismic waves to be detected at a distance are _____ waves.

Measuring Earthquakes (page 687)

15. What devices do geologists use to record seismic waves? _____

_____

Seismographic Data (page 689)

16. Most earthquakes are concentrated along _____.

17. Is the following sentence true or false? Some earthquakes will occur in the interior of plates. _____

18. Is the following statement true or false? When seismic waves interact with boundaries between different kinds of rock within Earth, they can be reflected, refracted, or diffracted.

_____

© Pearson Education, Inc., publishing as Pearson Prentice Hall. All rights reserved.

Chapter 22   Earth's Interior

Section 22.6 Volcanoes
(pages 690–696)

This section describes volcanoes, how they form, and the different ways they erupt. It also describes the different types of volcanoes and other features created by magma.

Reading Strategy (page 690)

Sequencing As you read, complete the flowchart to show how a volcano forms. For more information on this Reading Strategy, see the **Reading and Study Skills** in the **Skills and Reference Handbook** at the end of your textbook.

Formation of a Volcano

Magma forms and rises toward surface.

1. A mountain that forms when magma reaches the surface is called a(n) _____.

Formation of a Volcano (page 691)

2. Is the following sentence true or false? Liquid magma is formed when small amounts of mantle rock melt. _____

3. Describe how a volcano forms. _____

_____

4. Describe how a volcano erupts. _____

_____

5. Magma collects in a pocket called the _____ before a volcanic eruption.

Match each feature of a volcano to its correct description.

Feature	Description
_____ **6.** pipe	a. A narrow, vertical channel where magma rises to the surface
_____ **7.** vent	b. An opening in the ground where magma escapes to the surface
_____ **8.** crater	c. A huge depression created if the shell of the magma chamber collapses
_____ **9.** magma chamber	d. A bowl-shaped pit at the top of a volcano
_____ **10.** caldera	e. A pocket where the magma collects

© Pearson Education, Inc., publishing as Pearson Prentice Hall. All rights reserved.

Chapter 22   Earth's Interior

Quiet and Explosive Eruptions (page 692)

11. Is the following sentence true or false? How easily magma flows depends on its viscosity. _____

12. List three factors that determine the viscosity of magma.

   a. _____

   b. _____

   c. _____

13. Is the following sentence true or false? Magma with higher temperatures has higher viscosity. _____

14. Hot, fast-moving lava is called _____ and cooler, slow-moving lava is called _____ .

Location and Types of Volcanoes (page 693)

15. Where do most volcanoes occur? _____

_____

16. Is the following sentence true or false? A region where hot rock extends from deep within the core to the surface is called a hot spot. _____

17. Is the following sentence true or false? A composite volcano is produced by a quiet eruption of low-viscosity lava. _____

18. An eruption of ash and cinders will produce a volcano called a(n) _____ .

19. Is the following sentence true or false? A composite volcano is formed from an explosive eruption of lava and ash. _____

Other Igneous Features (page 696)

20. Circle the letters of the igneous features that are formed by magma.

   a. dikes

   b. sills

   c. volcanic necks

   d. batholiths

21. The largest type of intrusive igneous rock mass is called a(n) _____ .

22. Is the following sentence true or false? A crack that has been filled in by magma and hardens parallel to existing rock layers is called a dike. _____

© Pearson Education, Inc., publishing as Pearson Prentice Hall. All rights reserved.

Chapter 22   Earth's Interior

WordWise

Use the clues below to identify vocabulary terms from Chapter 22. Write the terms below, putting one letter in each blank. When you finish, the term enclosed in the diagonal will reveal an important process on Earth.

Clues

1. A solid combination of minerals or mineral materials

2. The central layer of Earth

3. A type of fracture in which a mineral tends to split along regular, well-defined planes

4. A movement of Earth's lithosphere that occurs when rocks shift suddenly, releasing stored energy

5. A region where plates collide

6. The type of rock that forms when small pieces of sediment are squeezed together

7. A mountain that forms when magma reaches the surface

8. A bend in layers of rock

9. Wegener's hypothesis in which continents move slowly across Earth's surface

Vocabulary Terms

1. Ⓞ _ _ _

2. _ Ⓞ _ _

3. Ⓞ _ _ _ _ _ _

4. _ _ _ _ _ _ _ Ⓞ _

5. Ⓞ _ _ _ _ _ _ _ _   _ _ _ _ _ _ _ _ _

6. _ _ _ _ _ _ _ _ _ _ Ⓞ _   _ _ _ _

7. _ _ _ Ⓞ _ _ _

8. _ _ Ⓞ _

9. _ _ _ _ _ Ⓞ _ _ _ _   _ _ _ _ _

Hidden Word: _ _ _ _   _ _ _ _ _

Definition: _____

_____

© Pearson Education, Inc., publishing as Pearson Prentice Hall. All rights reserved.

Chapter 22   Earth's Interior

Calculating Wavelength and Frequency

Math Skill:
Line Graphs

You may want to read more about this **Math Skill** in the **Skills and Reference Handbook** at the end of your textbook.

An earthquake occurs 1000 km from seismograph station B. What is the difference in time between the arrivals of the first P wave and the first S wave at station B?

1. Read and Understand

What information are you given in the problem?
   Station B is 1000 km from where an earthquake occurred.

2. Plan and Solve

What does the question ask you to find?
   The difference in time between the arrivals of the first P wave and the first S wave at station B

Find the amount of time it took the first P wave to reach station B by following the 1000-km line up to where it meets the P wave curve.
   2 minutes

Find the amount of time it took the first S wave to reach station B by following the 1000-km line up to where it meets the S wave curve.
   4 minutes

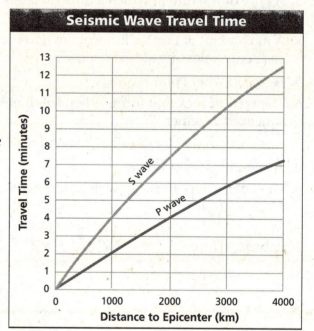

Subtract the amount of time it took the P wave to travel to station B from the amount of time it took the S wave to travel to station B.
   4 minutes − 2 minutes = 2 minutes

3. Look Back and Check

Is your answer reasonable? Yes, because S waves move slower than
                    P waves.

Math Practice

On a separate sheet of paper, solve the following problems. Use the graph.

1. An earthquake occurs 500 km from seismograph station B. What is the difference in time between the arrivals of the first P waves and the first S waves?

2. Station C is 2000 km from the epicenter of the earthquake. If P waves arrived there at 4:37 a.m., at approximately what time did the earthquake occur?

© Pearson Education, Inc., publishing as Pearson Prentice Hall. All rights reserved.

Chapter 23   Earth's Surface

Summary

23.1 Fresh Water

Almost three quarters of Earth's surface is covered with water. For this reason, Earth is sometimes called the "water planet." Water can exist on Earth as a liquid in oceans and lakes, as a solid in snow and ice, and as a gas in the atmosphere. Most of Earth's water is salt water found in the oceans. Very little of Earth's water is fresh water.

Water moves among the oceans, atmosphere, and land in the water cycle. The water cycle covers the entire planet and goes on continuously. It consists of several processes: evaporation, transpiration, condensation, precipitation, and return of flowing water to the oceans. Sunlight and gravity drive these processes.

- Evaporation is the process in which a liquid changes to a gas. Sunlight heats water and changes it into water vapor in the atmosphere. Most evaporation occurs over the oceans.
- Transpiration is the process in which the leaves of plants release water vapor to the atmosphere.
- Condensation is the process in which a gas changes to a liquid. When air rises and cools, it can hold less water vapor. Water droplets or ice crystals condense on small particles in the air. The droplets may combine to form clouds.
- Precipitation is the process in which water droplets or ice crystals fall from clouds to the ground. Precipitation has several forms, including rain and snow.
- Return of flowing water to the oceans is a process that starts with runoff. Runoff is water that flows over Earth's surface after it rains. Runoff flows into streams, rivers, ponds, and lakes. Some of this water eventually returns to the oceans.

A tiny part of Earth's fresh water exists as water vapor in the atmosphere. Most water enters the atmosphere by evaporation, mainly from the oceans. Some water vapor enters the atmosphere by transpiration from plants. Water vapor stays in the atmosphere for only a short time. It soon condenses and falls back to the surface as precipitation.

Even less of Earth's fresh water flows on the surface in streams and other bodies of surface water. A stream is any natural channel of flowing water. Streams flow together to form rivers. The streams that come together to form a river are called tributaries. Tributaries collect runoff and channel it into rivers. The area of land that contributes water to a river is called a watershed. Lakes and ponds usually drain into streams and rivers as well.

More of Earth's fresh water exists as groundwater. Groundwater is found in cracks in rocks and between particles of soil. Below the surface, there is a region where groundwater fills all the tiny spaces in soil and rocks. This is called the saturated zone. The top of the saturated zone is called the water table. Water flows through rocks underground. Rocks that water can easily flow through are called permeable. Rocks that water cannot easily flow through are called impermeable. An aquifer is a permeable rock layer that is full of water. People drill wells into aquifers to get water for drinking and agriculture.

Most of Earth's fresh water exists as snow and ice in glaciers. Glaciers are found in Earth's high mountains and in polar regions. They are formed when snow and ice pile up year after year. Glaciers slowly flow over the land. Icebergs are large pieces of ice that break off when a glacier reaches the ocean. Icebergs eventually melt.

© Pearson Education, Inc., publishing as Pearson Prentice Hall. All rights reserved.

Chapter 23   Earth's Surface

23.2 Weathering and Mass Movement

Erosion is a destructive process. It wears down and carries away rock and soil. Erosion has helped shape Earth's surface for millions of years. Erosion acts through several agents, including weathering, the force of gravity, and moving winds, water, and ice. Over time, erosion breaks down even the tallest mountains. The end product of erosion is sediment.

Weathering is the process of wearing away rocks. Weathering occurs at or near Earth's surface. There are two forms of weathering: mechanical weathering and chemical weathering.

- Mechanical weathering is the process of physically breaking rock into smaller pieces. The most common form of mechanical weathering is frost wedging. Water in cracks in a rock freezes and expands. This pries open the cracks. When the ice melts, the water seeps deeper into the rock. The process repeats over many years. Eventually, the rock cracks apart. Plant roots can also slowly pry apart cracks in rocks.
- Chemical weathering is the process of dissolving rock. Water is the main agent of chemical weathering. It can dissolve all minerals. Chemical weathering makes holes in rock. Eventually the rock crumbles and falls apart.

How fast weathering breaks down rock depends on the temperature, the amount of water, and the type of rock. Mechanical weathering occurs faster where the temperature keeps changing between freezing and thawing. Chemical weathering occurs faster where it is hot and wet. Chemical weathering also occurs faster with some rocks than with others. For example, limestone weathers quickly because of chemical weathering.

After weathering loosens particles of rock, the particles move downhill due to the force of gravity. Mass movement is the downward movement of rock and soil due to gravity. There are several types of mass movement, including landslides, mudflows, creep, and slumping.

- A landslide is a rapid movement of rock and soil down a slope. Landslides occur after heavy rains or earthquakes.
- A mudflow is a rapid movement of wet soil and other fine sediment down a slope. Mudflows occur after heavy rains in areas where there are deep layers of fine sediment.
- Creep is a gradual movement of soil down a slope. Creep occurs when water in soil repeatedly freezes and expands. Each time the cycle is repeated, the soil moves a small distance downhill.
- Slumping is a sudden movement of an entire layer of soil or rock down a slope. Slumping occurs when the ground is full of water. Slumping often leaves a curved scar on a hillside.

23.3 Water Shapes the Land

Most sediment is moved and deposited by flowing water. As a result, flowing water is the major agent of erosion that shapes Earth's surface. Erosion begins when runoff carries small particles of soil downhill to a stream. As the stream flows, the soil and other sediment scrape against the streambed and slowly wear it away. The speed of the stream determines the size and amount of sediment it can carry. A faster stream can carry more sediment and cause greater erosion. Erosion by flowing water creates features such as V-shaped valleys, waterfalls, meanders, and oxbow lakes.

- A V-shaped valley is a deep, narrow valley with steep sides. A V-shaped valley forms where a stream flows rapidly down a steep slope. The rushing water erodes the streambed into a V shape.

© Pearson Education, Inc., publishing as Pearson Prentice Hall. All rights reserved.

Chapter 23   Earth's Surface

- A waterfall is a sharp drop in a streambed that causes the water to fall from a higher level to a lower level. A waterfall forms where softer rock layers lie downstream from harder rock layers. The softer rock layers erode rapidly. The harder rock layers remain to form the top of the waterfall.
- A meander is a loop-like bend in a river. It forms where a river has a curve. The water moves faster on the outside of the curve and erodes the outside bank. The water moves slower on the inside of the curve and deposits sediment along the inside bank. Over time, this process turns the curve into a meander.
- An oxbow lake is a curved lake near a river. It forms when an old meander is cut off from the rest of the river. This happens because the river erodes a shorter, more direct path between the two ends of the meander.

As a stream or river slows down, it begins to deposit sediment. Deposition is the process in which sediment is laid down in new locations. The sediment creates features such as alluvial fans and deltas. An alluvial fan is a fan-shaped deposit of sediment on land. It occurs where a stream flows out of the mountains and onto the plains. A delta is a mass of sediment deposited in water. It occurs where a river enters a large body of water.

Erosion and deposition due to water occur below ground as well as at the surface. Groundwater mainly causes chemical erosion. Groundwater erosion leads to the formation of caves and sinkholes. A cave is an empty passage in rock that is left behind when the water table drops. A sinkhole is a hole in the ground that forms when a portion of ground suddenly collapses. Sinkholes occur because groundwater erosion weakens underground layers of rock.

23.4 Glaciers and Wind

Glaciers form in places where more snow falls than melts. As the layers of snow pile up, the weight on the lower layers increases. The pressure turns the lower layers into ice. The force of gravity pulls the glacier downhill. There are two types of glaciers: continental glaciers and valley glaciers. A continental glacier is a thick sheet of ice that forms over a huge area. Continental glaciers cover Antarctica and Greenland. A valley glacier is a smaller glacier that forms in a high mountain valley.

Although glaciers move very slowly, they cause a great deal of erosion. Like flowing water, a moving glacier picks up and carries sediment. The sediment acts like sandpaper as the glacier moves downhill. Erosion by glaciers creates features such as cirques, horns, U-shaped valleys, and glacial lakes.

- A cirque is a large bowl-shaped valley on a mountainside. It forms when a moving glacier scoops out rock.
- A horn is a pyramid-shaped peak. It forms when several cirques develop around the top of a mountain.
- A U-shaped valley is a V-shaped valley that has been widened by a glacier. It forms when a valley glacier follows a V-shaped valley down a mountainside.
- A glacial lake is a large lake left behind by a glacier. It forms when a natural depression is eroded and enlarged by a moving continental glacier. The Great Lakes are glacial lakes.

A glacier gathers and carries a huge amount of sediment. Glacial sediment is called till. It contains rock pieces in a wide range of sizes, from giant boulders to rock dust. When a glacier melts, it deposits its load of sediment and creates features such as moraines, erratics, and drumlins.

© Pearson Education, Inc., publishing as Pearson Prentice Hall. All rights reserved.

- Moraines are mounds of sediment deposited at the downhill end of a glacier and along its sides.
- Erratics are boulders that a glacier has carried away from their place of origin.
- Drumlins are long mounds of till. They often occur in groups.

Wind also causes erosion and deposition. The speed of the wind determines the size of the sediment it can carry. Most wind erosion occurs in dry areas such as deserts. Wind erodes the land in two ways: deflation and abrasion.

- Deflation occurs when wind picks up and carries away soil, sand, and pebbles. Over time, only the larger rocks are left behind.
- Abrasion occurs when the wind blows sand against rocks. The sand slowly wears away the rocks.

When the wind slows down, it deposits sediment. The sediment forms features such as sand dunes and loess deposits. Sand dunes are deposits of windblown sand. Loess deposits are deposits of windblown dust.

23.5 The Restless Oceans

Most of Earth's water exists as salt water in the oceans. Salinity is the proportion of dissolved salt in water. The most common salt in ocean water is table salt, or sodium chloride. Rain slowly dissolves salt out of surface rocks. This salt is washed into rivers, and rivers carry the salt to the oceans. Some salt is removed from the oceans by living things. Some salt is also deposited as sediment.

As you move from the surface of the ocean to the ocean floor, the water becomes darker and colder. The deep ocean is entirely dark and very cold. Water pressure also increases with depth. At a depth of 500 meters, pressure is about 50 times greater than pressure at sea level. Few living things can

withstand such great pressure. Along the edges of most continents is a gently sloping plain called the continental shelf. Over the continental shelf, the ocean is shallow. Beyond the continental shelf is the ocean floor. Here the ocean is deep. The ocean floor consists of a huge plain, dotted with volcanic peaks. The ocean floor also has mid-ocean ridges and deep trenches.

Water flows from one ocean to another in ocean currents. Ocean currents may be surface currents or deep currents.

- A surface current is a large stream of ocean water that moves continuously in the same path on the surface. Winds blowing across the surface of the ocean cause surface currents. The Gulf Stream is a surface current. It carries warm water from the Gulf of Mexico to the North Atlantic Ocean.
- A deep ocean current is caused by differences in density of ocean water. This is why deep currents are sometimes called density currents. Colder, saltier water is denser. It sinks into the deep ocean and pushes less dense water upward to the surface. This creates a density current. Density currents slowly mix the water between the surface and deeper ocean.

Upwelling is the movement of water from the deep ocean to the surface. It tends to occur along the western coasts of continents. Wind blows warm surface water aside. This allows cold water from the deep ocean to rise and take the place of the warm water. Upwelling brings nutrients from the deep ocean to the surface. The nutrients attract large populations of fish and other organisms.

Ocean waves are the major cause of erosion along coastlines. Over time, wave erosion can create features such as cliffs, arches, and caves. Wave erosion occurs through two processes: hydraulic action and abrasion.

- Hydraulic action occurs when waves pound on cracks in rock. The pressure

© Pearson Education, Inc., publishing as Pearson Prentice Hall. All rights reserved.

Chapter 23   Earth's Surface

from the repeated pounding causes the cracks to get bigger. Eventually, the rock breaks apart into smaller pieces.
- Abrasion occurs when sediment in waves acts like sandpaper. The sediment wears away rock.

Ocean waves deposit sediment as they wash over the shore and slow down. Over time, sediment can collect along the shore and form a beach. Longshore drift is the process in which ocean waves gradually move sand along a shore by repeated erosion and deposition. Longshore drift occurs when waves approach the shore at an angle.

23.6 Earth's History

Deposited sediment slowly turns into sedimentary rock. Remains of living things in the sediment turn into fossils. Fossils are the preserved remains or traces of once-living things. Scientists study rocks and fossils to learn more about Earth's history.

One of the most important facts about a rock is its age. The relative age of a rock is whether it is older or younger than other rocks. Generally, if rock layers are undisturbed, younger rocks lie above older rocks, and the oldest rocks are at the bottom. This is the law of superposition. Scientists use this law to determine the relative ages of rocks and the fossils they contain.

Most types of organisms preserved as fossils are now extinct. An extinct type of organism is one that no longer exists. Index fossils are fossils of certain extinct organisms. To be an index fossil, the organism must be easy to identify, and it must have occurred over a large area during a well-defined period of time. Index fossils are used to determine the relative ages of rocks from different places. If a rock contains an index fossil, the rock must have formed during the time period that the index organism lived.

The absolute age of a rock is the time that has passed since the rock formed. Geologists use radioactive dating to determine the absolute ages of rocks. When a rock forms, it contains known ratios of radioactive and stable forms of certain elements. Through time, the radioactive forms decay, or break down, into stable forms of other elements. Scientists can measure the ratios of radioactive and stable forms the rock now contains. From this, they can calculate how much time has passed since the rock formed.

The geologic time scale is a time line for the history of Earth. It is based on the relative and absolute ages of rock. It divides Earth's history into eras. Each era is a major stage in Earth's history. Eras are further divided into periods. The eras of the geologic time scale are Precambrian time, the Paleozoic Era, the Mesozoic Era, and the Cenozoic Era.

- Precambrian time is the earliest part of Earth's history. It began 4.6 billion years ago. During Precambrian time, planet Earth formed and early life forms evolved.
- The Paleozoic Era began 544 million years ago. During the Paleozoic Era, fish and land organisms evolved.
- The Mesozoic Era began 248 million years ago. During the Mesozoic Era, dinosaurs, mammals, and flowering plants evolved.
- The Cenozoic Era began 65 million years ago. It continues to the present. During the Cenozoic Era, mammals became widespread and humans evolved.

Between some eras, many different organisms became extinct in a short time. When this happens, it is called a mass extinction. Scientists have developed several theories to explain what causes mass extinctions. These theories include asteroids striking Earth, volcanoes erupting, widespread disease, and climate change.

© Pearson Education, Inc., publishing as Pearson Prentice Hall. All rights reserved.

Chapter 23   Earth's Surface

Section 23.1 Fresh Water
(pages 704–708)

This section describes where water is found on Earth. It also explains the water cycle.

Reading Strategy (page 704)

Build Vocabulary Copy the table on a separate sheet of paper. As you read, add terms and definitions from this section to the table. For more information on this Reading Strategy, see the **Reading and Study Skills in the Skills and Reference Handbook** at the end of your textbook.

Earth's Fresh Water	
Vocabulary Term	**Definition**
Groundwater	
Water cycle	
Transpiration	

1. Water found underground in soil and within cracks in rocks is called _____.

The Water Cycle (pages 705–706)

2. Name five major processes of the water cycle.

    a. _____

    b. _____

    c. _____

    d. _____

    e. _____

Match each process with its correct description.

Description

_____ 3. When water droplets or ice crystals fall to the ground

_____ 4. The process through which a liquid changes into a gas

_____ 5. The process that forms clouds

_____ 6. When water is released from a plant's leaves

Process

a. evaporation

b. transpiration

c. condensation

d. precipitation

7. What is a glacier? _____
_____

© Pearson Education, Inc., publishing as Pearson Prentice Hall. All rights reserved.

Chapter 23   Earth's Surface

Fresh Water (pages 706–708)

8. Circle the letters of the places where portions of Earth's fresh water are located.

    a. in streams

    b. in the atmosphere

    c. in the oceans

    d. in lakes

9. Most of Earth's fresh water is located in _____ and
   _____.

10. What is runoff? _____

11. A smaller stream that flows into a river is called a(n)
    _____.

12. Circle the letters of the sentences that are true about watersheds.

    a. Watersheds are areas of land that contribute water to a river system.

    b. Watersheds can be large or small.

    c. The Mississippi River watershed drains most of the central United States.

    d. Watersheds are also called drainage basins.

13. Where do lakes and ponds form? _____
    _____

14. Is the following sentence true or false? Ponds usually form in large, deep depressions, but lakes form in smaller depressions.
    _____

15. An area underground where the pore spaces are entirely filled with water is called the _____.

16. Is the following sentence true or false? The water table is found at the bottom of the saturated zone. _____

17. Water cannot pass through _____ rocks.

18. Circle the letters of the sentences that are true about aquifers.

    a. They are permeable rock layers that are saturated with water.

    b. They are recharged or refilled as rainwater seeps into them.

    c. They are often made of shale and unbroken granite.

    d. Many people rely on aquifers for drinking water.

19. Where do glaciers form? _____
    _____

20. Circle the letter of each word that describes how ice is removed from a glacier.

    a. melting

    b. sublimation

    c. precipitation

    d. formation of icebergs

21. A large piece of ice that breaks off when a glacier reaches the ocean is called a(n) _____.

© Pearson Education, Inc., publishing as Pearson Prentice Hall. All rights reserved.

Chapter 23   Earth's Surface

Section 23.2 Weathering and Mass Movement
(pages 709–712)

This section describes how land is changed by weathering and erosion. It also discusses mass movement.

Reading Strategy (page 709)

Concept Map As you read, complete the concept map showing the key factors which affect the rate of weathering. For more information on this Reading Strategy, see the **Reading and Study Skills** in the **Skills and Reference Handbook** at the end of your textbook.

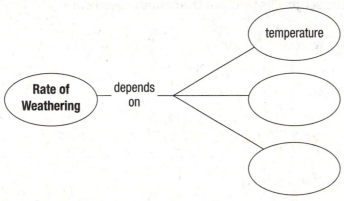

Erosion (page 709)

1. The process that wears down and carries away rock and soil is called _____.

2. Circle the letters of the sentences that are true about erosion.

    a. It acts through hoodoos.

    b. It acts through weathering.

    c. It acts through the force of gravity.

    d. It acts through the movement of glaciers, wind, or waves.

3. Is the following sentence true or false? The end product of erosion is sediment. _____

Weathering (pages 710–711)

4. The process by which rocks are chemically changed or physically broken into fragments is called _____.

5. Circle the letters of the sentences that are true about weathering.

    a. It can be mechanical.

    b. It can be chemical.

    c. It only breaks down soft rocks.

    d. It can break down rocks into fragments.

© Pearson Education, Inc., publishing as Pearson Prentice Hall. All rights reserved.

Chapter 23   Earth's Surface

6. Circle the letters of the sentences that are true about mechanical weathering.

   a. It occurs through frost wedging.

   b. It occurs from acidic rain.

   c. It occurs through rusting.

   d. It occurs through abrasion.

7. Is the following sentence true or false? Abrasion happens when rocks scrape against each other. _____

8. In the process of chemical weathering, rock is broken down by _____ .

9. Circle the letters of the sentences that are true about chemical weathering.

   a. Chemical weathering occurs because rain is slightly acidic.

   b. Rocks are broken down by chemical reactions.

   c. Water is the main agent of chemical weathering.

   d. Chemical weathering involves abrasion and frost wedging.

10. What happens to the minerals found in rocks during the process of chemical weathering? _____

Rates of Weathering (page 711)

11. What factors determine the rate at which mechanical and chemical weathering take place?

    a. _____   b. _____

    c. _____

12. The kind of weathering that most likely occurs in places where temperature conditions alternate between freezing and thawing is _____ weathering.

Mass Movement (page 712)

13. In mass movement, rocks and soil move downhill because of _____ .

Match each type of mass movement with its correct description.

Description	Mass Movement
_____ 14. Rapid mass movement of soil and other sediment mixed with water	a. creep
_____ 15. The rapid movement of large amounts of rock and soil	b. slumping
_____ 16. Weak layers of soil or rock suddenly moving down a slope as a single unit	c. mudflow
_____ 17. Soil gradually moving down a slope	d. landslide

© Pearson Education, Inc., publishing as Pearson Prentice Hall. All rights reserved.

Chapter 23   Earth's Surface

Section 23.3 Water Shapes the Land
(pages 713–717)

This section describes how water erodes the land. It also describes features created by water erosion and water deposition.

Reading Strategy (page 713)

Concept Map As you read, complete the concept map showing how moving water shapes the land. For more information on this Reading Strategy, see the **Reading and Study Skills** in the **Skills and Reference Handbook** at the end of your textbook.

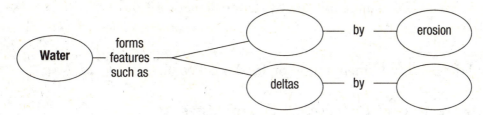

1. The process through which sediment is laid down in new locations is called _____.

Running Water Erodes the Land (pages 714–715)

Match each method that sediment is transported in streams with its correct description.

Description

_____ 2. Dissolved sediment is carried this way.

_____ 3. Large boulders can be moved this way during floods.

_____ 4. Tiny sediment grains move along with the water in a stream.

_____ 5. Large particles bounce along the bottom of a stream.

Method of Transportation

a. in suspension

b. in solution

c. by saltation

d. pushed or rolled

6. What does a stream's ability to erode mainly depend on? _____
_____

Features Formed by Water Erosion (pages 715–716)

7. A(n) _____ valley is formed by a fast-moving stream.

8. Is the following sentence true or false? A waterfall may develop where a stream crosses layers of rock that differ in hardness.
_____

© Pearson Education, Inc., publishing as Pearson Prentice Hall. All rights reserved.

9. A flat area alongside a stream or river that is covered by water only during times of flood is called a(n) _____.

10. A loop-like bend in a river is called a(n) _____.

11. Is the following sentence true or false? Oxbow lakes form when an old meander is cut off from the rest of a river. _____

12. Circle the letters of features that are formed by water erosion.

    a. oxbow lakes   b. V-shaped valleys

    c. meanders   d. waterfalls

Features Formed by Water Deposition (page 716)

13. Name two main features that are formed by deposits made by flowing water.

    a. _____   b. _____

14. A fan-shaped deposit of sediment found on land is called a(n) _____.

15. Is the following sentence true or false? Deltas are masses of sediment that form where rivers enter large bodies of water. _____

Groundwater Erosion (page 717)

16. What type of weathering causes groundwater erosion?

    _____

17. Name two features that are formed by groundwater erosion.

    a. _____   b. _____

a.

b.

18. Identify the two types of cavern formations shown in the figure above.

    a. _____   b. _____

© Pearson Education, Inc., publishing as Pearson Prentice Hall. All rights reserved.

Name _____ Class _____ Date _____

Chapter 23   Earth's Surface

Section 23.4 Glaciers and Wind
(pages 719–724)

This section describes how glaciers form and how landscape features are created. It also describes wind erosion and deposition.

Reading Strategy (page 719)

Sequencing As you read, complete the flowchart to show how a glacier forms and moves, and how it erodes and deposits sediment. For more information on this Reading Strategy, see the **Reading and Study Skills** in the **Skills and Reference Handbook** at the end of your textbook.

How Glaciers Form and Move (page 719)

1. Glaciers form in places where snow melts _____ than it falls.

Match the type of glacier to its description.

Description	Glacier Type
_____ **2.** Found in high mountain valleys	a. valley glacier
_____ **3.** Covers a continent or large island	b. continental glacier

Glacial Erosion and Deposition (pages 720–722)

4. What are the two ways through which glaciers erode rock?

a. _____   b. _____

5. Circle the letters of the sentences that are true about glacial erosion.

a. Glacial ice widens cracks in bedrock beneath a glacier.

b. Pieces of loosened rock stick to the top of a glacier.

c. Rocks stuck to the bottoms and sides of a glacier act like sandpaper, scraping rock and soil.

d. As a glacier moves, it gently brushes the rocks and soil underneath it.

6. What are four distinctive features caused by glacial erosion?

a. _____

b. _____

c. _____

d. _____

© Pearson Education, Inc., publishing as Pearson Prentice Hall. All rights reserved.

Chapter 23   Earth's Surface

7. Large bowl-shaped valleys carved high on a mountainside are called _____.

8. How does a U-shaped valley form? _____
_____

9. Is the following sentence true or false? Continental glaciers fill depressions in the surface with water, where they create cirques.
_____

10. How does a glacier create landforms? _____
_____

11. Mounds of sediment at the downhill end of a glacier are called
_____.

Match each feature formed by glacial deposition to its correct description.

Description	Feature Formed
_____ 12. Long teardrop-shaped mounds of till	a. outwash plain
_____ 13. A flat plain made of particles of rock that were deposited from glacial streams	b. erratics
	c. eskers
_____ 14. A lake formed where large blocks of glacial ice become buried and melt	d. drumlins
	e. kettle lake
_____ 15. Ridges made from sand and gravel that were deposited in the bed of a glacial stream	
_____ 16. Boulders that a glacier has carried away from their place of origin	

Wind Erosion and Deposition (pages 723–724)

17. Name two ways that wind erodes the land.

a. _____   b. _____

18. Is the following sentence true or false? Deflation happens when the wind picks up and carries away loose surface material.
_____

19. Circle the letters of the features deposited by wind.

a. cirques   b. glacial lakes

c. sand dunes   d. loess deposits

20. Is the following sentence true or false? Deposits formed from windblown dust are called loess deposits. _____

© Pearson Education, Inc., publishing as Pearson Prentice Hall. All rights reserved.

Chapter 23   Earth's Surface

Section 23.5 The Restless Oceans
(pages 725–729)

This section describes the oceans and ocean currents. It also describes water erosion and deposition in the oceans.

Reading Strategy (page 725)

Relating Cause and Effect Copy the table on a separate sheet of paper. After you read, complete the table to compare ways that ocean water can move. For more information on this Reading Strategy, see the **Reading and Study Skills** in the **Skills and Reference Handbook** at the end of your textbook.

Ways Ocean Water Moves		
Movement Type	**Causes**	**Effects**
Surface current		
Density current		
Upwelling		
Longshore drift		

Exploring the Ocean (pages 725–726)

1. The proportion of dissolved salts in water is called _____.

2. Is the following sentence true or false? Salt is removed from the ocean by animals and plants and through deposition as sediment.

   _____

3. Circle the letters of the conditions that decrease with the ocean's depth.

   a. pressure   b. light

   c. temperature   d. salinity

4. What is the continental shelf? _____

   _____

   _____

© Pearson Education, Inc., publishing as Pearson Prentice Hall. All rights reserved.

Chapter 23   Earth's Surface

Ocean Currents (pages 726–728)

Match each type of ocean current with its correct description.

Description	Ocean Current
_____ **5.** A current responsible for a slow mixing of water between the surface and deeper ocean	a. surface current
_____ **6.** Movement of water from the deep ocean to the surface	b. density current
_____ **7.** A large stream of ocean water that moves continuously in about the same path near the surface	c. upwelling

8. What causes the continuous flow of surface currents? _____

_____

9. Winds blow warm surface water aside, allowing cold water to rise, in the process of _____.

10. What does each letter in the diagram below represent?

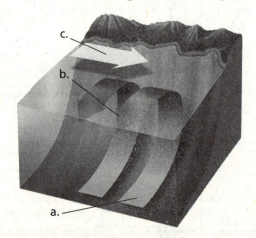

a. _____   b. _____   c. _____

Wave Erosion and Deposition (pages 728–729)

11. What are two hydraulic processes that can be responsible for wave erosion?

a. _____   b. _____

12. Circle the letters of the sentences that are true about hydraulic action.

a. A wave fills a crack with water.

b. Hydraulic action causes no changes to earth's coastlines.

c. Waves compress air as they slam into cracked rocks.

d. Pressure from waves causes cracks in rocks to get bigger.

13. Is the following sentence true or false? The process that moves sand along a shore is called hydraulic action. _____

© Pearson Education, Inc., publishing as Pearson Prentice Hall. All rights reserved.

Chapter 23   Earth's Surface

Section 23.6 Earth's History
(pages 732–738)

This section explains how scientists determine the age of rocks and how they use these methods to develop a time line for the history of Earth. It also describes the four major divisions of Earth history.

Reading Strategy (page 732)

Previewing Before you read, examine Figures 34 and 36 to help you understand geologic time. Write at least two questions about them in the table. As you read, write answers to your questions. For more information on this Reading Strategy, see the **Reading and Study Skills** in the **Skills and Reference Handbook** at the end of your textbook.

Questions on Geologic Time

1. What are fossils? _____

_____

Determining the Age of Rocks (pages 732–734)

2. Is the following sentence true or false? The relative age of a rock is its age compared to the ages of rocks above or below it. _____

3. Circle the letter that identifies the direction in which layers of sedimentary rocks form.

   a. vertically

   b. horizontally

   c. diagonally

   d. randomly

4. Circle the letter of the sentence that is true about the law of superposition.

   a. Younger rocks lie above older rocks if the layers are undisturbed.

   b. Older rocks lie above younger rocks if the layers are undisturbed.

   c. Rock layers are never disturbed.

   d. The youngest rock layers are typically at the bottom.

5. How do geologists use the law of superposition to determine the relative age of rocks?

   a. _____

   b. _____

© Pearson Education, Inc., publishing as Pearson Prentice Hall. All rights reserved.

6. Organize and write the letters of the layers of rock in the diagram from oldest to youngest. If two rock layers are the same age, write them as a pair. _____

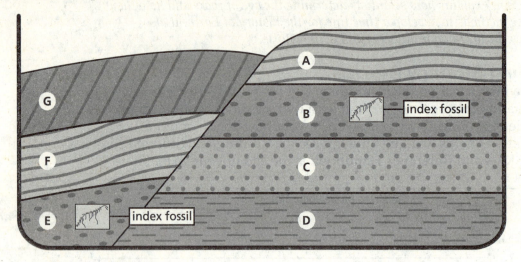

7. Circle the letters of the sentences that are true about index fossils.

   a. They can be easily identified.

   b. They help to determine the relative ages of rocks.

   c. The organisms that formed them occurred over a large area.

   d. The organisms that formed them lived during a well-defined time period.

8. Geologists use radioactive dating to determine the _____ of rocks.

A Brief History of Earth (pages 734–738)

9. What is the geologic time scale based on?

   a. _____   b. _____

10. What is a mass extinction? _____

_____

Match each division of Earth's history to its correct description.

Description	Time
_____ **11.** Dinosaurs appeared.	a. Precambrian time
_____ **12.** Fishes and other animals first developed in the oceans.	b. Mesozoic Era
_____ **13.** Humans first appeared in Africa.	c. Cenozoic Era
_____ **14.** Earth was formed.	d. Paleozoic Era

© Pearson Education, Inc., publishing as Pearson Prentice Hall. All rights reserved.

Chapter 23   Earth's Surface

WordWise

Solve the clues to determine which vocabulary terms from Chapter 23 are hidden in the puzzle. Then find and circle the terms in the puzzle. The terms may occur vertically, horizontally, or diagonally.

```
t  a  v  f  n  o  l  k  w  e  f  r  z  h
g  b  i  m  e  t  l  o  e  s  s  k  d  r
s  i  y  b  r  r  w  f  a  d  u  o  l  u
b  a  x  a  s  a  d  q  t  w  i  d  m  j
p  r  l  l  c  n  p  t  h  r  p  e  p  d
s  j  e  i  n  s  g  i  e  a  q  p  y  e
u  a  k  p  n  p  j  p  r  u  n  o  f  f
p  x  l  v  c  i  b  x  i  a  b  s  c  l
w  g  i  t  q  r  t  c  n  s  f  i  p  a
e  z  e  f  a  a  z  y  g  q  a  t  j  t
l  n  b  o  r  t  x  f  o  s  s  i  l  i
l  f  p  j  g  i  i  o  p  d  f  o  g  o
i  d  a  n  b  o  l  o  e  m  k  n  c  n
n  z  g  d  e  n  r  q  n  i  g  f  s  d
g  l  j  q  c  i  s  o  n  a  z  l  x  j
m  a  s  s  m  o  v  e  m  e  n  t  n  a
```

Clues	Hidden Words
When water is released from the leaves of plants	_____
Water that flows over Earth's surface	_____
The process by which rocks are broken down into fragments	_____
The downward movement of rock and soil due to gravity	_____
The process through which sediment is laid down in new locations	_____
The process wherein pieces of sediment bounce and skip	_____
When wind picks up and carries away loose surface material	_____
Deposits formed from windblown dust	_____
The proportion of dissolved salts in water	_____
The movement of water from the deep ocean to the surface	_____
A preserved remain or trace of a once living thing	_____
A smaller unit of an era	_____

© Pearson Education, Inc., publishing as Pearson Prentice Hall. All rights reserved.

Chapter 23   Earth's Surface

Exploring Radioactive Dating

A fossil contains 100.0 milligrams of Thorium-232, which has a half-life of 14.0 billion years. How much Thorium-232 will remain after three half-lives?

Math Skill:
Fractions
You may want to read more about this **Math Skill** in the **Skills and Reference Handbook** at the end of your textbook.

1. Read and Understand

How many milligrams of Thorium-232 does the fossil contain?
   100.0 milligrams

What is the half-life of Thorium-232?   14.0 billion years

What are you asked to find?   the amount of Thorium-232 that will remain in the fossil after three half-lives

2. Plan and Solve

During a half-life, one half of the original amount of a radioisotope decays. To find the amount of Thorium-232 left in the fossil after three half-lives, begin by multiplying $\frac{1}{2}$ by the number of half-lives.

$$\frac{1}{2} \times \frac{1}{2} \times \frac{1}{2} = \frac{1}{8}$$

This is the fraction of Thorium-232 that will be left in the fossil after three half-lives. Multiply this fraction by the original amount of Thorium-232 to find the amount of Thorium-232 that will remain.

   100.0 milligrams $\times \frac{1}{8}$ = 12.5 milligrams

3. Look Back and Check

Is your answer reasonable?

   To check your answer, divide the number of milligrams in the fossil after three half-lives by the fraction of Thorium-232 left after three half-lives. Your answer should equal the original amount of Thorium-232 in the fossil.   100.0 milligrams

Math Practice

On a separate sheet of paper, solve the following problems.

1. A fossil contains 40.0 milligrams of Uranium-238, which has a half-life of 4.5 billion years. How much Uranium-238 will remain after two half-lives?

2. How long will it take for 50.0 milligrams of Thorium-232 in a rock to decay to 25.0 milligrams?

3. How long will it take for the amount of Rubidium-87 (which has a half-life of 48.8 billion years) in a rock to decay from 80.0 milligrams to 10.0 milligrams?

© Pearson Education, Inc., publishing as Pearson Prentice Hall. All rights reserved.

Name _____ Class _____ Date _____

Summary

24.1 The Atmosphere

The atmosphere is the layer of gases that surrounds Earth. The atmosphere helps protect Earth from meteoroids and radiation from space. The atmosphere also provides conditions on Earth that are suitable for life. It keeps Earth's temperature relatively constant. It also contains gases, such as oxygen, that are needed by living things.

Earth's atmosphere is a mixture of nitrogen, oxygen, water vapor, and many other gases. Nitrogen and oxygen are the major gases in the atmosphere. The atmosphere also contains tiny solid and liquid particles.

The atmosphere has weight because of Earth's gravity. As a result, the atmosphere exerts pressure. Air pressure is the force exerted by the weight of a column of air above a surface. Air pressure is highest at sea level, because the height of the column of air is greatest at sea level. Air pressure decreases at higher altitudes as the column of air becomes shorter. Air pressure is measured with a barometer.

The density of the atmosphere also decreases at higher altitudes. The temperature of the atmosphere changes with altitude as well. Scientists use differences in temperature to divide the atmosphere into four layers: the troposphere, stratosphere, mesosphere, and thermosphere.

- The troposphere is the lowest layer of the atmosphere. It begins at the surface and rises to an average height of 12 kilometers above the surface. In this layer, temperature generally falls as altitude increases.
- The stratosphere is the next layer of the atmosphere. It lies between 12 and 50 kilometers above the surface. In the upper part of the stratosphere, temperature rises as altitude increases.

- The mesosphere is the third layer of the atmosphere. It lies between 50 and 80 kilometers above the surface. In this layer, temperature falls as altitude increases.
- The thermosphere is the highest layer of the atmosphere. It begins at 80 kilometers above the surface and extends outward into space. In this layer, temperature rises as altitude increases.

The ionosphere is a region of charged particles that overlaps the lower thermosphere. In this region, gas molecules lose electrons when they absorb radiation from the sun. The molecules become charged particles, called ions.

24.2 The Sun and the Seasons

Earth is constantly moving in space. Earth moves in two major ways: rotation and revolution. Earth spins like a top around an imaginary line called its axis. This motion is rotation. At the same time, Earth also follows a path that circles around the sun. This motion is revolution. Earth makes one complete rotation on its axis each day. It makes one complete revolution around the sun each year.

Latitude measures distance north or south of the equator. At the equator, sunlight strikes Earth's surface directly. At higher latitudes, sunlight strikes the surface at a slant. Where sunlight is more slanted, the surface is generally cooler. Scientists use latitude to divide Earth's surface into three major temperature zones: tropic, temperate, and polar. The warm tropic zone is around the equator. The cold polar zones include the North and South poles. The cool temperate zones lie between the tropic zone and the polar zones.

© Pearson Education, Inc., publishing as Pearson Prentice Hall. All rights reserved.

Chapter 24   Weather and Climate

The seasons are caused by the tilt of Earth's axis as Earth moves around the sun. The Northern Hemisphere is tilted toward the sun and receives more direct sunlight from about March to September. The Southern Hemisphere is tilted toward the sun and receives more direct sunlight from September to March. For one day in March and one day in September, the sun is directly over the equator. The two days are called equinoxes.

24.3 Solar Energy and Winds

Energy from the sun is called solar energy. A great deal of solar energy strikes Earth's atmosphere. Some solar energy is reflected by the atmosphere back out into space. Some solar energy is absorbed by the gases and particles in the atmosphere. The rest of the solar energy is absorbed by Earth's surface. Most energy absorbed by Earth's surface radiates back into the troposphere. Gases such as carbon dioxide and water vapor absorb most of this reradiated energy and warm the lower atmosphere. The process is called the greenhouse effect.

Within the troposphere, solar energy moves in three ways: radiation, convection, and conduction.

- Radiation occurs when Earth's surface gives off infrared rays to the troposphere.
- Convection occurs when heated air rises and creates currents that move heat through the troposphere.
- Conduction occurs when the surface directly passes heat to molecules of air near the surface.

Wind is the natural flow of air from areas of higher pressure to areas of lower pressure. Large differences in air pressure produce strong winds. Differences in air pressure are often caused by unequal heating of Earth's surface. Winds may be local or global.

Local winds blow over short distances. They are caused by unequal heating of Earth's surface over small regions. Examples of local winds are sea breezes and land breezes.

- Sea breezes blow during the day from the ocean to the land. The land heats up more than the ocean during the day, so the air over the land becomes warmer and rises. The cooler air over the ocean flows in to take its place.
- Land breezes blow during the night from the land to the ocean. The land cools off more than the ocean at night, so the air over the land becomes cooler. The warmer air over the ocean rises. The cooler air over the land flows out to take its place.

Global winds blow over long distances. They are caused by unequal heating of Earth's surface over large regions. Examples of global winds are trade winds, westerlies, and polar easterlies. All of these global winds move in a curved path because of Earth's rotation. The curving effect of Earth's rotation is called the Coriolis effect. Monsoons are global winds that occur in Asia. They are like land and sea breezes on a bigger scale. They blow from the ocean toward land in the summer, bringing heavy rain. They blow from the land toward the ocean in the winter, bringing dry weather.

24.4 Water in the Atmosphere

The amount of water vapor in the air is called humidity. How much water vapor the air can hold depends on the temperature of the air. Warm air can hold more water vapor than cold air. If the temperature falls, some of the water vapor in the air may condense. Water vapor in air may condense as dew, frost, clouds, or fog. Dew is water vapor that condenses on Earth's surface. Frost forms instead of dew in cold weather. In frost, the water vapor condenses as ice crystals instead of droplets.

© Pearson Education, Inc., publishing as Pearson Prentice Hall. All rights reserved.

Chapter 24   Weather and Climate

Clouds form as warm, moist air rises and cools. Water vapor in the rising air condenses around tiny solid particles in the atmosphere. The water vapor may condense as water droplets or ice crystals. A visible mass of billions of droplets or crystals is a cloud. There are three basic cloud forms: stratus, cumulus, and cirrus.

- Stratus clouds are flat layers of clouds that cover much or all of the sky.
- Cumulus clouds are puffy white clouds that look like piles of cotton balls.
- Cirrus clouds are thin, white, wispy clouds with a feathery appearance.

Other cloud forms are variations on these three basic forms. For example, adding -nimbus to the name of a basic form means that the cloud produces precipitation. Cumulonimbus clouds are cumulus clouds that produce precipitation. Cumulonimbus clouds are sometimes called thunderheads. Clouds on or near the ground are called fog. Precipitation occurs when water droplets or ice crystals in clouds fall to the ground. The most common types of precipitation are rain, snow, hail, sleet, and freezing rain.

- Rain is liquid precipitation.
- Snow is precipitation in the form of ice crystals.
- Hail consists of ice pellets that form in storm clouds.
- Sleet is rain that freezes as it falls. Sleet consists of smaller ice particles than hail.
- Freezing rain is rain that freezes after hitting the surface. It occurs when the surface is colder than the air.

24.5 Weather Patterns

Weather results from the movement and interactions of air masses. An air mass is a large body of air that has about the same temperature and moisture content throughout. An air mass can cover a very large area. An air mass forms when air stays over one region for a long time, or when air moves over a uniform region like an ocean. An air mass has the same properties as the region where it forms. For example, an air mass that forms over the Arctic is cold, and an air mass that forms over the ocean is moist.

Air masses move around the globe. As they move, they meet other air masses. A boundary usually forms between different air masses. This boundary is called a front. There are four types of fronts: cold fronts, warm fronts, stationary fronts, and occluded fronts.

- A cold front forms when a cold air mass overtakes a warm air mass. The advancing cold air mass sinks down under the warm air mass. Cold fronts usually produce high winds and heavy precipitation.
- A warm front forms when a warm air mass overtakes a cold air mass. The advancing warm air mass rises up over the cold air mass. Warm fronts usually produce steady rain.
- A stationary front forms when a warm air mass and a cold air mass form a boundary but neither air mass moves. Stationary fronts usually produce clouds and steady precipitation for several days.
- An occluded front forms when a warm air mass is caught between two cold air masses. The cold air masses force the warm air mass to rise. Occluded fronts usually produce cloudy skies and precipitation.

Weather systems are huge areas containing more than one air mass. Each weather system has a center of either low or high air pressure. A weather system with a center of low air pressure is called a cyclone, or a low. A weather system with a center of high air pressure is called an anticyclone, or a high. An area covered by a cyclone tends to have windy, wet weather. An area covered by an anticyclone tends to have calm, sunny weather.

© Pearson Education, Inc., publishing as Pearson Prentice Hall. All rights reserved.

Chapter 24 Weather and Climate

Storms have strong winds and heavy precipitation. Major types of storms include thunderstorms, tornadoes, and hurricanes.

- Thunderstorms are storms that have thunder and lightning. They may also have strong winds and heavy rain or hail. Thunderstorms form when warm moist air rises rapidly in cumulonimbus clouds.
- Tornadoes are small but intense windstorms. They develop in some thunderstorms. A tornado forms when a rapidly spinning column of air touches the ground. A tornado's winds can reach more than 500 kilometers per hour.
- Hurricanes are large storms with winds that blow at least 119 kilometers per hour. They form over warm ocean water.

Ocean waves deposit sediment as they wash over the shore and slow down. Over time, sediment can collect along the shore and form a beach. Longshore drift is the process in which ocean waves gradually move sand along a shore by repeated erosion and deposition. Longshore drift occurs when waves approach the shore at an angle.

24.6 Predicting the Weather

The study of Earth's atmosphere is called meteorology. Meteorologists are scientists who study weather. Meteorologists try to predict what the weather will be in the next few hours or days. They use many technologies to help them predict the weather, including Doppler radar, automated weather stations, weather satellites, and high-speed computers.

Doppler radar is a technology based on the Doppler effect. Radio waves are bounced off particles of precipitation in a moving storm. The returning waves are detected, and the information is used to track the path of the storm. Automated weather stations gather weather data without a human observer being present.

This allows weather stations to be placed in harsh regions. The data are sent to weather centers. Weather satellites also send data to weather centers. Weather satellites collect information about weather from space. They collect data that cannot be gathered from Earth's surface. High-speed computers help meteorologists make sense of all the data from these different sources.

Weather maps show weather patterns of different regions. They typically show temperature, amount of cloud cover, and type of precipitation. Isotherms are lines on weather maps that connect places with the same temperature. Isotherms help meteorologists see temperature patterns. Isobars are lines on weather maps that connect places with the same air pressure. Isobars help meteorologists identify fronts and centers of high and low pressure.

24.7 Climate

Climate is a description of a region's pattern of weather over many years. Scientists classify all the world's climates into six major climate groups: tropical, temperate marine, temperate continental, polar, dry, and highland. Scientists further divide the six major climate groups into many different specific climates. A region's climate depends mostly on its temperature and precipitation.

Several factors affect a region's temperature. Some of the factors are latitude, distance from large bodies of water, and altitude. Latitude is probably the most important factor. Regions farther away from the equator have lower temperatures than regions near the equator. Regions near large bodies of water tend to have less variation in their temperatures from season to season. Regions at high altitudes have lower temperatures than low-altitude regions at the same latitude.

© Pearson Education, Inc., publishing as Pearson Prentice Hall. All rights reserved.

Chapter 24   Weather and Climate

Several factors affect a region's precipitation. Some of the factors are latitude, air pressure, and global winds. Latitude affects precipitation because it affects temperature. Warm air can hold more water and produce more precipitation than cool air. Therefore, tropical regions tend to receive more precipitation than temperate regions. Regions that have almost constant high air pressure receive very little rain. These regions may be deserts. A desert is an extremely dry region receiving less than 25 centimeters of rain per year. Regions that usually receive winds from the ocean generally have more precipitation than regions that usually receive winds from inland.

Climates change over time. Some climate changes are due to natural forces. Ice ages are examples of climate changes due to natural forces. Ice ages were periods when Earth's climate was much colder. During those periods, glaciers covered a large part of Earth's surface. Ice ages have occurred many times in the past. A change in the angle of Earth's axis may have caused the ice ages.

Some climate changes are due to human activities. Global warming is an example of a climate change due to human activities. By burning fossil fuels, humans add a great deal of carbon dioxide to the atmosphere. The added carbon dioxide contributes to the greenhouse effect, causing Earth's temperature to rise. The rising temperature is called global warming. The effects of global warming include rising sea levels and floods in low areas.

© Pearson Education, Inc., publishing as Pearson Prentice Hall. All rights reserved.

Chapter 24 Weather and Climate

Section 24.1 The Atmosphere
(pages 746–751)

This section describes Earth's atmosphere, its composition, and its different layers. It also explains air pressure and the effects of altitude on air pressure.

Reading Strategy (page 746)

Relating Text and Diagrams As you read, refer to Figure 5 and the text to complete the table on the layers of the atmosphere. For more information on this Reading Strategy, see the **Reading and Study Skills** in the **Skills and Reference Handbook** at the end of your textbook.

Layers of the Atmosphere		
Layer	**Altitude Range**	**Temperature Change**
Troposphere		
	12–50 km	
		Temperature decreases as altitude increases.
Thermosphere		

Earth's Protective Layer (page 747)

1. Is the following sentence true or false? The layer of gases that surrounds Earth is called the atmosphere. _____

2. How does the atmosphere make Earth's temperatures suitable for life? _____

3. Name two gases in the atmosphere that are essential for life.

   a. _____   b. _____

Composition of the Atmosphere (page 747)

4. Is the following sentence true or false? The composition of the atmosphere changes every few kilometers as you move away from Earth. _____

5. Earth's atmosphere is a mixture of _____

   _____.

6. What two gases together make up about 99% of Earth's atmosphere? a. _____   b. _____

7. Is the following sentence true or false? Both water droplets and solid particles are suspended in the atmosphere. _____

Air Pressure (page 748)

8. What is air pressure? _____

   _____

9. As altitude increases, air pressure and density _____.

© Pearson Education, Inc., publishing as Pearson Prentice Hall. All rights reserved.

Chapter 24   Weather and Climate

10. Circle the letter of the instrument used to measure air pressure.

    a. a thermometer

    b. a barometer

    c. a psychrometer

    d. Doppler radar

Layers of the Atmosphere (pages 749–751)

11. Scientists divide the atmosphere into layers based on variations in

    _____.

12. List the four layers of the atmosphere.

    a. _____   b. _____

    c. _____   d. _____

13. Is the following sentence true or false? Weather is the average condition of the atmosphere in a particular place over a period of many years. _____

14. What is the ozone layer? _____

    _____

15. How is ozone formed? _____

16. Is the following sentence true or false? Infrared radiation in sunlight is absorbed by ozone before it reaches Earth.

    _____

17. The layer above the stratosphere is the _____.

18. Is the following sentence true or false? The temperature of the outer thermosphere is quite high. _____

Match the layer of the atmosphere with a characteristic that would best describe it.

	Layer of the Atmosphere	Characteristic
_____	19. troposphere	a. Contains the ozone layer
_____	20. stratosphere	b. The outermost layer of the atmosphere
_____	21. mesosphere	c. The layer where most meteoroids burn up
_____	22. thermosphere	d. The layer where most weather occurs

23. What is the ionosphere? _____

    _____

24. When charged particles from the sun are attracted to Earth's magnetic poles, a(n) _____ may appear.

© Pearson Education, Inc., publishing as Pearson Prentice Hall. All rights reserved.

Chapter 24   Weather and Climate

Section 24.2 The Sun and the Seasons
(pages 752–754)

This section describes the two major ways Earth moves. It also explains what causes the seasons.

Reading Strategy (page 752)

Building Vocabulary Copy the table on a separate sheet of paper. As you read, complete it by defining each vocabulary term from the section. For more information on this Reading Strategy, see the **Reading and Study Skills** in the **Skills and Reference Handbook** at the end of your textbook.

Vocabulary Term	Definition
Rotation	
Revolution	

1. What are the two major ways Earth moves?

   a. _____

   b. _____

2. The spinning of Earth on its axis, called _____, causes day and night.

3. Is the following sentence true or false? It takes Earth one year to complete one rotation. _____

4. The movement of one body in space around another is called

   _____.

5. Earth completes a full revolution around the sun in

   _____.

6. The path Earth takes around the sun is called its _____.

Earth's Latitude Zones (pages 752–753)

7. What is latitude? _____

8. Circle the letter that identifies the latitude of the North Pole.

   a. 70° north

   b. 80° south

   c. 90° north

   d. 100° south

© Pearson Education, Inc., publishing as Pearson Prentice Hall. All rights reserved.

Chapter 24   Weather and Climate

9. The part of Earth that receives the most direct sunlight is near the _____.

10. Is the following sentence true or false? Scientists use lines of latitude to mark out three different types of regions on Earth. _____

Match each type of region to its latitude.

Region	Latitude
_____ **11.** temperate zone	a. Falls between latitudes of 23.5° south and 23.5° north
_____ **12.** tropic zone	
_____ **13.** polar zone	b. From 66.5° north to the North Pole, and 66.5° south to the South Pole
	c. From 23.5° north to 66.5° north, and 23.5° south to 66.5° south

The Seasons (pages 753–754)

14. In which type of region is most of the United States located?
_____

15. Is the following sentence true or false? Earth's axis of rotation is tilted at an angle of about 25.3°. _____

16. The north end of Earth's axis points to _____.

17. The _____ are caused by the tilt of Earth's axis as it moves around the sun.

18. Circle the letter of each sentence that is true about a solstice.

    a. A solstice occurs when the sun is directly above the North Pole.

    b. A solstice occurs when the sun is directly above the South Pole.

    c. A solstice occurs when the sun is directly above the latitude 23.5° north or 23.5° south.

    d. A solstice occurs when the sun is directly above the latitude 66.5° north or 66.5° south.

19. Is the following sentence true or false? When the winter solstice begins in the Northern Hemisphere, the Southern Hemisphere is tilted toward the sun. _____

20. Is the following sentence true or false? Earth is closer to the sun when it is summer than when it is winter in the Northern Hemisphere. _____

21. Circle the letter that identifies the season that begins with the vernal equinox.

    a. summer   b. spring

    c. autumn   d. winter

© Pearson Education, Inc., publishing as Pearson Prentice Hall. All rights reserved.

Chapter 24   Weather and Climate

Section 24.3 Solar Energy and Winds
(pages 755–759)

This section explains what happens to solar energy that reaches Earth's atmosphere and how it is transferred within the troposphere. It also describes the different winds on Earth and what causes them.

Reading Strategy (page 755)

Comparing and Contrasting After you read, complete the table to compare and contrast sea and land breezes. For more information on this Reading Strategy, see the **Reading and Study Skills** in the **Skills and Reference Handbook** at the end of your textbook.

Sea and Land Breezes		
	Day or Night?	**Direction of Air Movement**
Sea breeze		
Land breeze		

Energy in the Atmosphere (page 755)

1. What happens to the solar energy that reaches Earth's atmosphere?

   a. _____   b. _____

   c. _____

2. Is the following sentence true or false? The atmosphere is heated mainly by energy that is reradiated by Earth's surface. _____

3. The process where certain gases in the atmosphere radiate absorbed energy back to Earth's surface, warming the lower atmosphere, is called the _____.

4. Circle the letter of each way energy can be transferred within the troposphere.

   a. convection   b. radiation

   c. precipitation   d. conduction

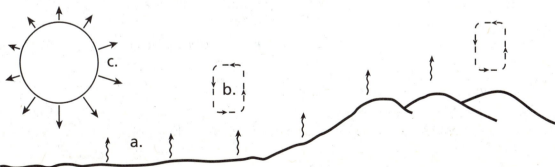

5. Name the type of energy transfer in the troposphere that each type of arrow on the diagram represents.

   a. _____   b. _____   c. _____

© Pearson Education, Inc., publishing as Pearson Prentice Hall. All rights reserved.

Name _____ Class _____ Date _____

Chapter 24   Weather and Climate

6. Is the following sentence true or false? The air that directly contacts Earth's surface is heated by conduction. _____

7. Heat is circulated through the troposphere by _____.

Wind (page 757)

8. Is the following sentence true or false? Air flows from areas of high pressure to areas of low pressure. _____

9. What causes winds? _____

10. Is the following sentence true or false? The equal heating of Earth's surface causes differences in air pressure. _____

11. What happens to air as it warms, expands, and becomes less dense? _____

Local Winds (page 757)

12. Is the following sentence true or false? A local wind blows over a long distance. _____

13. Circle the letter of each example of a local wind.

   a. a sea breeze   b. a trade wind

   c. a jet stream   d. a land breeze

14. Would you expect to find a land breeze on the beach during the day or during the night? _____

Global Winds (pages 758–759)

15. Is the following sentence true or false? Winds that blow over short distances from a specific direction are global winds. _____

16. Global winds move in a series of circulating air patterns called _____.

Match the global winds to their locations.

Global Winds	Location
_____ **17.** polar easterlies	a. Just north and south of the equator
_____ **18.** tradewinds	b. Between 30° and 60° latitude in both hemispheres
_____ **19.** westerlies	c. From 60° latitude to the poles in both hemispheres

20. The curving effect that Earth's rotation has on global winds is called the _____.

21. A wind system characterized by seasonal reversals of direction is called a(n) _____.

22. Is the following sentence true or false? A jet-stream is a belt of high-speed wind in the upper troposphere. _____

© Pearson Education, Inc., publishing as Pearson Prentice Hall. All rights reserved.

Chapter 24   Weather and Climate

Section 24.4 Water in the Atmosphere
(pages 760–764)

This section discusses the water in the atmosphere. It explains the effect water has on processes in the atmosphere such as cloud formation and precipitation.

Reading Strategy (page 760)

Sequencing As you read, complete the flowchart to show how a cloud forms. For more information on this Reading Strategy, see the **Reading and Study Skills** in the **Skills and Reference Handbook** at the end of your textbook.

Cloud Formation

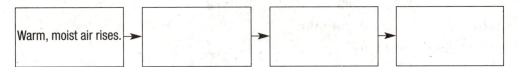

Warm, moist air rises.

Humidity (pages 760–761)

1. The amount of _____ in the air is called humidity.

2. Is the following sentence true or false? The ratio of the amount of water vapor in the air to the amount of water vapor the air can hold at that temperature is relative humidity. _____

3. What is the dew point? _____

4. Name what water vapor may condense into.

   a. _____   b. _____

   c. _____   d. _____

5. When water vapor in air changes directly from a gas to a solid, _____ forms.

Cloud Formation (page 761)

6. What is a cloud? _____

   _____

7. Is the following sentence true or false? Clouds are formed when cool, dry air rises and water vapor condenses. _____

8. Clouds may form when moist air rises and the temperature cools below the _____.

9. Besides water vapor, what must be present for a cloud to form?

   _____

Classifying Clouds (pages 762–763)

10. Scientists classify clouds based on their form and

    _____.

© Pearson Education, Inc., publishing as Pearson Prentice Hall. All rights reserved.

11. What are the three basic cloud forms?

a. _____   b. _____   c. _____

12. A cloud that is near or touching the ground is called _____.

13. Is the following sentence true or false? Flat layers of clouds that cover much of the sky are stratus clouds. _____

14. The letters _____ are added to a cloud's name to mean that the cloud produces precipitation.

15. Is the following sentence true or false? Altostratus clouds are low-level clouds similar to fog. _____

16. Circle the letter of the cloud form that looks like puffy, white clouds with flat bottoms.

a. fog   b. stratus

c. altostratus   d. cumulus

17. What do cirrus clouds look like? _____

_____

18. Circle the letter of each type of cloud you often see on sunny days.

a. cumulonimbus   b. cumulus

c. altostratus   d. cirrus

Match each cloud to its description.

Cloud	Description
_____ **19.** cumulus	a. Thin, high-altitude clouds that generally produce no rain
_____ **20.** cirrus	b. "Fair-weather clouds" that look like piles of cotton balls
_____ **21.** altostratus	c. Clouds that produce heavy precipitation and are sometimes called thunderheads
_____ **22.** cumulonimbus	d. Middle-level clouds that can produce light rain

Forms of Precipitation (page 764)

23. What are the five most common types of precipitation?

a. _____   b. _____

c. _____   d. _____

e. _____

24. Is the following sentence true or false? Snow is precipitation in the form of ice crystals. _____

25. How does hail form? _____

_____

26. Rain that freezes as it falls is called _____.

© Pearson Education, Inc., publishing as Pearson Prentice Hall. All rights reserved.

Name _____ Class _____ Date _____

Chapter 24 Weather and Climate

Section 24.5 Weather Patterns
(pages 765–771)

This section describes the weather patterns on Earth. It explains how air masses form and create fronts, low and high-pressure systems, and storms.

Reading Strategy (page 765)

Outlining Complete the outline with information from the section. Use the green headings as the main topics and the blue headings as subtopics. As you read, add supporting details to the subheadings. For more information on this Reading Strategy, see the **Reading and Study Skills** in the **Skills and Reference Handbook** at the end of your textbook.

Weather Patterns
I. Air Masses
II. Fronts
A. Cold fronts
B.
C.
D.

Air Masses (pages 765–766)

1. A large body of air that has fairly uniform physical properties such as temperature and moisture content at any given altitude is a(n) _____.

2. When do air masses form? _____

_____

Match the classifications of air masses to where they form.

Classification of Air Mass	Where They Form
_____ 3. maritime	a. Originates where it is very warm
_____ 4. tropical	b. Forms over water transpiration
_____ 5. polar	c. Forms over land
_____ 6. continental	d. Originates where it is very cold

Fronts (pages 767–768)

7. When a continental polar air mass collides with a maritime tropical air mass, a(n) _____ forms.

8. Circle the letters of the weather conditions often associated with cold fronts.

    a. large amounts of precipitation   b. clear skies

    c. severe thunderstorms   d. strong winds

© Pearson Education, Inc., publishing as Pearson Prentice Hall. All rights reserved.

Chapter 24   Weather and Climate

Match each front to the way it forms.

Front	How It Forms
_____ **9.** cold front	**a.** Occurs when a warm air mass is caught between two cooler air masses
_____ **10.** warm front	
_____ **11.** stationary front	**b.** Occurs when a warm air mass overtakes a cold air mass
_____ **12.** occluded front	
	c. Occurs when a cold air mass overtakes a warm air mass
	d. Occurs when two unlike air masses have formed a boundary and neither is moving

Low- and High-Pressure Systems (page 769)

13. A weather system around a center of low pressure is called a(n) _____.

14. Circle the letter of each weather condition associated with cyclones.

    a. precipitation   b. clouds

    c. stormy weather   d. clear skies

15. Is the following sentence true or false? An anticyclone is a weather system with a swirling center of low pressure. _____

16. What kind of weather conditions are associated with an anticyclone?

_____

_____

Storms (pages 770–771)

17. Is the following sentence true or false? A thunderstorm is a small weather system with thunder and lightning. _____

18. Circle the letter of each characteristic of a thunderstorm.

    a. strong winds and heavy rain or hail

    b. only occurs on cool days

    c. forms when columns of air rise within a cumulonimbus cloud

    d. thunder and lightning

19. Is the following sentence true or false? A tornado is a small, intense windstorm in the shape of a rotating column that touches the ground. _____

20. How does a tornado form? _____

_____

21. A hurricane is a large tropical _____ with winds of at least 119 kilometers per hour.

© Pearson Education, Inc., publishing as Pearson Prentice Hall. All rights reserved.

Chapter 24   Weather and Climate

Section 24.6 Predicting the Weather
(pages 774–777)

This section explains some of the technology meteorologists use to predict the weather. It also explains some of the symbols found on weather maps.

Reading Strategy (page 774)

Identifying the Main Idea As you read the text, write the main idea for each heading of this section in the table. For more information on this Reading Strategy, see the **Reading and Study Skills** in the **Skills and Reference Handbook** at the end of your textbook.

Heading	Main Idea
Weather forecasting	
Weather maps	

Weather Forecasting (pages 774–776)

1. What is meteorology? _____

2. Is the following sentence true or false? Scientists who study weather are called weatherologists. _____

3. What are four technologies that help meteorologists predict the weather?

   a. _____   b. _____

   c. _____   d. _____

4. With Doppler radar, _____ waves are bounced off particles of precipitation in moving storms.

5. Scientists can calculate a storm's _____ by calculating how much the frequency of Doppler radar waves changes.

6. The types of weather data that can be collected by a typical weather station include _____.

7. Meteorologists use high-speed computers to analyze data and create short- and long-term _____.

8. Meteorologists can accurately forecast the movement of large weather systems for a period of _____ days.

9. Why is it difficult for meteorologists to predict the weather beyond a week? _____

   _____

Weather Maps (pages 776–777)

10. What does a weather map show? _____

   _____

© Pearson Education, Inc., publishing as Pearson Prentice Hall. All rights reserved.

Chapter 24   Weather and Climate

11. Circle the letter of each type of information that a typical weather map shows.

   a. temperatures   b. mountain altitudes

   c. symbols for cloud cover   d. areas of precipitation

12. Is the following sentence true or false? Weather maps often
    include symbols for fronts and areas of high and low pressure.

    _____

Look at the weather map and the key to answer questions 13–15.

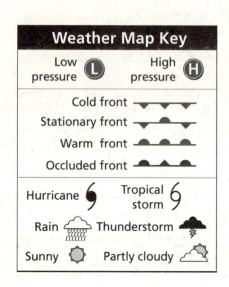

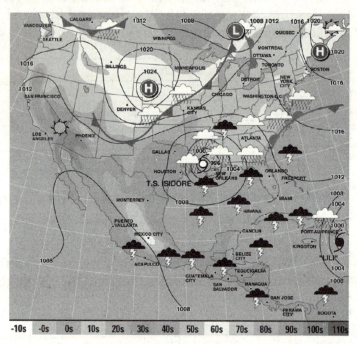

13. What type of front is shown near Calgary, Canada?

    _____

14. What are the weather conditions in Los Angeles?

    _____

15. What is the highest air pressure shown on the map?

    _____

16. A line on a map that connects points of equal air temperatures is
    called a(n) _____.

17. How is a map with isotherms helpful to meteorologists? _____

    _____

18. Is the following sentence true or false? An isobar is a line that connects points of
    unequal air pressure. _____

19. Circle the letter of each type of weather information that isobars
    help meteorologists to identify.

    a. areas of cloud cover   b. centers of low-pressure systems

    c. locations of fronts   d. centers of high-pressure systems

© Pearson Education, Inc., publishing as Pearson Prentice Hall. All rights reserved.

Chapter 24   Weather and Climate

Section 24.7 Climate
(pages 778–782)

This section describes climate and climate changes. It also describes factors that affect the patterns of temperature and precipitation of a region.

Reading Strategy (page 778)

Building Vocabulary As you read, complete the concept map with terms from this section. For more information on this Reading Strategy, see the **Reading and Study Skills** in the **Skills and Reference Handbook** at the end of your textbook.

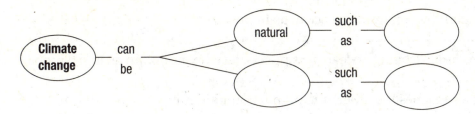

1. What is climate? _____

Classifying Climates (pages 778–779)

2. What are the six major climate groups?

   a. _____   b. _____

   c. _____   d. _____

   e. _____   f. _____

3. Circle the letters of the two main factors that determine a region's climate.

   a. elevation   b. temperature

   c. precipitation   d. winds

Factors Affecting Temperature (pages 779–780)

4. What are four factors that affect a region's temperature?

   a. _____   b. _____

   c. _____   d. _____

5. What factors influence the temperature of coastal regions? _____

   _____

6. Is the following sentence true or false? As altitude increases, temperature generally increases. _____

Factors Affecting Precipitation (page 780)

7. Circle the letter of each factor that can affect a region's precipitation.

   a. the existence of a mountain barrier   b. distribution of air pressure systems

   c. distribution of global winds   d. latitude

8. Precipitation is generally higher near the _____ than the poles.

© Pearson Education, Inc., publishing as Pearson Prentice Hall. All rights reserved.

Chapter 24   Weather and Climate

Use the diagram below to answer the questions that follow.

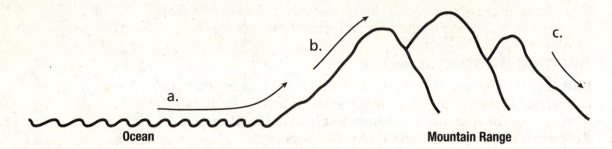

9. What type of air blows in from the ocean as in position a?
   _____

10. What happens as air from the ocean gets pushed up the mountain as in position b?
    _____

11. What type of air reaches the other side of the mountain range as in position c?
    _____

Natural Climate Change (page 781)

12. Is the following sentence true or false? The climate of a region never changes. _____

13. Circle the letters of two factors that may contribute to changes in climate.

    a. human activities   b. animal activities

    c. meteorologists   d. natural forces

14. Glaciers covered a portion of Earth's surface and temperatures were colder than usual during _____.

15. Is the following sentence true or false? El Niño is the periodic cooling of water in the central and eastern Atlantic Ocean.
    _____

Global Warming (page 782)

16. The addition of _____ and certain other gases to the atmosphere may cause global warming.

17. The _____ effect occurs when certain gases absorb radiation from Earth's surface and then radiate energy back toward the surface.

18. The process called _____ refers to an increase in the worldwide temperature of the lower atmosphere.

19. Circle the letters that identify some possible strategies to limit the effects of global warming.

    a. increasing use of fossil fuels

    b. increasing use of solar and geothermal energy

    c. increasing use of nuclear energy

    d. increasing energy conservation efforts

© Pearson Education, Inc., publishing as Pearson Prentice Hall. All rights reserved.

Name _____ Class _____ Date _____

Chapter 24   Weather and Climate

WordWise

Complete the sentences by using one of the scrambled vocabulary terms from Chapter 24.

mertpoheas	ria superers	prehopotres
trainoot	quieoxn	hoeusegren tefefc
ase zebere	rilocosi ceteff	wed tinpo
rai sams	dunterh	mosthrei
emailtc		

The lower-most layer of the atmosphere is called the
_____.

A description of the pattern of weather over many years in a place
or region is its _____.

A time when neither hemisphere is tilted toward the sun and lengths
of daylight and sunlight are approximately equal is called a(n)
_____.

A large body of air that has fairly uniform physical properties such
as temperature and moisture content at any given altitude is a(n)
_____.

The process by which gases in the atmosphere radiate absorbed
energy back to Earth's surface, warming the atmosphere is known
as the _____.

The layer of gases that surrounds Earth is called the _____.

The spinning of Earth on its axis is called its _____.

A local wind that blows from sea to land is a(n) _____.

The curving effect that Earth's rotation has on all free-moving objects
is the _____.

A line on a map that connects points of equal air temperature is called
a(n) _____ .

The force exerted by the weight of a column of air on a surface
is called _____.

The temperature at which air becomes saturated is its _____.

The sound produced by rapidly expanding air along the path of a
lightning discharge is called _____.

© Pearson Education, Inc., publishing as Pearson Prentice Hall. All rights reserved.

Chapter 24   Weather and Climate

Calculating Volume of Gases

About 78% of the volume of dry air is composed of nitrogen. About how much nitrogen would there be in a 500 m³ volume of dry air?

Math Skill: Percents and Decimals

You may want to read more about this **Math Skill** in the **Skills and Reference Handbook** at the end of your textbook.

1. Read and Understand

What information are you given in the problem?

Dry air = 78% nitrogen

2. Plan and Solve

What unknown are you trying to calculate?

500 m³ volume of dry air contains ___?___ m³ of nitrogen

Convert the percent of nitrogen in dry air (78%) to a decimal.

Move the decimal point in 78% two places to the left and drop the percent sign. = 0.78

To find the amount of nitrogen in a 500 m³ volume of dry air, multiply 500 by the decimal conversion of 78%. $0.78 \times 500 \text{ m}^3 = 390 \text{ m}^3$

About how much nitrogen will a 500 m³ volume of dry air have?

500 m³ volume of dry air contains about 390 m³ nitrogen

3. Look Back and Check

To check your answer, find what percent of 500 m³ your answer is. To do this, first divide your answer by 500.

$$\frac{390 \text{ m}^3}{500 \text{ m}^3} = 0.78$$

Then, convert the decimal to a percent by moving the decimal point two places to the right and placing a percent symbol after the number. If the percent is the same as the percentage of nitrogen found in dry air, your answer is correct.   0.78 becomes 78%

Math Practice

On a separate sheet of paper, solve the following problems.

1. Helium makes up 0.00052% of dry air. About how much helium would there be in a 10,000 m³ volume of dry air?

2. A 500 m³ volume of dry air contains 0.185 m³ of carbon dioxide. What percent of this sample of air is made up of carbon dioxide?

3. Oxygen makes up 20.946% of dry air. Argon makes up 0.934% of dry air. About much more oxygen than argon would you find in a 1000-m³ volume of dry air?

© Pearson Education, Inc., publishing as Pearson Prentice Hall. All rights reserved.

Chapter 25   The Solar System

Summary

25.1 Exploring the Solar System

There have been two major models of the solar system: the geocentric model and the heliocentric model. In the geocentric model, Earth is in the center and the sun and the other planets circle around it. Ptolemy developed a complex version of this model around 140 A.D. The geocentric model was widely accepted until the early 1500s. In the heliocentric model, the sun is in the center and all the planets circle around it. Nicolaus Copernicus supported this model in the early 1500s. Scientists later proved that the heliocentric model is correct.

In 1600, Johannes Kepler discovered that the orbits of planets are ellipses, not circles. An ellipse has an oval shape. Isaac Newton discovered that the forces of gravity and inertia keep the planets in orbit. Inertia alone would cause the planets to fly into space. Gravity alone would cause them to fall into the sun. The two forces together keep the planets orbiting around the sun.

The solar system consists of the sun, the planets, their moons, and some smaller objects. Only the sun produces its own light. We can see planets and moons because they reflect sunlight. The first four planets are Mercury, Venus, Earth, and Mars. They are closest to the sun. The outer planets are Jupiter, Saturn, Uranus, Neptune, and Pluto. They are much farther from the sun. Except for Mercury and Venus, all the planets have moons. A moon is a small natural body that revolves around a planet.

Distances between objects in space are very great. As a result, astronomers often use astronomical units to measure distances. One astronomical unit (AU) equals the distance from Earth to the sun, or about 150 million kilometers.

Modern technology has allowed scientists to explore the solar system in new ways. Starting in the 1960s, astronauts could use spacecraft to orbit Earth and visit the moon in order to learn about the solar system. Today, scientists mainly use space probes and telescopes to learn about the solar system. Space probes are spacecraft without people on board. The probes carry scientific instruments and cameras into space and send data back to Earth. Space probes have photographed most of the planets and moons of the solar system. Telescopes, such as the Hubble Space Telescope, have provided new views of the solar system.

25.2 The Earth-Moon System

The moon is Earth's nearest neighbor in space. The moon is much smaller than Earth. It also has much less mass. As a result, the force of gravity on the moon is far less than the force of gravity on Earth. The moon's gravity is too weak even to hold onto gas molecules. Therefore, the moon has no atmosphere. Without an atmosphere, the moon's surface temperature varies greatly. When the surface is sunny, it is extremely hot. When the surface is dark, it is extremely cold.

The major features on the surface of the moon are maria, highlands, and craters.

- Maria are low, flat plains. They were formed by ancient volcanoes.
- Highlands are rough, mountainous regions. They cover most of the moon's surface.
- Craters are round dents in the surface caused by meteoroids hitting the moon. Meteoroids are chunks of rock that move through the solar system.

Scientists think that the moon formed from Earth about 4.6 billion years ago. They think that a huge object slammed

© Pearson Education, Inc., publishing as Pearson Prentice Hall. All rights reserved.

into Earth and broke off chunks of the planet. The chunks gradually came together to form the moon.

Recall that the moon does not produce its own light. You can see the moon because it reflects light from the sun. The different shapes of the moon visible from Earth are called phases. The moon's phases are caused by changes in the relative positions of the moon, Earth, and sun. The moon revolves around Earth.

Sunlight illuminates half of the moon. The phase of the moon depends on how much of the sunlit portion of the moon is facing Earth. During a full moon phase, you can see the entire sunlit half, so the moon looks like a circle. During other phases, you can see less of the sunlit half, so the moon takes different shapes, such as a half circle or a crescent.

The moon takes almost 30 days to complete one full revolution around Earth. In this time, the moon goes through a full cycle of phases.

An eclipse occurs when an object in space, such as the moon, casts a shadow on another object in space, such as Earth. Eclipses in the Earth-moon system can occur only when the sun, moon, and Earth are in a straight line. There are two different types of eclipses in the Earth-moon system: solar eclipses and lunar eclipses.

- A solar eclipse occurs when the moon casts a shadow on Earth. All or part of the sun disappears for a short time as the moon's shadow passes over Earth.
- A lunar eclipse occurs when Earth casts a shadow on the moon. All or part of the moon disappears for a short time as the moon passes through Earth's shadow.

Tides are the regular rise and fall of ocean waters. Tides are caused mainly by differences in the moon's gravitational pull on Earth. The moon's gravity affects the liquid oceans more than it does solid

Earth. The pull of the moon causes the oceans to bulge at places closest to and farthest from the moon. High tides occur when an area moves through either of these two bulges. Low tides occur halfway between high tides. Most coastal areas have two high tides and two low tides each day. The sun's gravity also influences the tides. However, the sun's gravity has less influence than the moon's gravity, because the sun is so much farther away from Earth.

25.3 The Inner Solar System

Mercury, Venus, Earth, and Mars are called the terrestrial planets. All the terrestrial planets are similar in structure to Earth. All are relatively small and dense, and all have rocky surfaces. All of them also have a crust, mantle, and iron core. The terrestrial planets are much warmer on average than the outer planets. This is because they are closer to the sun. Unlike the outer planets, the terrestrial planets have few, if any, moons.

Mercury is the smallest planet and the planet closest to the sun. Mercury also has the shortest year of any planet. Mercury is a dense planet with a very large iron core. Its surface has many craters. Mercury is geologically dead. This means that volcanism and other geological forces no longer act on the planet. Mercury has no water and virtually no atmosphere. Without an atmosphere, Mercury's surface temperature ranges between extremely hot and extremely cold. Mercury also has no moons.

Venus is called the "evening star" or the "morning star." Except for the moon, Venus is the brightest object in Earth's night sky. Venus is almost as large as Earth. It has a very thick atmosphere, which contains mostly carbon dioxide. The carbon dioxide absorbs heat and raises the planet's temperature. Venus is

© Pearson Education, Inc., publishing as Pearson Prentice Hall. All rights reserved.

Chapter 25   The Solar System

too hot to have liquid water on its surface. The atmosphere of Venus also contains sulfur, probably from volcanoes. Some volcanoes may still be active. Venus has no moons.

Earth is unique among the terrestrial planets in several ways. One of the most important ways is that liquid water can exist on Earth's surface. Earth has a suitable atmosphere and temperature range for water to remain in liquid form. Water makes it possible for life to survive on Earth. Living things use carbon dioxide. As a result, Earth's atmosphere contains relatively little carbon dioxide. Without much carbon dioxide, the atmosphere does not overheat the planet. Water on Earth also causes erosion. This has shaped Earth's land surface in many ways. Earth has one moon.

Mars is the planet that is most like Earth. Mars looks red because of rusty iron in the rocks on the surface. The surface of Mars also has huge volcanoes, but they are no longer active. Mars has a very thin atmosphere, which contains mostly carbon dioxide. It is very cold on Mars because of the thin atmosphere and relatively great distance from the sun. Mars may have had liquid water on its surface at one time. It still has water frozen in ice caps at the poles. Like Earth, Mars has a tilted axis. This causes Mars to have seasons. The changing seasons cause dust storms on Mars.

Beyond Mars is a belt of asteroids that orbit the sun. Asteroids are small, rocky bodies. They range in diameter from about 1 kilometer to 500 kilometers. Scientists think that asteroids are parts of the early solar system that never came together to form a planet.

25.4 The Outer Solar System

The outer solar system consists of the rest of the planets: Jupiter, Saturn, Uranus, Neptune, and Pluto. All of these planets, except Pluto, are called gas giants. The gas giants are very different

from the terrestrial planets. The gas giants are much colder because they are farther from the sun. They are also much larger and more massive. In addition, the gas giants have a different composition from terrestrial planets. The gas giants consist mainly of liquid hydrogen and helium, with small dense cores of metal and rock. They do not have solid surfaces. Also unlike the terrestrial planets, the gas giants have many moons.

Jupiter is the largest and most massive planet in the solar system. Its surface is covered with colorful clouds. Huge storms on Jupiter's surface may last for hundreds of years. Jupiter has more than 50 moons.

Saturn is the second-largest planet in the solar system. It is best known for its rings. The rings are made of particles of ice and rock. Most of the particles are the size of snowballs. Saturn has the thickest atmosphere in the solar system. It contains mostly hydrogen and helium. Saturn has more than 30 moons.

Uranus is the third-largest planet in the solar system. The atmosphere of Uranus also contains mostly hydrogen and helium, but it contains some methane gas as well. The methane gas makes Uranus look blue-green from Earth. Uranus has rings, but they are not as visible as Saturn's. The most unusual characteristic of Uranus is its tilt. Its axis is tilted nearly into the plane of the planet's orbit. Uranus has at least 20 moons.

Neptune is slightly smaller than Uranus. It has clearly visible clouds in its atmosphere. The clouds are made of methane ice crystals. The methane crystals make Neptune look blue from Earth. Neptune has huge storms in its atmosphere. It also has rings, similar to the rings of Uranus. Neptune has at least eight moons.

Pluto is the ninth planet. Pluto is much smaller and denser than the other outer planets. Pluto's orbit is also

© Pearson Education, Inc., publishing as Pearson Prentice Hall. All rights reserved.

unusual. It is very elliptical. Sometimes Pluto is closer to the sun than Neptune. At other times, Pluto is much farther from the sun than Neptune. Like Uranus, Pluto has a very tilted axis. Pluto has only one moon.

In addition to the planets and their moons, other objects move through the solar system. These objects include comets and meteoroids.

- A comet is a piece of ice and rock. Some of the comet vaporizes when the comet passes close to the sun. The gas and dust from the comet stream out behind the comet to form a tail.
- A meteoroid is a piece of rock that travels through the solar system. Most meteoroids are no bigger than grains of sand. Some meteoroids are as old as the solar system itself.

The solar system does not end with Pluto. Beyond Pluto thousands of pieces of ice, dust, and rock orbit the sun in a region called the Kuiper belt. Beyond the Kuiper belt is a huge area of comets called the Oort Cloud. These comets are thought to circle the solar system.

25.5 The Origin of the Solar System

Scientists have developed a theory about how the solar system formed. It is called the nebular theory. It is accepted by most astronomers.

The nebular theory states that the solar system formed from a rotating cloud of dust and gas, called a nebula.

The dust and gas may have come from previous stars. The explosion of a nearby star may have started the nebula rotating. The gravitational attraction among particles made the nebula shrink. As the nebula got smaller, it rotated faster. Eventually, the nebula began to flatten out like a disk. The disk was thicker in the middle than at the edges. The sun developed from the middle part of the disk. The sun formed when heat and pressure increased and began to cause nuclear reactions. The planets developed from the edge of the disk. The planets gradually formed as particles of dust and gas collided and combined into larger objects.

The nebular theory also helps explain some of the differences between the terrestrial planets and the gas giants. When the solar system formed, it was very hot near the sun. Rock-forming materials such as iron were able to condense at high temperatures. These materials formed the terrestrial planets. In the outer solar system, it was much cooler. It was cool enough for ice-forming materials such as methane and ammonia to condense. Therefore, these materials formed the gas giants. Much more material was available for planet formation in the outer solar system. This allowed the gas giants to become much larger than the terrestrial planets. Large size gave the gas giants strong gravity. The gravity attracted hydrogen and helium gas from space to form the atmospheres of the gas giants.

© Pearson Education, Inc., publishing as Pearson Prentice Hall. All rights reserved.

Chapter 25   The Solar System

Section 25.1 Exploring the Solar System
(pages 790–794)

This section explores early models of our solar system. It describes the components of the solar system and scientific exploration of the solar system.

Reading Strategy (page 790)

Comparing and Contrasting After you read, compare the geocentric and heliocentric systems by completing the table below. For more information on this Reading Strategy, see the **Reading and Study Skills** in the **Skills and Reference Handbook** at the end of your textbook.

Solar System Models			
	Location of Earth	**Location of Sun**	**Developer(s) of Theory**
Geocentric System	Center of universe		
Heliocentric System			Aristarchus, Copernicus

Models of the Solar System (pages 790–791)

1. Is the following sentence true or false? In the Northern Hemisphere, the stars appear to circle around the North Star.
   _____

2. Name the five planets besides Earth that ancient observers could see with the unaided eye.

   a. _____   b. _____

   c. _____   d. _____

   e. _____

3. Many ancient Greeks thought _____ was the center of the universe.

4. Circle the letter of each sentence that is true about a geocentric model.

   a. Earth is stationary at the center.

   b. Objects in the sky move around Earth.

   c. The sun is the center of the solar system.

   d. The planets revolve around the sun.

5. Name the center of the solar system in a heliocentric model.
   _____

6. Is the following sentence true or false? The first heliocentric model was widely accepted by most ancient Greeks. _____

© Pearson Education, Inc., publishing as Pearson Prentice Hall. All rights reserved.

Chapter 25   The Solar System

7. Is the following sentence true or false? The sun, moon, and stars appear to move because the Earth is rotating on its axis. _____

Planetary Orbits (page 792)

8. Planets move around the sun in orbits that are in the shape of a(n) _____.

9. The plane containing Earth's orbit is called the _____.

10. Name the two factors that combine to keep the planets in orbit around the sun. _____

    _____

Components of the Solar System (pages 792–793)

11. Circle the letters that identify objects in our solar system.

    a. moons of the planets   b. nine planets

    c. the sun   d. the stars other than the sun

12. Name three planets that were identified after the invention of the telescope in the early 1600s.

    a. _____ b. _____ c. _____

13. Is the following sentence true or false? All of the planets have moons. _____

14. Unlike the sun, planets and moons do not produce their own _____.

15. Is the following sentence true or false? The sun's mass is smaller than the combined mass of the rest of the solar system. _____

Exploring the Solar System (pages 793–794)

16. Name three examples of types of modern technology that scientists use to explore the solar system.

    a. _____ b. _____ c. _____

17. Circle the letter that identifies the first person to walk on the moon.

    a. Alan Shepard   b. Yuri Gagarin

    c. Chuck Yeager   d. Neil Armstrong

18. An unpiloted vehicle that sends data back to Earth is called a(n) _____.

19. Describe the space shuttle. _____

    _____

20. Is the following sentence true or false? The International Space Station is a permanent laboratory designed for research in space. _____

© Pearson Education, Inc., publishing as Pearson Prentice Hall. All rights reserved.

Chapter 25   The Solar System

Section 25.2 The Earth-Moon System
(pages 796–801)

This section describes Earth's moon, how it was formed, and its phases. It also explains solar and lunar eclipses and tides on Earth.

Reading Strategy (page 796)

Building Vocabulary As you read, complete the concept map with terms from this section. Make similar concept maps for eclipses and tides. For more information on this Reading Strategy, see the **Reading and Study Skills** in the **Skills and Reference Handbook** at the end of your textbook.

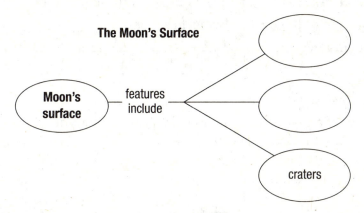

The Moon's Surface

1. What is the force of gravity on the moon's surface compared to the force of gravity on Earth's surface? _____
_____

Earth's Moon (pages 796–797)

2. How does the moon's lack of an atmosphere affect its temperatures? _____
_____

3. Evidence of ice on the moon has been found near the moon's _____.

Surface Features (page 797)

4. Circle the letter of each major surface feature of the moon.

    a. highlands   b. maria

    c. seas   d. craters

Match each lunar surface feature with its correct description.

Description	Surface Feature
_____ 5. A round depression caused by a meteoroid	a. maria
_____ 6. Low, flat plains formed by ancient lava flows	b. crater
_____ 7. A rough, mountainous region	c. highland

© Pearson Education, Inc., publishing as Pearson Prentice Hall. All rights reserved.

Chapter 25   The Solar System

Formation of the Moon (page 798)

8. Explain the leading hypothesis of how the moon formed. _____
_____

Phases of the Moon (pages 798–799)

9. Circle the letter of each sentence that is true about phases of the moon.

   a. The moon's phases change according to an irregular cycle.

   b. Phases are the different shapes of the moon visible from Earth.

   c. Phases are caused by changes in the relative positions of the moon, sun, and Earth as the moon revolves around Earth.

   d. The sunlit portion of the moon always faces Earth.

10. When does a full moon occur? _____
_____

Eclipses (pages 799–800)

11. When the shadow of a planet or moon falls on another body in space, a(n) _____ occurs.

Solar Eclipse

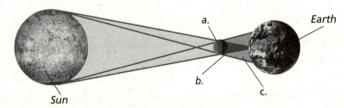

12. Look at the diagram showing a solar eclipse and label the parts.

   a. _____   b. _____   c. _____

13. Circle the letter of each sentence that is true about a lunar eclipse.

   a. A lunar eclipse occurs when Earth casts a shadow on the moon.

   b. A lunar eclipse occurs when the moon casts a shadow on a portion of Earth's surface.

   c. A lunar eclipse occurs during a full moon, when Earth is between the sun and moon.

   d. A lunar eclipse occurs during a new moon, when the moon is between the sun and Earth.

Tides on Earth (page 801)

14. Describe the cause of tides. _____
_____

15. Is the following sentence true or false? A spring tide is produced when the change between daily high and low tides is the greatest.
_____

© Pearson Education, Inc., publishing as Pearson Prentice Hall. All rights reserved.

Chapter 25   The Solar System

Section 25.3 The Inner Solar System
(pages 803–809)

This section describes the terrestrial planets found in the inner solar system.

Reading Strategy (page 803)

Summarizing Copy the table on a separate sheet of paper. Write all the headings for the section in the table. Write a brief summary of the text for each heading. For more information on this Reading Strategy, see the **Reading and Study Skills** in the **Skills and Reference Handbook** at the end of your textbook.

The Terrestrial Planets

I. The Terrestrial Planets
- Four planets closest to the sun
- Small, dense, with rocky surfaces

II.

  a.

III. Venus

  b. Thick atmosphere, very hot surface, many volcanoes

The Terrestrial Planets (pages 803–804)

1. Identify the four terrestrial planets.

   a. _____   b. _____

   c. _____   d. _____

2. Circle the letter of each sentence that is true about the terrestrial planets.

   a. They all are relatively small and dense.

   b. They all have rocky surfaces.

   c. They all have thick atmospheres.

   d. They all have a crust, mantle, and iron core.

Mercury (pages 804–805)

3. Circle the letter of each sentence that is true about Mercury.

   a. It is the closest planet to the sun.

   b. It is the smallest of the terrestrial planets.

   c. It is geologically dead.

   d. It is the slowest-moving planet.

4. Is the following sentence true or false? Mercury has a large number of craters, suggesting that the surface has been largely unchanged for billions of years. _____

© Pearson Education, Inc., publishing as Pearson Prentice Hall. All rights reserved.

Chapter 25   The Solar System

Venus (page 805)

5. Circle the letter of each sentence that is true about Venus.

   a. It rotates in the direction opposite to which it revolves.

   b. It is the brightest object in Earth's night sky besides the moon.

   c. It rotates once every 24 hours.

   d. Its rotation rate is very fast.

6. Describe the effect that carbon dioxide in Venus's atmosphere has on its temperature. _____

   _____

Earth (pages 805–806)

7. Circle the letter of each sentence that is true about Earth.

   a. Its atmosphere is very thin and composed mostly of carbon dioxide.

   b. It supports millions of different species of living things.

   c. It has a suitable atmosphere and temperature for liquid water to exist.

   d. Its core has cooled down to the point where it is geologically dead.

8. Why does Earth's surface continue to change? _____

   _____

Mars (pages 807–808)

9. Circle the letter of each sentence that is true about Mars.

   a. The largest volcano in the solar system is on Mars.

   b. Iron-rich rocks on Mars's surface give it a reddish color.

   c. It has a thick atmosphere that keeps the planet warm.

   d. The surface of Mars is colder than Earth's surface.

10. Is the following sentence true or false? Mars shows evidence of once having liquid surface water. _____

Asteroids (page 809)

11. Small, rocky bodies in space are called _____.

12. Circle the letter of each sentence that is true about asteroids.

    a. Most small asteroids have irregular forms.

    b. The asteroid belt formed when a giant planet was shattered by a collision with a meteoroid.

    c. Most asteroids are found in the asteroid belt between Earth and Mars.

    d. Most asteroids are less than 1 kilometer in diameter.

13. What do scientists hypothesize about how the asteroids formed? _____

    _____

© Pearson Education, Inc., publishing as Pearson Prentice Hall. All rights reserved.

Chapter 25   The Solar System

Section 25.4 The Outer Solar System
(pages 810–815)

This section describes the planets in the outer solar system. It also describes comets and meteoroids and the edge of the solar system.

Reading Strategy (page 810)

Summarizing Copy the table on a separate sheet of paper. Fill in the table as you read to summarize the characteristics of the outer planets. For more information on this Reading Strategy, see the **Reading and Study Skills** in the **Skills and Reference Handbook** at the end of your textbook.

The Outer Planets	
Outer Planets	**Characteristics**
Jupiter	Largest; most mass; most moons; Great Red Spot

Gas Giants (page 811)

1. Circle the letter of each sentence that is true about Jupiter, Saturn, Uranus, and Neptune compared to the terrestrial planets.
   a. Their years are shorter than the terrestrial planets.
   b. They are colder than the terrestrial planets.
   c. They are further from the sun than the terrestrial planets.
   d. They are much larger than the terrestrial planets.

2. Why are the outer planets called the gas giants? _____

   _____

3. Describe the cores of the gas giants. _____

   _____

Jupiter (pages 811–812)

4. The _____ is a huge storm on Jupiter.

5. Circle the letter of each sentence that is true about Jupiter's moons.
   a. Callisto and Ganymede are Jupiter's largest moons.
   b. Scientists hypothesize that Europa could support life.
   c. Ganymede has a metal core and rocky mantle.
   d. Io is covered with ice.

© Pearson Education, Inc., publishing as Pearson Prentice Hall. All rights reserved.

Chapter 25 The Solar System

Saturn (pages 812–813)

6. Saturn has the largest and most visible _____ in the solar system.

7. Is the following sentence true or false? Saturn has the largest atmosphere and the lowest average density of all the planets in the solar system. _____

Uranus (page 813)

8. Is the following sentence true or false? Uranus gets its distinctive blue-green appearance from large amounts of methane in its atmosphere. _____

9. Uranus's _____ is tilted more than 90°.

Neptune (page 814)

10. Circle the letter of each sentence that is true about Neptune.

   a. It has visible cloud patterns in its atmosphere.

   b. It has only five known moons.

   c. It has large storms in its atmosphere.

   d. It has no rings.

11. The _____ in Neptune's atmosphere causes its bluish color.

Pluto (page 814)

12. Is the following sentence true or false? Pluto is both larger and denser than the other outer planets. _____

13. Describe Pluto's probable composition. _____
_____

Comets and Meteoroids (page 815)

14. A(n) _____ is made of ice and rock that partially vaporizes when it passes near the sun.

15. Chunks of rock, usually less than a few hundred meters in size, that travel through the solar system are called _____.

16. The radioactive dating of ancient meteoroids has allowed scientists to establish that the age of the solar system is
_____.

The Edge of the Solar System (page 815)

17. The _____ contains tens of thousands of objects made of ice, dust, and rock that orbit the sun beyond Pluto.

18. The thick sphere of comets encircling the solar system out to a distance of about 50,000 AU is called the _____.

© Pearson Education, Inc., publishing as Pearson Prentice Hall. All rights reserved.

Chapter 25   The Solar System

Section 25.5 The Origin of the Solar System
(pages 818–820)

This section explains a theory of how the solar system originated. It also describes how this theory explains the composition and size of the planets.

Reading Strategy (page 818)

Identifying Main Ideas As you read, write the main idea for each topic. For more information on this Reading Strategy, see the **Reading and Study Skills** in the **Skills and Reference Handbook** at the end of your textbook.

Theories on the Origin of the Solar System	
Topic	**Main Idea**
The Nebular Theory	
Formation of the protoplanetary disk	
Planetesimals and protoplanets	
Composition and size of the planets	

The Nebular Theory (pages 818–819)

1. The generally accepted explanation for the formation of the solar system is called the _____.

2. Circle the letter of each sentence that is true about the nebular theory.

   a. The solar nebula formed from the remnants of previous stars.

   b. The explosion of a nearby star likely caused the solar nebula to start to contract.

   c. As the solar nebula contracted, it began to spin more slowly.

   d. The solar system formed from a rotating cloud of dust and gas.

3. Describe a solar nebula. _____

   _____

4. A large, spherical cloud of dust and gas in space is called a(n)

   _____.

5. Is the following sentence true or false? Most planets and moons are revolving now in the direction that the protoplanetary disk was spinning. _____

© Pearson Education, Inc., publishing as Pearson Prentice Hall. All rights reserved.

Chapter 25   The Solar System

6. Circle the letter of each sentence that is true about the formation of the protoplanetary disk.

   a. The disk was densest in the center and thinner toward the edges.

   b. At the center of the disk, nuclear reactions fused hydrogen and helium and the sun was formed.

   c. The temperature at the center of the disk was extremely low.

   d. Nearly all of the mass of the solar nebula became concentrated near the outer edge of the disk.

7. Asteroid-like bodies that combined to form planets were called

   _____.

8. The process by which planetesimals grew is called

   _____.

9. Put the following events about the formation of planetesimals and protoplanets in correct order. Number the events 1–5 in the order that they occurred.

   _____ Balls of gas and dust collided and grew larger.

   _____ Planetesimals became large enough to exert gravity on nearby objects.

   _____ Planetesimals grew by accretion.

   _____ Protoplanets joined to form the current planets in a series of collisions.

   _____ Planetesimals grew into protoplanets.

Composition and Size of the Planets (page 820)

10. At _____ pressures, such as those found in space, cooling materials can change from a gas directly into a solid.

11. Ice-forming materials _____ at temperatures between 500 K and 1200 K.

12. Why are the terrestrial planets relatively small and rocky? _____

    _____

    _____

13. Circle the letter of each sentence that is true about the formation of the gas giants.

    a. The gravity of the gas giants decreased as they grew larger.

    b. Ice-forming material could condense in the outer solar system.

    c. The planets grew large and were able to capture hydrogen and helium from nearby space.

    d. Less material was available for the gas giants to form than was available for the terrestrial planets.

14. Is the following sentence true or false? Scientists have found planets in orbit around distant stars that provide support for the nebular theory.

    _____

© Pearson Education, Inc., publishing as Pearson Prentice Hall. All rights reserved.

Chapter 25   The Solar System

WordWise

Test your knowledge of vocabulary words from Chapter 25 by completing this crossword puzzle.

Clues across:

3. A model where Earth is stationary while objects in the sky move around it
4. A small natural body in space that revolves around a planet
6. Asteroid-like bodies that eventually combined to form planets
9. The regular rise and fall of ocean waters
10. A chunk of rock that moves through the solar system

Clues down:

1. The event that occurs when the shadow of one body in space falls on another
2. Dusty pieces of ice and rock that partially vaporize when they pass near the sun
5. Small, rocky bodies that travel through the solar system
7. Low, flat plains on the moon
8. A disk made of many small particles of rock and ice in orbit around a planet

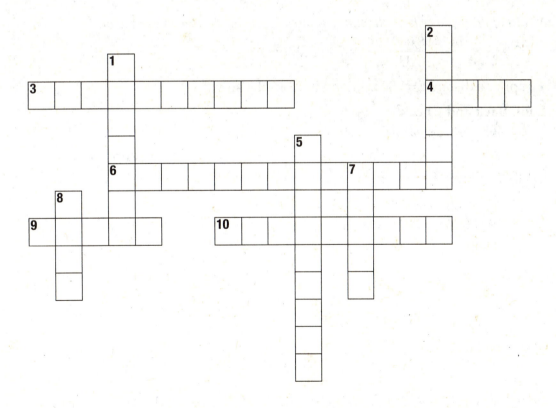

© Pearson Education, Inc., publishing as Pearson Prentice Hall. All rights reserved.

Chapter 25   The Solar System

Calculating Distances Between Objects in Space

Math Skill:
Conversion Factors
You may want to read more about this **Math Skill** in the **Skills and Reference Handbook** at the end of your textbook.

Jupiter is, on average, 5.2 astronomical units (AU) from the sun. About how many kilometers is Jupiter from the sun?

1. Read and Understand

What information are you given?

Jupiter's distance = 5.2 AU from the sun

2. Plan and Solve

What are you asked to find?

Jupiter's distance = ? kilometers from the sun

How many kilometers are in one AU?

149,598,000 kilometers

Write a conversion factor that can be used to change AU to kilometers.

$$\frac{149{,}598{,}000 \text{ km}}{1 \text{ AU}}$$

Multiply the distance from the sun to Jupiter in AU by the conversion factor.

$$5.2 \text{ AU} \times \frac{149{,}598{,}000 \text{ km}}{1 \text{ AU}} = 780 \text{ million km}$$

Jupiter's distance = 780 million km from the sun

3. Look Back and Check

Is your answer reasonable?

To check your answer, convert the distance between the sun and Jupiter in kilometers back to AU.

$$\frac{780{,}000{,}000 \text{ km}}{149{,}598{,}000 \text{ km/AU}} = 5.2 \text{ AU}$$

Math Practice

On a separate sheet of paper, solve the following problems.

1. Pluto is an average distance of 39.5 AU from the sun. How many kilometers from the sun is Pluto?

2. Mercury is 58.3×10^6 km from the sun on average. How many AU is Mercury from the sun?

3. Mars is 1.52 AU from the sun on average. Saturn is 9.54 AU. About how far apart, in kilometers, are Mars and Saturn when they are closest to each other?

© Pearson Education, Inc., publishing as Pearson Prentice Hall. All rights reserved.

Chapter 26   Exploring the Universe

Summary

26.1 The Sun

The sun gives off tremendous amounts of energy. The sun's energy is in the form of electromagnetic radiation. The source of the sun's energy is nuclear fusion. Inside the sun, hydrogen nuclei fuse, or combine, to form helium nuclei. These reactions convert mass to energy. The energy from nuclear fusion moves outward from the center of the sun. It exerts outward thermal pressure. At the same time, the sun's center exerts inward gravitational force. These two opposing forces balance each other. As a result, the sun remains stable.

The sun has an interior and an atmosphere. The sun's interior consists of the core, the radiation zone, and the convection zone.

- The core is the central region of the sun. Nuclear fusion produces energy in the core.
- The radiation zone is the next layer of the sun's interior. It is a region of gas under pressure. Energy from the core passes into the radiation zone. The energy takes thousands of years to pass through the radiation zone because the zone is so dense.
- The convection zone is the outer layer of the sun's interior. Energy from the radiation zone passes into the convection zone. Energy passes through the convection zone to the atmosphere by convection currents.

Outside the convection zone is the sun's atmosphere. The sun's atmosphere consists of three layers: the photosphere, the chromosphere, and the corona.

- The photosphere is the innermost layer of the sun's atmosphere. It is the visible surface of the sun. It has a bubbly appearance. The bubbles are the tops of convection currents in the convection zone.

- The chromosphere is the middle layer of the sun's atmosphere. It is hotter than the photosphere.
- The corona is the outermost layer of the sun's atmosphere. It is hotter than the chromosphere. The corona is very thin. It extends outward into space for millions of kilometers.

The corona gradually thins into the solar wind. The solar wind is a stream of electrically charged particles. The stream flows outward from the sun through the solar system.

The sun's atmosphere has some striking features, including sunspots, prominences, and solar flares.

- Sunspots are relatively cool areas in the photosphere. They look like dark spots on the sun's surface. They are often found in groups, and they occur in cycles.
- Prominences are huge loops of gas that erupt from sunspot regions. They start in the photosphere. They may extend upward into the corona.
- Solar flares are sudden bursts of energy released from the sun. They usually occur near sunspots. They heat the corona and increase the solar wind.

26.2 Stars

A star is a large, glowing ball of gas in space. It produces energy through nuclear fusion in its core. The sun is the closest star to Earth.

Although stars appear to be close together in the night sky, they are actually very far apart. In fact, stars are so far apart that astronomers measure distances between them in units called light-years. A light-year is the distance light travels in one year (in a vacuum), or about 9.8 trillion kilometers.

© Pearson Education, Inc., publishing as Pearson Prentice Hall. All rights reserved.

Chapter 26   Exploring the Universe

Astronomers cannot directly measure the distance of stars from Earth. Instead, they must use an indirect method. To find a star's distance, astronomers first measure its parallax. Parallax refers to how an object appears to change position, relative to its background, when you view it from different angles. As Earth moves in its orbit, astronomers can view stars from different angles. The more a star appears to change position relative to its background, the closer the star is to Earth. The parallax method works best for nearby stars.

There are many different types of stars. Astronomers classify stars by their color, size, and brightness. A star's color depends on its surface temperature. The hottest stars appear blue. The coolest stars appear red. In between are yellow stars, like the sun. Stars vary greatly in how bright they are. Absolute brightness is how bright a star really is. Apparent brightness is how bright a star appears from Earth. A star's apparent brightness depends on its absolute brightness and its distance from Earth. Stars appear dimmer when they are farther away. Astronomers can measure a star's apparent brightness and distance. Then, they can use the information to calculate the star's absolute brightness. Astronomers also have methods for calculating the diameter, volume, and mass of stars.

Astronomers use a spectrograph to identify the elements in a star's atmosphere. A spectrograph is an instrument that spreads light from a hot, glowing object into a spectrum. Different elements absorb light of different colors. Colors that are absorbed by elements in a star's atmosphere are absent from the star's spectrum. In their place are dark lines, called absorption lines. The absorption lines show where light has been absorbed. The absorption lines can be used to identify the elements in the star's atmosphere. Astronomers have

found that the atmospheres of most stars consist mainly of hydrogen and helium.

A graph that shows the surface temperature of stars on one axis and the absolute brightness of stars on the other axis is called a Hertzprung-Russell diagram, or an H-R diagram. H-R diagrams are used to estimate the size and distance of stars. The diagrams also help scientists understand how stars change over time.

Most stars fall within a diagonal band on an H-R diagram. This diagonal band is called the main sequence. It shows that cooler stars are generally dimmer and that brighter stars are generally hotter. Some stars fall outside the main sequence on an H-R diagram. Stars called giants or supergiants fall above the main sequence. They are very bright because they are large, not because they are very hot. Stars called white dwarfs fall below the main sequence. They are very dim because they are small, not because they are very cool.

26.3 Life Cycles of Stars

Scientists think that an H-R diagram represents the life cycle of stars. The first and longest part of the life cycle of a star is spent as a main-sequence star. As stars age, they become giants or supergiants. Some giants eventually become white dwarfs.

A star first forms from a nebula. A nebula is a large cloud of gas and dust spread out over space. Gravity pulls a nebula's gas and dust into a denser cloud. As the nebula shrinks, its pressure and temperature rise. Eventually, it becomes so dense and hot inside the nebula that nuclear fusion begins. At this point, a star has formed. Outward pressure from fusion balances the inward pull of gravity. These two opposing forces keep the star stable. It is now a main-sequence star.

How long a star lasts as a main-sequence star depends on its mass. High-

© Pearson Education, Inc., publishing as Pearson Prentice Hall. All rights reserved.

Chapter 26   Exploring the Universe

mass stars have greater internal heat and pressure. As a result, they burn more brightly and use up fuel more quickly. They do not last as long as low-mass or medium-mass stars. High-mass stars may last only a few million years. In contrast, low-mass stars may last over 100 billion years.

Even low-mass stars do not last forever. Eventually, hydrogen in the core is used up, and energy can no longer be produced by fusion. Without the outward energy of fusion to counter the inward force of gravity, the star shrinks. This causes temperature and pressure to rise inside the star. Fusion begins again, but now in a shell outside the core. Energy flows outward from the shell and causes the star to expand. The star's atmosphere also expands. It moves away from the hot core and cools. The star becomes a red giant or a red supergiant.

Low-mass and medium-mass stars become red giants. A red giant eventually blows off much of its mass. It becomes surrounded by a glowing cloud of gas called a planetary nebula. All that remains of the star itself is its hot, dense core. This core is called a white dwarf.

High-mass stars become red supergiants. A red supergiant rapidly uses up fuel, so fusion slows and outward thermal pressure drops. Gravity causes the star's outer layers to collapse inward. This collapse produces a giant explosion, called a supernova. The dense core that remains after the explosion is called a neutron star. A neutron star is much smaller and denser than a white dwarf. Very massive stars may collapse beyond the neutron star stage and form black holes. A black hole is an object with such strong gravity that light cannot escape from it.

26.4 Groups of Stars

A group of stars that appear to form a pattern is called a constellation. The stars in a constellation are not necessarily close

together. They just happen to lie in the same general direction as seen from Earth. Constellations help astronomers form maps of the sky.

Most stars actually do occur in groups. A star system is a group of two or more stars. A star system is held together by gravity. The majority of stars are members of star systems. A star system with two stars is called a binary star.

Groups of thousands or even millions of stars are called star clusters. There are three basic types of star clusters: open clusters, associations, and globular clusters.

- Open clusters are the smallest type of star cluster. They are loose groupings of stars. The stars are generally spread out. Open clusters often contain bright supergiants.
- Associations are typically larger than open clusters. Associations are temporary groupings of bright, young stars. Gravity from neighboring stars eventually breaks up associations.
- Globular clusters are large groups of older stars. The clusters are shaped like spheres, with a dense concentration of stars in the center. There may be more than a million stars in a globular cluster.

A galaxy is a huge group of individual stars, star systems, star clusters, dust, and gas. All the parts of a galaxy are bound together by gravity. There are billions of galaxies in the universe. Astronomers classify galaxies into four main types based on their shape: spiral, barred-spiral, elliptical, and irregular.

- Spiral galaxies have a bulge of stars at the center. They have arms extending outward from the center like a pinwheel.
- Barred-spiral galaxies are spiral galaxies with a bar through the center. They have arms extending outward from the bar on either side.

© Pearson Education, Inc., publishing as Pearson Prentice Hall. All rights reserved.

- Elliptical galaxies are spherical or oval. They do not have arms.
- Irregular galaxies come in many shapes. They look disorganized.

Our own galaxy is called the Milky Way. It is a spiral galaxy with billions of stars. In the arms of the Milky Way, stars are still forming. At the center of the Milky Way, there may be a huge black hole.

Quasars are extremely bright centers of distant young galaxies. Quasars produce more light than hundreds of galaxies the size of the Milky Way. In a quasar, matter is pulled into a massive black hole. As matter falls into the black hole, its gravitational potential energy is changed into electromagnetic radiation.

26.5 The Expanding Universe

As a light source moves toward or away from an observer, its wavelength appears to change. This is due to the Doppler effect. This effect can be used to determine how fast stars or galaxies are moving toward or away from Earth. Because of the Doppler effect, a star or galaxy moving toward Earth would have its spectrum shifted toward shorter (bluer) wavelengths. On the other hand, a star or galaxy moving away from Earth would have its spectrum shifted toward longer (redder) wavelengths. The shift to longer wavelengths is a red shift.

Edwin Hubble discovered that the spectra of most galaxies undergo a red shift. This means that most galaxies are moving away from Earth. Hubble also found that more-distant galaxies have greater red shifts. This means that more-distant galaxies are moving away from Earth faster than closer galaxies. From these data, astronomers know that the universe is expanding.

Most astronomers think that the universe came into being at a single moment, in an explosion called the big bang. According to the big bang theory, all the matter and energy of the universe were at one time concentrated into a tiny, incredibly hot region. Then, about 14 billion years ago, an enormous explosion occurred, and the universe began in an instant. After the explosion, the universe expanded quickly and cooled. Eventually, the temperature dropped enough for atoms to form. Gravity pulled the atoms together into clouds of gas. Gradually, the clouds of gas evolved into stars and galaxies.

The big bang theory is the best current scientific explanation for the formation and development of the universe. The theory is supported by the red shift, which shows that the universe is expanding. The theory is also supported by cosmic microwave background radiation. This radiation can be detected from every direction in space. Scientists think that cosmic background radiation is energy that was produced during the big bang.

Scientists wonder if the universe will continue to expand. If the universe has enough mass, gravity might reverse the outward expansion. However, it is hard to determine the amount of mass in the universe. Much of the matter in the universe cannot be seen. It is called dark matter. Dark matter does not give off radiation, so it cannot be detected directly. It can only be detected by observing how its gravity affects visible matter. Some astronomers think that much of the universe is made of dark matter.

Recently, astronomers discovered that the universe may be expanding faster than before. The reason is not known. A mysterious force, called dark energy, may be causing the rate of expansion to increase. If the rate of expansion is increasing, it is likely that the universe will expand forever.

© Pearson Education, Inc., publishing as Pearson Prentice Hall. All rights reserved.

Chapter 26   Exploring the Universe

Section 26.1 The Sun
(pages 828–833)

This section describes how the sun produces energy. It also describes the sun's interior and atmosphere.

Reading Strategy (page 828)

Build Vocabulary Copy the table on a separate sheet of paper and add more lines as needed. As you read, write a definition of each vocabulary term in your own words. For more information on this Reading Strategy, see the **Reading and Study Skills** in the **Skills and Reference Handbook** at the end of your textbook.

The Sun	
Vocabulary Term	**Definition**
Core	
Radiation zone	
Convection zone	

Energy from the Sun (pages 828–829)

1. The sun gives off a large amount of energy in the form of _____ radiation.

2. Circle the letter of each sentence that is true about nuclear fusion in the sun.

   a. Less massive nuclei combine into more massive nuclei.

   b. The end product of fusion is hydrogen.

   c. Fusion is a type of chemical reaction.

   d. Hydrogen nuclei fuse into helium nuclei.

Forces in Balance (page 829)

3. For the sun to be stable, inward and outward forces within it must be in _____.

4. Is the following sentence true or false? The sun remains stable because the inward pull of gravity balances the outward push of thermal pressure from nuclear fission. _____

The Sun's Interior (pages 830–831)

5. Circle the letter of each layer of the sun's interior.

   a. the radiation zone   c. the convection zone

   b. the photosphere   d. the core

© Pearson Education, Inc., publishing as Pearson Prentice Hall. All rights reserved.

Chapter 26   Exploring the Universe

6. Circle the letter of each way that energy moves through the sun.

a. gravity   b. convection

c. radiation   d. nuclear fusion

7. List the layers of the sun's interior shown on the diagram.

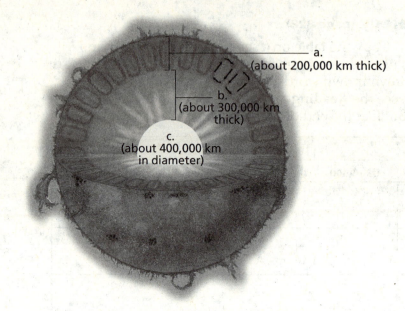

a. _____

b. _____

c. _____

The Sun's Atmosphere (page 831)

8. Circle the letter of each layer of the sun's atmosphere.

a. photosphere   b. chromosphere

c. corona   d. core

9. When can the corona be seen? _____

_____

Features of the Sun's Atmosphere (pages 832–833)

Match each description to a feature of the sun's atmosphere.

Description	Feature of Sun's Atmosphere
_____ **10.** Spectacular features of the sun's atmosphere that occur near sunspots	a. solar flares
_____ **11.** Areas of gas in the atmosphere that are cooler than surrounding areas	b. prominences
_____ **12.** Sudden releases of energy that produce X-rays and hurl charged particles into space	c. sunspots

© Pearson Education, Inc., publishing as Pearson Prentice Hall. All rights reserved.

Chapter 26   Exploring the Universe

Section 26.2 Stars
(pages 834–839)

This section discusses how scientists classify stars. It also describes other important properties of stars.

Reading Strategy (page 834)

Using Prior Knowledge Add what you already know about stars to the concept map. After you read, complete your concept map, adding more ovals as needed. For more information on this Reading Strategy, see the **Reading and Study Skills** in the **Skills and Reference Handbook** at the end of your textbook.

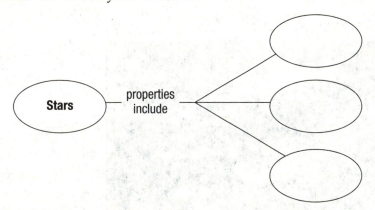

Distances to the Stars (pages 834–836)

1. Circle the letter of each sentence that is true about a light-year.

    a. It is a typical unit of measure for distances on Earth.

    b. It is a distance of about 9.5 trillion kilometers.

    c. It is the distance that light travels in a vacuum in a year.

    d. It is a unit of time.

2. Is the following sentence true or false? Parallax is the apparent change in position of an object with respect to a distant background. _____

3. Astronomers measure the parallax of a nearby star to determine its _____.

Properties of Stars (pages 836–837)

4. Circle the letter of each property that astronomers use to classify stars.

    a. brightness   b. distance

    c. color   d. size

5. Is the following sentence true or false? The brightness of a star as it appears from Earth is called its absolute brightness. _____

6. A star's _____ can be used to identify different elements in the star.

© Pearson Education, Inc., publishing as Pearson Prentice Hall. All rights reserved.

Name _____ Class _____ Date _____

Chapter 26 Exploring the Universe

7. Describe the chemical makeup of most stars. <u>Hydrogen and helium combine to make up</u>

_____

The Hertzsprung-Russell Diagram (pages 838–839)

8. Circle the letter of each way that Hertzsprung-Russell (H-R) diagrams might be used.

   a. to study sizes of stars

   b. to study distant planets

   c. to determine a star's absolute brightness

   d. to determine a star's surface temperature or color

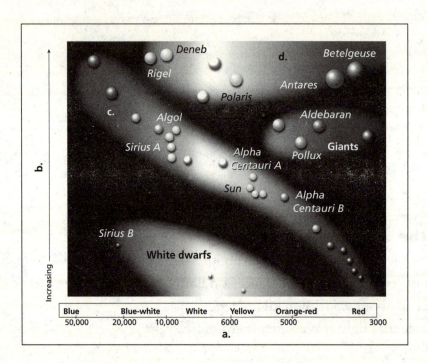

9. Provide labels for each of the letters shown on the H-R diagram above.

   a. _____   b. _____

   c. _____   d. _____

10. Circle the letter of each sentence that is true about supergiants.

    a. They are found at the upper right of the H-R diagram.

    b. They are much brighter than main sequence stars of the same temperature.

    c. They are 100 to 1000 times the diameter of the sun.

    d. They are smaller and fainter than giants.

11. How does the brightness of white dwarfs compare to the brightness of main sequence stars? _____

_____

© Pearson Education, Inc., publishing as Pearson Prentice Hall. All rights reserved.

Chapter 26   Exploring the Universe

Section 26.3 Life Cycles of Stars
(pages 840–844)

This section explains how stars form, their adult stages, and how they die.

Reading Strategy (page 840)

Sequencing Copy the flowchart on a separate sheet of paper. As you read, extend and complete it to show how a low-mass star evolves. For more information on this Reading Strategy, see the **Reading and Study Skills** in the **Skills and Reference Handbook** at the end of your textbook.

Evolution of a Low-Mass Star

How Stars Form (pages 840–841)

1. A large cloud of dust and gas spread out over a large volume of space is called a(n) _____.

2. Circle the letter of each sentence that is true about a protostar.

   a. Nuclear fusion is taking place within it.

   b. It has enough mass to form a star.

   c. Its internal pressure and temperature continue to rise as it contracts.

   d. It is a contracting cloud of dust and gas.

3. Describe how a star is formed. _____

_____

Adult Stars (page 841)

4. A star's _____ determines the star's place on the main sequence and how long it will stay there.

5. Circle the letter of each true sentence about adult main-sequence stars.

   a. High-mass stars become the bluest and brightest main-sequence stars.

   b. Low-mass stars are usually short-lived.

   c. Yellow stars like the sun are in the middle of the main sequence.

   d. Red stars are the hottest and brightest of all visible stars.

The Death of a Star (pages 842–844)

6. The core of a star starts to shrink when the core begins to run out of _____.

© Pearson Education, Inc., publishing as Pearson Prentice Hall. All rights reserved.

Name _____ Class_____ Date _____

Chapter 26   Exploring the Universe

7. Name three possible end stages of a star.

   a. _____ b. _____ c. _____

8. Is the following sentence true or false? The final stages of a star's life depend on its mass. _____

9. Circle the letter of each sentence that is true about the death of low-mass and medium-mass stars.

   a. The dying stars are called planetary nebulas.

   b. They remain in the giant stage until their supplies of helium and hydrogen are gone and there are no other elements to fuse.

   c. The energy coming from the stars' interiors decreases and the stars eventually collapse.

   d. The cores of the stars shrink and only their atmospheres remain.

10. The glowing cloud of gas that surrounds a dying low- or medium-mass star is called a(n) _____.

11. List the stages in the evolution of a low-mass star shown in the diagram below.

EVOLUTION OF STARS   Later stages of a low-mass star

a.   b.   c.   Red giant   d.   e.   f.

   a. _____ b. _____

   c. _____ d. _____

   e. _____ f. _____

12. Is the following sentence true or false? A high-mass star dies quickly because it consumes fuel rapidly. _____

13. An explosion so brilliant that a dying high-mass star becomes more brilliant than an entire galaxy is called a(n) _____.

Match each final stage of a high-mass star to its correct description.

Description

_____ 14. Surface gravity so great that nothing can escape from it

_____ 15. A spinning neutron star that gives off strong pulses of radio waves

_____ 16. The remnant of a high-mass star that has exploded as a supernova, which begins to spin more and more rapidly as it contracts

Final Stage of a High-Mass Star

a. pulsar

b. black hole

c. neutron star

© Pearson Education, Inc., publishing as Pearson Prentice Hall. All rights reserved.

Chapter 26   Exploring the Universe

Section 26.4 Groups of Stars
(pages 846–849)

This section describes star systems, star clusters, and galaxies.

Reading Strategy (page 846)

Comparing and Contrasting After you read, compare types of star clusters by completing the table. For more information on this Reading Strategy, see the **Reading and Study Skills** in the **Skills and Reference Handbook** at the end of your textbook.

Types of Star Clusters		
Cluster Type	**Appearance**	**Age and Type of Stars**
Open cluster		
		Bright, young stars
	Spherical, densely packed	

1. A group of stars that seems to form a pattern as seen from Earth is called a(n) _____.

2. Is the following sentence true or false? Constellations are important to astronomy because they help to form a map of the sky. _____

Star Systems (pages 846–847)

3. A group of two or more stars that are held together by gravity is called a(n) _____.

4. Is the following sentence true or false? Astronomers have concluded that more than half of all stars are members of groups of two or more stars. _____

5. A star system with two stars is called a(n) _____.

Star Clusters (page 847)

Match each basic kind of star cluster to its description.

Description	Star Cluster
_____ 6. A loose grouping of no more than a few thousand stars that are well spread out	a. globular cluster
_____ 7. Loose groupings of bright, young stars	b. open cluster
_____ 8. A large group of older stars	c. associations

© Pearson Education, Inc., publishing as Pearson Prentice Hall. All rights reserved.

Chapter 26   Exploring the Universe

9. Is the following sentence true or false? Astronomers estimate that the oldest globular clusters are at least 20 billion years old.
_____

Galaxies (pages 848–849)

10. A huge group of individual stars, star systems, star clusters, dust, and gas bound together by gravity is called a(n) _____.

11. Our galaxy is called the _____.

12. Galaxies that have a bulge of stars at the center with arms extending outward like a pinwheel are called
_____.

13. Is the following sentence true or false? The arms of spiral galaxies contain very little gas and dust. _____

14. A spiral galaxy that has a bar through the center with the arms extending outward from the bar on either side is called a(n)
_____.

15. Circle the letter of each sentence that is true about elliptical galaxies.

   a. They are spherical or oval shaped.

   b. They typically have lots of dust and gas.

   c. They come in a wide range of sizes.

   d. They usually contain only old stars.

16. A(n) _____ galaxy has a disorganized appearance and is typically smaller than other types of galaxies.

Match each type of galaxy to its description.

Description	Galaxy
_____ 17. Spherical or oval, no spiral arms, and usually contains only old stars	a. barred-spiral galaxy
	b. elliptical galaxy
_____ 18. Bulge of stars at the center with arms extending outward like a pinwheel	c. spiral galaxy
	d. irregular galaxy
_____ 19. Composed of many young stars, comes in many shapes, and has a disorganized appearance	
_____ 20. Has a bar through the center with arms extending outward from the bar on either side	

21. Is the following sentence true or false? The Milky Way appears as a band from Earth because we are looking at it edgewise.
_____

22. The enormously bright centers of distant galaxies are called
_____.

© Pearson Education, Inc., publishing as Pearson Prentice Hall. All rights reserved.

Chapter 26   Exploring the Universe

Section 26.5 The Expanding Universe
(pages 852–855)

This section describes Hubble's Law. It also explains the big bang theory.

Reading Strategy (page 852)

Previewing Before reading, examine Figure 26 and write at least two questions to help you understand the information in it. As you read, write answers to your questions. For more information on this Reading Strategy, see the **Reading and Study Skills** in the **Skills and Reference Handbook** at the end of your textbook.

The Evolution of the Universe
Questions on the Evolution of the Universe

Hubble's Law (pages 852–853)

1. Is the following sentence true or false? The apparent change in frequency and wavelength of a wave as it moves towards or away from an observer is known as the Doppler effect.

   _____

2. How can astronomers use the Doppler effect? _____
   _____

3. Circle the letter of each sentence that is true about spectrums of stars or galaxies.

   a. As a star or galaxy circles the Earth, the lines in its spectrum shift toward the middle of the spectrum.

   b. As a star moves toward Earth, the lines in its spectrum are shifted toward shorter wavelengths.

   c. As a star or galaxy moves away from Earth, the lines in its spectrum are shifted toward longer wavelengths.

   d. The greater the observed shift in spectrum, the greater the speed the star or galaxy is moving.

4. The shift in the light of a galaxy toward the red wavelengths is called a(n) _____.

5. Describe Hubble's Law. _____
   _____

6. Is the following sentence true or false? The most distant galaxies that can be seen from Earth are moving away at more than 90% of the speed of light. _____

© Pearson Education, Inc., publishing as Pearson Prentice Hall. All rights reserved.

Name _____ Class _____ Date _____

Chapter 26   Exploring the Universe

7. Describe what the observed red shift in the spectra of galaxies shows.

_____

_____

The Big Bang Theory (page 854)

8. Astronomers theorize that the universe came into being in an event called the _____.

9. Circle the letter of each sentence that is true according to the big bang theory.

   a. The matter and energy in the universe was once concentrated in a very hot region smaller than a sentence period.

   b. The universe began billions of years ago with an enormous explosion.

   c. The universe came into existence in an instant.

   d. The matter and energy in the universe has taken billions of years to form.

10. After the big bang, it is theorized that the universe _____.

11. How large was the universe when the sun and solar system formed?

_____

12. Circle the letter of each sentence that gives evidence that supports the big bang theory.

   a. The existence of cosmic microwave background radiation.

   b. The red shift in the spectra of distant galaxies.

   c. The fact that the sun is about 20 billion years old.

   d. The pulling of atoms together into gas clouds by gravity.

13. Recent measurements of the microwave background radiation have led astronomers to estimate that the universe is _____.

Continued Expansion (page 855)

14. Matter that does not give off radiation is known as _____.

15. Circle the letter of each sentence that is true about dark matter.

   a. Astronomers currently don't know what it is or how it is distributed.

   b. It cannot be seen directly.

   c. It can be measured using the Doppler effect.

   d. It can be detected by observing how its gravity affects visible matter.

16. Why is it significant that the galaxies contain as much as ten times more dark matter than visible matter? _____

_____

© Pearson Education, Inc., publishing as Pearson Prentice Hall. All rights reserved.

Chapter 26   Exploring the Universe

WordWise

Answer the questions by writing the correct vocabulary terms from the chapter in the blanks. Use the circled letter in each word to find the hidden word.

Clues

Vocabulary Terms

What is the central region of the sun?

Ⓞ _ _ _

What is the surface layer of the sun?

_ Ⓞ _ _ _ _ _ _ _ _ _

What is a dramatic eruption on the sun that produces X-rays and hurls charged particles into space at nearly the speed of light?

_ _ _ _ Ⓞ _ _ _ _ _

What is a contracting cloud of gas and dust with enough mass to form a star?

_ _ Ⓞ _ _ _ _ _

What is the diagonal band of stars on the H-R diagram?

Ⓞ _ _ _   _ _ _ _ _ _ _ _

What is the dense remnant of a high-mass star that has exploded as a supernova?

_ _ _ _ _ Ⓞ _   _ _ _ _ _

What are the very bright stars at the upper right of the H-R diagram?

Ⓞ _ _ _ _ _ _ _ _ _

What is the apparent change in position of an object with respect to a distant background?

Ⓞ _ _ _ _ _ _ _

What is an object whose surface gravity is so great that nothing, not even light, can escape from it?

_ _ _ _ _ Ⓞ _ _ _

What is the distance that light travels in a vacuum in a year?

_ _ _ _ _ - _ Ⓞ _ _

What is a large glowing ball of gas in space?

_ _ _ Ⓞ

What is a large cloud of gas and dust spread out over a large volume of space?

_ Ⓞ _ _ _ _

Hidden Word: _ _ _ _ _ _ _ _ _ _ _ _ _

Definition: _____

_____

© Pearson Education, Inc., publishing as Pearson Prentice Hall. All rights reserved.

Chapter 26   Exploring the Universe

Calculating Distances to Stars

A star is 3.6×10^{19} kilometers from Earth. How many light-years is this?

Math Skill: Exponents

You may want to read more about this **Math Skill** in the **Skills and Reference Handbook** at the end of your textbook.

1. Read and Understand

How many kilometers from Earth is the star?

Star $= 3.6 \times 10^{19}$ kilometers from Earth

What are you asked to find?

Star $= ?$ light-years from Earth

2. Plan and Solve

Write the number of kilometers in a light-year using scientific notation.

9.5×10^{12} kilometers

To find the number of light-years the star is from Earth, divide its distance by the number of kilometers in a light-year. Begin by dividing 3.6 by 9.5. Round your answer to the nearest hundredth.

0.38

To divide numbers with exponents, subtract the exponents. What will the exponent of the answer be?

7

To write your answer in scientific notation, a number other than zero must be in the ones place. Move the decimal one place to the right and subtract one from the exponent. How many light-years is the star from Earth?

3.8×10^{6} light-years

3. Look Back and Check

Is your answer reasonable?

To check your answer, multiply the number of light-years away the star is by the number of kilometers in a light-year. Remember to add the exponents when you multiply. Your answer should be the distance from Earth to the star in kilometers.

3.6×10^{19} kilometers

Math Practice

On a separate sheet of paper, solve the following problems.

1. A star is 8.6×10^{14} kilometers from Earth. How many light-years away is the star? Round your answer to the nearest tenth.

2. The star Proximi Centauri is about 4.3 light-years from Earth. How many kilometers from Earth is it?

3. A star is 6.8×10^{8} light-years from Earth. How many kilometers from Earth is the star?

© Pearson Education, Inc., publishing as Pearson Prentice Hall. All rights reserved.